GROWING
SLOWLY
NOWHERE

IWAN ROSS

This one's for all the doubters and naysayers who wished to see me fall. I'm still standing strong, alive and kicking.

PROLOGUE

When the author with no name first approached me, his request seemed ordinary—a mere task amidst my usual projects. Yet, as the days turned into nights, and my once serene evenings were invaded by restless contemplation, I found myself grappling with a profound challenge. My desk became a battlefield of thoughts, my screen a canvas of unspoken truths and fabrications. Little did I realize the depth of the darkness that enveloped the world he came from, a world so intricately woven with shadows and half-truths that it blurred the lines between reality and fiction.

In those fleeting moments of clarity, when I would glance at the blank page, the weight of his story seemed almost surreal. I had to immerse myself in his voice, navigating a labyrinth of deception and raw emotion. What follows in these pages is presented as truth—a narrative steeped in genuine pain and unrelenting struggle. Yet, as you delve deeper, remember this: Every word you read is indeed true, but the reality it portrays may be an illusion.

This is not merely a story of survival and despair; it is a reflection of perceptions, a mirror held up to the complexities of the human condition. The line between truth and fabrication is deliberately blurred. So as you journey through this account, ask yourself—where does the truth end and fiction begin?

Welcome to "Growing Slowly Nowhere," a tale where the boundaries of reality and imagination are deliberately, and perhaps dangerously, intertwined.

And remember this, to protect the truly guilty, the initials of his wrongdoers have been cleverly employed.

Chapter One

Hello, dear readers. I am the author with no name known for my expertise in crafting chilling ghost suspense and supernatural tales. Take a moment of your precious time to listen to my story, a shocking reality that will captivate you. Brace yourselves, for it is about to get interesting.

Let's begin this adventure without any more delay. Hold on tight as I take you back to Hillbrow, Johannesburg, in the late months of the early 1970s. This suburb, known to all, was a rundown neighborhood infested with crime and controlled by greasy mob bosses. The air was thick with tension and the stench of decay.

My mother, who I only came to realize late in life, was a narcissist. Her presence was suffocating, like the heavy smog that hung over the city. My brother, on the other hand, was a genuine psychopath. The sound of his unsettling laughter still echoes in my mind.

In the midst of this chaos, my father, a Scottish citizen, fought tirelessly against the apartheid regime as an "Apartheids Stryder." He was a courageous soul, but his defiance came at a cost. Suddenly, he vanished without a trace, leaving me with unanswered questions that haunt me to this day.

I won't bore you with the details of my childhood, but let's fast forward. Against all odds, I fought tooth and nail in a relentless battle and managed to graduate from high school, defying all expectations. Meanwhile, my brother's life spiraled out of control. Expelled from schools, fired from jobs, his existence was a whirlwind of chaos and destruction. The sound of his violent outbursts still rings in my ears.

Amid our turmoil, my mother, a social worker by trade, mysteriously accumulated great wealth. The scent of money and deceit lingered around her, like a sweet but rotten perfume. Her tactics, shrouded in secrecy, remain unknown to me. I suspect her seductive allure played a role in her success.

She indulged in relationships with wealthy, married men as if it were a twisted hobby. One such affair involved my best friend's father, who lived in a grand home across the road from us. The tension between my mother and my best friend's mother was palpable. It filled the air with an uncomfortable electricity, like a storm waiting to break.

My mother reveled in the pain she caused to these women, her victims. The suffering she inflicted was an open secret, staining our neighborhood with a sense of betrayal and resentment.

Stay tuned for more, dear readers. The tale of my life unfolds, revealing the intricate web of deceit, pain, and survival that shaped me into the person I am today.

Despite my mother's protests, I decided to join the army, fully aware of her co-dependency issues. The reasons were valid. Firstly, I wanted to mature, like a fine wine, before pursuing further studies. Secondly, it was the final year in our country where military service was compulsory, as the Afrikaner government, on the verge of collapse, faced mounting external pressures. However, my mother, consumed by her longing for my absent brother and her aversion to being alone, vehemently objected. She threatened to use my study funds against me if I enlisted.

Undeterred, I packed my bags and boarded the army train, nicknamed "Wors Masjien" in Afrikaans, symbolizing the cramped conditions with its sausage-like carriages. As the train whistle pierced the air at Kimberley station, I peered out the window, hoping for a farewell from someone. Yet, as expected, the platform stood empty. At that very moment, my mother lounged on a beach, flaunting her yellow bikini alongside a wealthy man, one of her victims.

Ironically, it was during my time in the monotonous army that my love for literature blossomed. Unlike those around me, I relished every moment. The army became a sanctuary, shielding me from the reach of my mother and brother. Over the next two years, they made no effort to contact me, not even a birthday wish or a care package like my comrades received from their loved ones. Nevertheless, I rejoiced, for I had an abundance of books at my disposal. Like an insatiable beast, I scoured every library, stacking my arms with literature, a luxury I had never known.

However, my solitary tendencies did not go unnoticed by those with brass epaulettes, and I was soon called to meet the army psychologist. In a nutshell, she became my first girlfriend, and we shared our intimate moments together. She was a petite blonde, genuinely fond of me, and our first date involved shooting pool balls. But, hold on a second, what was her diagnosis of my condition? I solemnly admit that I have no clue, as our time was consumed by intimacy, reading books, and playful moments. Shh, this secret remained hidden, until now.

Two years later, I arrived back home, greeted by an eerily quiet house, ready to resume my studies at college. The scent of familiarity wafted through the air as I stepped inside. Liesbet, our beloved household servant, opened the front door, enveloping me in a warm embrace. Her touch was reassuring, and I couldn't help but feel a surge of affection for her. She informed me that my mother was out and had left a letter for me.

Excitement rushed through me as I rushed to my bedroom, my footsteps echoing through the empty hallways. I hastily threw my bags onto the bed, the soft landing muffled by the plush duvet. My eyes eagerly scanned the room, searching for the elusive letter. Finally, I spotted it, lying there without an envelope. Stinginess radiated from its exposed state.

My heart pounded in my chest, and my hands trembled slightly as I unfolded the letter, the paper rustling under my touch. The words, written in Afrikaans, stared back at me. "I told you," my mother's voice echoed through the ink, "I will use your tuition money if you join the army. And I did. I am in France, on holiday, with [the name of one of her victims]. I will be in Paris for six weeks. Find a job, or move out. You have two weeks."

Unsurprisingly, the contents of the letter failed to surprise me. I crumpled it up, the sound of paper crunching in my hand, and tossed it into the bin. Determination filled my being as I made my way to the study, the creaking floorboards accompanying each step. I reached for the phone, its plastic surface cool against my fingertips, eager to find a job and escape this suffocating environment.

However, as I reached for the phone, my eyes caught sight of another handwritten letter from my mother. Its presence felt mocking, a reminder of her control. "Phone calls cost money. I know you saved up during your time in the army. Leave the change on the counter." The bitterness in her words hung heavy in the air.

I couldn't help but scoff at her assumption. If she knew the extent of my savings, she would have never left. With determination fueling my actions, I packed my bags, the sound of zippers closing echoing in the room, and left, finding my way to a commune.

Please forgive me for this short deviation from my journey. The words may sound simple, but it was anything but easy to leave the house I had grown to love with all my heart. As a young teenager, I had a peculiar habit that I was unaware of at the time. With my mom often working late or spending evenings with her lovers, I would become a scavenger, roaming the streets in search of food. On this particular day, I found myself on a long street lined with grand houses and expansive gardens. My eyes darted from one house to another, marveling at their majestic details. It reminded me of my home in Durban, the city we had left behind for this smaller city filled with mine rubble.

Then, my gaze fell upon a sign next to a foreboding gate: "Klein Boland," meaning 'Little Cape Winelands' in English. My lips parted in awe, uttering a silent "wow!" Intrigued, I felt a magnetic pull drawing me closer to the low boundary wall, allowing me a glimpse into the garden. It was a paradise. Leaning against the brick wall, I soaked in every majestic detail, my mouth agape. The growls of hunger in my stomach became a distant murmur as my attention was captured by the mesmerizing sight.

Suddenly, the lady of the manor, whom we shall call Auntie H, caught sight of me. With an elegant wave of her hand, she invited me inside, saying, "Come in." Her beauty made my knees weak, and to add to the magic of the moment, she spoke English. She introduced me to her two sons, E and N, and we spent the afternoon splashing about in the crystal-clear swimming pool, indulging in delicious snacks and homemade lemonade. For a brief period, I felt like I was in heaven.

Over time, the estate's ownership shifted, and my mother

eventually became the proud owner when my 'new family' left for their hometown. A decision I deeply regret, as it meant that in addition to my schoolwork, I would now have to take on the role of a full-time gardener. My curiosity had earned me a fair reward—a mix of satisfaction and remorse for the embarrassment I had caused my mother. Nonetheless, my unwavering instinct to scavenge and prowl for food brought me into contact with intriguing people, some of whom were part of a family my mother had always wished I would avoid.

I often wonder where my mother got the money for such a property, but I know I will never find out. Regardless, I am grateful for that experience, and now it is time to continue on my journey.

A friend's dad, aware of my valuable Information Technology experience gained during my time in the army, swiftly contacted me. He informed me that the local government was actively reaching out for help with their decentralization efforts, specifically for benefit payout grants.

Before I continue, let me take a moment to remind you of the civil unrest that plagued our country just before Nelson Mandela's release from prison. The tension was palpable, especially among white Afrikaners who feared losing their positions to qualified black individuals. I was told that even my English father faced difficulties in finding a job. I silently honor his perseverance wherever he may be.

Returning to my story, I agreed to the job opportunity and conveyed my interest to my friend's father. He arranged an interview and informed me that I would face a panel of experts the following day. I couldn't help but give them a nickname, the "Boere Maffia," or Boer Mafia in English, the true beneficiaries of apartheid.

And so, he invited me over for a beer to prep me. The dimly lit room smelled of stale cigarette smoke and old beer. The wooden table was sticky to the touch, evidence of countless spills and neglect. He leaned in close, his voice a low rumble, as he shared his instructions. I should tell them that I am a member of the NGK "N.G. Kerk," meaning Dutch Reformed Church. If they ask, I should also mention that I play rugby. And the most delicate part, if they inquire about my surname Ross, I should confidently explain that it is actually Roos, a popular Afrikaans surname, but there was a typo on my ID book.

He lent me his son's church clothing, the fabric crisp and freshly pressed. The familiar routine from my army days kicked in, and I meticulously made my bed and tidied my small room. Arriving at the interview, I settled onto a cold wooden bench in a long, brightly lit corridor. The constant ticking of the clock on the wall marked the passing seconds, minutes, and hours. Eventually, the lunch break arrived, and the boisterous laughter of the Boer Maffia spilled into the hallway, their flushed faces revealing their indulgence in alcohol.

Finally, a voice boomed, calling out my name, "Iwan Roos!" The deep resonance startled me, but I held firm to the deception we had planned. Though my last name is Ross, this deceit was carefully orchestrated. I stuck to my fabricated story, relaying everything my friend's dad had instructed me. To my astonishment, I was offered the job and started working the very next day.

As time passed, I found myself immersed in my new role, forging strong friendships and even encountering my first actual girlfriend. The office buzzed with activity, the sounds of ringing phones and keyboard clicks creating a rhythmic symphony. Despite my accomplishments, I couldn't help but feel a pang of frustration. My mother, who had returned from her vacation in France, had yet to reach out to me, unaware of my recent success. Yearning to share my joy, I dialed my friend's dad, seeking solace in his company and a celebratory drink.

That moment marked a turning point in my life. We sat together, sipping our beers, our bond growing stronger. He became the father figure I had never known, guiding me, even in the art of deception, to secure a job. And though I cherished my newfound employment and the connections I had made, little did I know that a complicated love affair with a married woman would soon test the boundaries of my newfound happiness. But that's a tale for another time. My fingers ache from typing, and I crave the comfort of a cold beer.

And that, my dearest reader, is how my journey of becoming the most destitute and industrious person I know began.

As the sun set on the final day of apartheid, my life took a turn I could never have anticipated. The shadows of my past were about to collide with an unexpected revelation. What came next changed everything.

Thank you for reading, and until next time, my friend. Stay tuned, for the story is about to heat up, sizzle. Keep an eye out for the full story to uncover the depths of my journey's secrets and triumphs. 'Growing Slowly Nowhere' is available on Amazon Kindle and all digital platforms, allowing readers to access the full story.

Farewell, but only for now.

Chapter Two

My journey continues, inching toward startling revelations. You see, dearest reader, during my employment with the government, dark forces were at play, unbeknownst to my fragile mind. Where to begin? Yes, I landed my first job, leveraging IT skills honed by my father. I soared through the ranks to become a senior paymaster and accounting clerk. My role was to computerize manual grant payouts, and I excelled. The government rewarded me with extensive travel, a car, and a housing subsidy.

Strutting around the office, I felt like a peacock, brimming with newfound success. I decided to visit the house of my youth, longing to reconnect with my mother. However, upon arriving, unfamiliar cars greeted me. Consumed by my self-importance, I overlooked the changes in my once-familiar surroundings.

Bursting through the front door, I called out her name with anticipation. Her sanctuary was her bed, where she unwound with minimal clothing, a good book, and a bottle of red wine. But as I entered, a deep voice boomed, "Hey!" I turned, expecting to confront her latest lover, but the man's sorrowful eyes revealed a painful truth. My mother had sold the house and moved to a small town in the Cape Winelands—a place I jokingly called "Boer Maffia Headquarters." Her past had finally caught up with her, and she had left in haste.

Years before, in Durban, a similar scene unfolded. Arriving home from school, I was met with the sight of a removal truck in our driveway. The engine's roar drowned out my racing heartbeat, and the air was thick with the scent of exhaust and fear. The sight of the truck filled me with dread.

My hands trembled, and anxiety gripped me. The once-vibrant colors of our home seemed dull and lifeless, mirroring my heavy heart. Each room, now empty, echoed with bittersweet memories. The impending loss of my childhood home and connection to my mother felt like a cruel twist of fate.

Despite the despair, I managed a poker face, having learned to navigate challenges from a young age. Taking a deep breath, I straightened my shoulders and faced the future with renewed purpose. As I turned away from the empty house, the creaking floorboards seemed to echo my shattered dreams. I embarked on a journey of self-discovery and redemption, or so I believed.

Rejection triggers various responses in individuals. Personally, it sends me spiraling into a state of panic. Drawing on my army days, I'd learned that beer supposedly eases heartache and loneliness. So, I hastily retrieved my car, raced to my favorite hangout spot, and rendezvoused with my friends. As we congregated, I pretended the world around us was nothing but pure bliss. I generously spent a significant portion of my salary on rounds of drinks for my eager companions and indulged them with mouthwatering hamburgers from a nearby roadhouse until the early hours of the morning.

With the bass pulsating, we embarked on our journey; the wind whispering secrets in our ears. The engine roared as I accelerated down the empty roads, without a care in the world. Our voices melded together in the car, harmonizing the lyrics to our favorite tune by the Pet Shop Boys.

Traffic light? Who cared? Tires screeched as I careened through it. Suddenly, there was a deafening crash as my car collided with a delivery truck at a staggering speed of 120 kilometers per hour. Astonishingly, no one sustained any injuries. It was nothing short of a miracle, considering I had four passengers with me.

No one knows how I managed to extricate myself from the predicament I had caused, but I suspect my friend's influential father, a prominent figure in the police force, played a role. If they had tested my alcohol levels at the scene, I would have only had one destination: jail.

However, just like the time I escaped unscathed during my high school years, this incident propelled my social status to the heights of celebrity. The accident became the talk of the town, and people went to great lengths to catch a glimpse of the wreckage. One of my closest friends, whose sister was in the car during the accident, even fainted upon seeing the mangled remains.

Everyone clamored for a piece of my attention. It was during this time that I met my new girlfriend, a young and attractive clerk who had previously paid me no mind at work. For the purposes of this story, let's call her B.

Oh, how my friends seethed with jealousy over my stunning new companion. Even the bartenders at my beloved watering hole suddenly served me free drinks. I was the man of the hour! No, I was THE man. With B by my side, the world was my oyster, a fleeting twist of fate woven by the gods into the tapestry of my life.

I traveled extensively, immersing myself in different cultures and places, while B often ventured out on weekends, causing us to have limited time together. However, one Friday night stands out vividly in my memory. It was unlike any other. B's parents entrusted us with the keys to their expansive home, creating an opportunity we had long yearned for—a moment filled with anticipation and desire that consumed us entirely.

Yet, as the night unfolded, uncertainty clouded my mind. I had previously shared with B about my intimate encounters during therapy sessions with my army psychologist, but those experiences were innocent, devoid of the darkness that was about to unfold.

You see, I carried within me a reluctance towards intimacy, a result of a haunting childhood memory. It was a time when a female family member came to visit. She was aware of my deep affection for my spud gun, a constant companion resting beside me on the bed. Seizing upon this knowledge, she enticed me into the dimly lit depths of the basement, where slivers of sunlight pierced through the gaps in the walls, casting a surreal glow.

My heart raced as I frantically searched for my beloved spud gun, oblivious to the sinister intentions that lurked beneath her undressing. And then, in a voice that sent shivers down my spine, she commanded me to "Screw me."

Conflicted by my own insecurities and low self-esteem, I felt trapped, devoid of choice. The longing for my spud gun fueled my compliance, even though the true nature of her request eluded my young mind. As she clutched onto my bare backside, her nails digging into my flesh, an unsettling mixture of pain and pleasure coursed through me. Her moans, haunting echoes that reverberate within my soul to this day. And when she finally reached her climax, laughter pierced the air, a chilling sound that accompanied her as she rose from the soiled floor, her depravity exposed.

And now, I found myself alone with B, our fingertips intertwining as we reveled in the moment. The atmosphere was charged with a sense of enchantment, though my past encounters with intimacy cast a shadow over our time together. I did what I believed was necessary, but alas, I fumbled and stumbled, tarnishing my reputation as a Casanova. Even now, the memory makes me flinch, a knot tightening in my stomach.

Needless to say, I was certain she had shared our peculiar nocturnal habits with colleagues at work. As I maneuvered through the dimly lit corridors, junior clerks would pass by, their murmurs of astonishment piercing my ears, their giggles fading into the background.

My boss, whom we shall refer to as W, noticed my discomfort at work and simply uttered, "I warned you." Yet, fate, a god I believed to lurk in the shadows, ever present, ever watchful, once again conspired against me. One Friday afternoon, I remained behind, compelled to prepare for my upcoming trip the following morning. From the window, I observed a sleek, impeccably clean car glide into the parking lot. A slender figure ascended the stairs. I watched, captivated, as B retrieved a shimmering diamond ring from her drawer and delicately slipped it onto her finger. They embraced, their passion clear in a shared kiss.

Hand in hand, they descended the stairs, while I stood there, wide-eyed, a silent witness to their union. In that moment, B introduced me to her husband, V, who lived in a distant city. The smirk etched upon her face remains eternally etched in my memory, haunting me to this very day.

My celebrity status faded with my ego, like a dimming spotlight on a stage. I could feel the eyes of the town on me, their laughter echoing in my ears. It was a bitter pill to swallow, realizing that everyone else knew about my fall from grace long before I did. The weight of my own mistakes crushed me, leaving me with no grounds to blame my mother for her indiscretions. I was becoming the person I had always despised, a painful truth that consumed me.

The rejection I experienced was suffocating, like a heavy fog that enveloped me wherever I went. To make matters worse, I had to face the person who had hurt me deeply every day at work, her presence a constant reminder of the pain. B, with her smirks and fleeting glances, turned our office into a twisted game of power. Each look she gave me was a dagger, a silent message saying, "You're not good enough" or "You're a fool for trying."

No one seemed to understand the turmoil I was going through. I threw myself into my work, seeking solace in long hours and constant travel, even sacrificing my weekends. I teetered on the edge of burnout, dangerously close to losing myself completely. Work became my only refuge, my way of coping with the pain, though the memories of my mistakes haunted me daily.

Then, a minor miracle appeared in the form of an angel. K, a junior clerk assigned to my team, brought a breath of fresh air into my life. I can still remember the way her legs seemed to go on forever, a sight that etched itself into my memory. She was oblivious to my past mistakes, and her arrival at the office seemed to bring out the worst in B. Finally, I saw B for who she truly was—a heartless snake in disguise.

K was different, a tomboy with a playful spirit who enjoyed spending time with the boys, especially me. We shared moments of laughter and camaraderie, but it never crossed the line into intimacy. She would crack jokes, and we would share stories, her presence a balm to my wounded soul. Yet, despite her efforts to break through my walls, I foolishly pushed her away. It's another regret added to the ever-growing list, and I continue to despise myself for it.

To me, at that time, it felt like I was sailing smoothly as long as I steered clear of relationships. There was a recurring pattern in my thoughts, but the words to describe it eluded me. I couldn't quite understand why, but every time I became entangled in a relationship, I sensed a suffocating confinement. And so, my instinctive response was to push back, at times resorting to verbal abuse. It seemed safer to reject others before they could reject me, and tragically, I ended up sabotaging a potentially blossoming connection with K.

Once again, I found myself single, believing that I was content, embracing the only thing I knew how to do well—work. It was just me and my friends, but one by one, they embarked on the journey of marriage, inviting me to be their best man or capture their special moments as their photographer. My circle of friends was gradually thinning, and it alarmed me. To exacerbate matters, some of their new wives either wanted me out of their lives, clinging possessively to their husbands, or flirted with me, despite their husbands being my closest companions.

I can recall two specific instances where this occurred, and in one, it led to a fleeting but intense kiss. However, I swiftly turned her away, remaining loyal to my friend. Nowadays, their son lives nearby, and he has become a cherished friend in our household. I often ponder how he would react if I were to disclose his mother's indiscretions. Yet, I know this secret remains buried deep within the recesses of my mind, along with countless others, until the day I reach the conclusion of my tale and share it with the world.

But working too hard at your job, just like in a relationship, can have the opposite reaction. The warning signs were unmistakable, like neon lights flashing in every corner of my life. The concerned voices of friends and colleagues echoed in my ears, both at work and outside. Even my own actions screamed of self-destruction. Yet my mother and brother remained distant, unaffected by my downward spiral.

To numb the pain, I sought solace in my familiar refuge—the nights spent drowning in alcohol, be it alone or with anyone willing to join me in squandering my hard-earned wages. It was a tragic blend, mixing excessive work with the intoxicating allure of booze.

But for now, I'll let my weary fingers find respite, teasing you with the tantalizing details that await in my next installment. What will become of my reckless path? Will I find redemption, or sink further into the abyss? I am grateful for your presence and endurance throughout this tumultuous journey. I wish I could address you by name. Please, take a moment to leave a comment and share your own experiences. I yearn to discover more about you. Until next time, adieu.

Chapter Three

Welcome back, dearest mortal reader, and thank you for joining me on part 3 of my exciting journey. I am delighted that you are here. Let's continue.

Over the last couple of months, I worked diligently to achieve my goals at work. I painstakingly liaised with banks to develop integration solutions, the sound of ringing phones filling the air. We arranged meetings with biometric companies to work on solutions for storing fingerprints and expediting recognition processes. In Africa, due to apartheid, not everyone had the ability to write, so we had to rely on traditional methods to identify those who regularly received grants.

Fraud was a prevalent issue, the lingering scent of deceit always present, and that is exactly why the government had decided to implement computer-based solutions. At the time, it seemed like an almost impossible feat. Despite the challenges, we persisted, and our small branch emerged as a pioneering force in inventing this technology. But I'll delve into that later.

The end was drawing near, a faint light at the far end of the dark tunnel. Little did I know, this light would transform into a thundering train hurtling towards me at alarming speed, derailing the life I had grown so comfortably accustomed to. If only I had known.

As I grew closer to computerizing the government grants, the atmosphere at work grew increasingly peculiar. For some inexplicable reason, I found myself regularly summoned to the office on the tribune. A group of overweight individuals, their bellies protruding, faces flushed red, and sneers of scorn etched upon their features. The sound of their condescending chuckles filled the room, echoing in my ears. I developed a clever trick to shield myself from their piercing gazes and intimidating scoffs. I imagined them as helpless infants, sucking on dummies and clad only in diapers. It helped to some extent, but the sight of my grin often elicited raised eyebrows. So, there I stood, summoned before the tribunal of excellency, my heart pounding in my chest. This time around, they accused me of having an affair with a married woman at work, their accusatory words hanging in the air like a noxious scent, threatening immediate dismissal. The last time I stood in exactly the same spot, gaping at their insinuations, they blamed me for using the government car to participate in an illegal street race.

In my desperation, I sought legal assistance from my close friend, whose father, with his eye on a judge's seat, was nothing short of an advocate. His name, when spoken in the community, was met with hushed whispers. With his wife practically raising me during the last two years of high school, he saw me as a son, his protective presence always felt. There was an unmistakable air of sacredness surrounding him, as if he personified the law itself.

I will never forget the look of shock on the faces of the tribune as he accompanied me to a hearing. Their gasps for air echoed through the room, mixing with the scent of smoke from their quickly extinguished cigarettes. The accusing glances they usually threw my way faded, their eyes now fixed on their shoes. It still amazes me how swiftly they dropped the charges against me, claiming that the evidence had mysteriously vanished. Need I say more? Over the next few months, I noticed a noticeable shift in how my coworkers treated me—with unwavering respect. There were even whispers of a potential promotion if I continued excelling in my work.

Finally, we had a fully functional computerized alternative in place. And we decided to embark on a road trip to test it out. We began in small towns, just in case any glitches arose. Fortunately, everything went smoothly. However, when we arrived in Upington, a television crew eagerly awaited us at the community center. I found myself appearing on television, being interviewed by a stunning blonde reporter, whose presence alone was captivating. Later that evening, she even took me on a date. The details of what ensued are best left censored, I apologize.

For the first time since I started this job, we had an escort of media vans closely tailing us, their presence adding to the excitement. Perhaps it had something to do with the events of the previous night, or perhaps not. Before this pivotal moment, I had pleaded with our superiors to provide police escorts due to the large amounts of cash we transported. Thankfully, no incidents were ever reported, and for that, I am grateful.

Next stop, Colesberg, where the first glitch introduced itself. We arrived early, the anticipation in the air was palpable. Eagerly, we walked through the heavy doors of the bank, only to be met with disappointment. The scent of frustration lingered as we learned that they did not have enough cash. Yes, we computerized the systems, but the payouts were still in cash, or parts thereof, depending on the size of the grant.

We waited for what felt like an eternity, the ticking of the clock mocking us. We set a deadline: three in the afternoon. Yet, counting the stacks of cash was a painstaking task, each bill creating a soft rustle. It took hours to complete, the sound of shuffling money becoming a monotonous symphony. Finally, we left the bank at four in the afternoon, our footsteps quickening as we rushed towards the pay site.

A rundown community center on the outskirts of the small town awaited us, its dilapidated walls echoing with the sounds of discontent. The grant beneficiaries, filled with impatience, greeted us with piercing gazes that seemed to penetrate right through us. They unleashed a torrent of insults, their foreign language punctuated by rapid tongue clicking and deep guttural sounds that echoed through the air. It was total mayhem; the chaos drowning out any other sound. Thousands of locals blocked access, their presence suffocating. The police cordoned off the area, their stern faces a stark contrast to the chaos unfolding. News vans trailed behind, their engines humming softly in the background.

Clutching the cases tightly, our knuckles turning white, we fought our way through the angry crowd. The push and pull of bodies created a physical storm, our senses overwhelmed. Into the small hall we stumbled, our hearts pounding in our chests, the rhythm like thunder. Our eyes widened, taking in the scene before us. More angry, shouting beneficiaries awaited, their voices merging into a cacophony of anger. My heart raced, adrenaline coursing through my veins. In one hand, I carried a case filled with millions in rands, its weight a constant reminder of the responsibility. In the other, the computer equipment, its cold metal pressing against my palm.

It was utter chaos. The police struggled desperately to restore order, their commands drowned out by the chaos. To this day, I have no idea why the senior paymaster had not postponed the payout to the next day. A fateful decision, indeed.

Surrounded by the masses, I lost sight of my peers, the sea of bodies overwhelming. I kept my gaze fixed on the stage, where we would set up our equipment. The angry roars of the crowd became a deafening symphony assaulting my senses. Bang! Suddenly, a gunshot echoed through the air, its deafening sound reverberating in my ears. Panic surged through me as my eyes darted around, desperately searching for bodies. But all I found was silence, a sudden tranquility that hung in the air. If only the media had not been present on that day. I wish I had been more cautious with my words when the reporter asked me about our upcoming destination. What had started as a night of innocent fun quickly descended into a terrifying nightmare. Darn.

We worked tirelessly until the late evening, the dim lights of the room casting long shadows on the walls, ensuring that each person present received their grant. The air was filled with a mix of anticipation and exhaustion, the excitement of reaching the end of our testing journey lingering around us.

As the night wore on, we encountered a minor glitch that still puzzles me to this day. It was a strange occurrence, a thumbprint going undetected, resulting in a young man receiving a grant meant for a pensioner. Perplexing, indeed. However, we eventually unraveled the mystery and discovered that it was not a flaw in our systems.

In the end, our road trip proved to be a resounding success. Just before the doors of a local steakhouse closed, we managed to make our way inside. The aroma of sizzling meat filled the air, and the owners, a kind-hearted couple, graciously invited us in, sensing the money we would spend. They kindly gave their waiters a break and attended to our requests themselves.

Amidst laughter and joy, we celebrated well into the early hours of the morning, the sounds of clinking glasses and lively conversations echoing through the restaurant. Eventually, I made my way back to the hotel, fatigue weighing heavily on my shoulders. To my surprise, a letter awaited me, wedged through the gap beneath the door, adding an element of intrigue to the night.

Blondie, my reporter companion, had requested that I wake her up, no matter how late I returned. It was a night filled with promises whispered in my ears, fueling dreams of fame. If only those promises could become a reality, the world would surely take notice.

When we returned to the office the next day, eagerly anticipating praise and celebration for our success, we were met with a heavy, solemn atmosphere. Unbeknownst to us, the incident that had unfolded at Colesberg had become front-page news. The tension in the air was palpable, causing a knot to form in my stomach. It was as if the whispers of Blondie, who had previously showered me with affectionate words, were now laced with bitterness. That treacherous woman.

This time, it wasn't just a simple gathering of colleagues; it felt like an entire army had assembled. They followed proper protocol, making it clear that I was not alone in this predicament. All of us who had been present at the Colesberg massacre, as the media had dubbed it, were immediately suspended. Right then and there, on that icy spot, our professional lives were put on hold.

However, I was singled out as the one responsible for firing a weapon, despite my vehement denial. The others had conspired against me, their betrayal lingering in the air. A security guard was summoned, and he led me to my office, taking possession of my gun, car keys, and computer. As I walked out, I felt a profound emptiness, as if I had been stripped of everything I held dear. It was a feeling akin to that of a newborn baby entering the world with nothing.

"Are you satisfied now, Blondie?" I muttered under my breath. "Just wait until I inform your husband about our affair." A mischievous chuckle escaped my lips, muffled by the fabric of my sleeve. Little did I know that three agonizing months of misery lay ahead of me.

Without a safety net, I could not stay in the small city whose people I loved with all my heart. I deeply regret my cowardice, knowing that I always take the easy way out, fleeing instead of fighting. Without a safety net and the absence of a father, I believe there are exceptional circumstances at play. What else was I supposed to do? Despite my denial, deep down, I knew that staying and facing the situation head-on would have been the better choice instead of fleeing.

Wait! Please allow me to introduce one of my many puns. One of the reasons I think the army psychologist fell for me was because of my humor. When she introduced the concept of denial, I abruptly raised a hand, cutting her short, and said, "No way! I am not in De-Nile, I am in de-Orange river," referring to the largest river in South Africa. With a mischievous giggle, she playfully settled onto my lap; the rest is a secret.

In any case, I packed my stuff, handed over my keys, and traveled to the shitty town where my mum resided. Let's call the town the Boer Mafia Headquarters for the purpose of this story. Or we could also call it the pram pusher capital, as my friend playfully dubbed it on his first and only visit, never to return again.

Back in the day, the town stood out for two things. Firstly, the abundance of education, with an educational college, social studies college, and bible college, the latter reigning supreme. The towering buildings reflected the town's dedication to knowledge. Secondly, the town is well rehearsed for its religious endeavor, with the statue of a famous religious scholar guarding the towering mother church, as the locals call it.

It was the first thing I noticed when I moved here. As I went on my long walks, biding my time, the picturesque surroundings were accompanied by a chorus of "God Bless" and "Bless you" as pram pushers exchanged greetings. The sound of their cheerful greetings filled the streets, mingling with the sound of children's laughter. Every time I walked by, they would slyly wink at me, as if sharing a secret. Do you understand the image I'm trying to paint?

Let's rewind a little, shall we? Apologies for the brief sidetrack. So, I landed on my mother's doorstep, defeated, ready to face her wrath. But it was a stranger with an insincere smile who greeted me at the door, beckoning me inside, and extending an invitation for a cup of coffee. It turned out my mother had embraced a Jewish alternative for her first names. Good heavens.

Engaged in a hushed discussion, I stood at the threshold with the lady who opened the creaky door. The truth slowly revealed itself. Like most of the locals, my mother rented out the spare bedrooms to hordes of students, filling our home with a diverse mix of biblical scholars from all walks of life. My mother's insatiable greed never failed to surprise me, and her own inability to work had led her to find a job at the local bible school.

As frustration consumed me, I felt a knot forming in my throat, desperate to scream out my discontent. But my astonishment grew even greater when I discovered that the very same female family member who had seduced me in the dimly lit attic of our house was among the students. Regret flooded over me, drowning my thoughts.

Throughout the afternoon, the front door swung open and slammed shut repeatedly as the students came and went, creating a symphony of noise that filled the air. And it was in that exact moment, amidst the commotion, when I first laid eyes on L, another alluring brunette. She introduced a pivotal moment in my life, her presence casting a spell that captivated my senses.

But that, my friend, is a tale for another time. For now, my fingers ache for the cool touch of an ice-cold beer. Stay tuned for the next installment, where L will teach me profound lessons about faith and more.

Chapter Four

As I stepped into the opulent living room of my mother's house, the sight of four beautiful women surrounded me. They bombarded me with a barrage of questions, their voices filling the air with a cacophony of noise. I fought back, answering their squeaky-mouthed inquiries with determination.

"How long have you been away?" one asked, her curiosity almost accusatory.

"Are you staying for good?" another chimed in, eyes wide with interest.

Somehow, I managed to verbally wrestle myself out of the situation, my astonishment evident on my face, which silenced them momentarily.

Finally, I seized a moment to inquire about their identities. Unsurprisingly, their answers did not astonish me. The leader of the group, the one who had opened the front door, gripped my hand and guided me down the corridor and into the kitchen. Halting abruptly, she stood tall like a sentinel before Ceaser, her finger pointing towards the refrigerator door. There, a montage of vibrant photographs greeted my gaze, capturing my attention.

"That's not you," she stated, but I couldn't help but notice the striking resemblance between the guy in the photograph and myself. Recognition flickered across her face, and no further explanation was needed. Behind me, a chorus of astonished murmurs filled the air. It became clear that my mother had only spoken of having one son.

"You look exactly like your dad," one of the women remarked, her eyes fixed on a faded wedding photograph on the fridge door. The truth struck me, and I whispered to the unresponsive group of eight women, their eyes filled with amazement, "Now I understand why my mother refuses to have a photo of me."

Suddenly, a bellowing voice echoed from the front of the house, causing my stomach to churn. I instantly recognized it as my mother's. With her usual flair, she gracefully entered the kitchen, flailing her arms flamboyantly. The women rushed towards her, embracing her and singing her praises. She had a knack for making an entrance, a trick I had yet to decipher.

"Oh," she exclaimed, locking eyes with me, "I see you've met my Prodigal Son." Giggles filled the air, and I stood there in confusion. In that moment, my first punishment was bestowed upon me. In my mind, I pictured a judge with a stern expression, raising his gavel high before bringing it down with a resounding thud. It became my responsibility to cook for the women and my mother that evening. Just like that.

My mind raced, a whirlwind of thoughts as I pondered the idea of treating everyone to dinner. However, the constraints of my budget forced me to come up with an alternative plan. With a burst of inspiration, I suggested a "braai," a South African barbecue, which was met with an enthusiastic chorus of exclamations. The ladies exchanged glances filled with delight, their nods and widening grins showing their approval as they eagerly scribbled down a menu.

In my mind, I calculated the costs, realizing that I had to be frugal. But as I glanced at my mother's expression, I knew she had ulterior motives. From the determined look on her face, it was clear that she intended to even the score.

As the girls excitedly piled into the bright yellow Volkswagen Beetle, affectionately named Tweety Pie, with its vibrant red bumper sticker, the engine roared to life, belching thick clouds of black smoke into the air. With that, they set off on their mission to procure the meat for our barbecue.

Left alone, I busied myself by stacking the fireplace and setting it ablaze. It was then that my mother emerged, holding a note tightly in her hand. With her piercing, snake-eyed gaze fixed upon me, she awaited my full attention before delivering her verdict.

"You can stay," she said, her tone icy, "but only in the servant's quarters."

I remained unfazed, meeting her stern gaze head-on. Her eyes, filled with pure hatred, briefly flickered to the note. She proceeded to read aloud the exorbitant price I was expected to pay for my accommodation, a sum that left me astounded. No provision for food or water was included. I cleared my throat nervously, sensing that there was more to come.

And indeed, I knew she had meticulously compiled her list of demands long before this moment. The dinner suggestion had merely been a ploy to lure the girls out of the house, leaving me vulnerable to her wrath.

To make matters worse, I discovered that I was also responsible for covering the costs of water and electricity, in addition to my rent. Furthermore, I was tasked with tending to the garden, maintaining a clean room, and washing her car. It was then that my eyes caught sight of something new, something I had not noticed before. A regal white poodle stood poised beside my mother, seemingly aware of its privileged position in this female-dominated society.

I need not ask, the dog's name turned out to be "Mephibosheth." Go figure. It sat their, eyeballing me in a way that I felt like a burglar. Strange thing though, it was the first dog my mother ever owned. And she chose a bloody poodle and gave it a biblical name.

Before I proceed, I want to quickly share something with you. You see, I am not a believer in miracles. Not the type where a figure appears through the clouds, draped in white, wielding a magic wand, with thunder echoing in the distance. Nor do I believe in metaphorical miracles. However, I firmly believe that the universe, or other unseen forces, watches over us and present us with the right outcome or strategy at precisely the right time. We cannot foresee the future, and though it pained me to return to my mother's house, I cannot speculate on what would have occurred had I stayed in my job.

It was perilous work, traveling with millions of rands in cash and visiting remote settlements. Anything could have transpired. But things unfolded as they did, and now I find myself here, with no power to change it. Yes, we make choices, but each of us is exactly where we are, right here, right now, and regardless of circumstances, it would have led to the same outcome. I am not attempting to convey a message about dealing with regrets in our decisions. However, you will soon have the opportunity to witness it firsthand.

Yet, one thing I could never unravel was which force presented itself at the opportune moment. The benevolent one or the not-so-benevolent one. And in that very moment, I was on the verge of encountering such a force when I needed it. Or did I?

In walked the ladies, their arms cradling shopping bags, one after another, their laughter permeating the air. It was then that I noticed the transformation in my mother. The cold-hearted snake morphed into the kindest, fluffiest, most gentle teddy bear. She joyfully threw her arms up in the air, twirling her wrists gracefully like a ballerina, while singing their praises for returning.

The situation made me feel like she had been taken captive by an armed robber. Personally, I believe it was the sight of the wine that stirred her emotions. Each lady held either a box or a large bottle of wine. And I knew it wasn't to celebrate my homecoming. Meanwhile, L, the quiet one, cradled a six-pack of beer and an expensive-looking bottle of wine. The beer caught my attention, and I observed as she placed it in the refrigerator before joining us outside. The scent of her invigorating perfume trailed behind her, teasing my senses, as she passed by with a mischievous smile. While the others were dressed casually, she remained in her elegant dress, its fabric billowing around her like a petal enveloping a rose.

I took the wine orders, effortlessly navigating from left to right, filling glasses and popping corks with a satisfying "pop" sound. My mother, always one to indulge in a sneaky habit, sat with her wineglass held at shoulder length, a mischievous smirk on her lips. Her silence spoke volumes, silently demanding to be topped up. Obliging her request, I poured the wine, the liquid cascading into the glass, almost reaching the brim. Her satisfaction was evident as she took an elegant sip, smacking her lips in approval, granting permission to everyone else to enjoy the festivities she had orchestrated.

The braai area of my mom's house stood outside, sheltered by a canopy. It was a lively and social space, typical of South African braai's, which are cherished outdoor events, especially during our sun-soaked summers. The word "braai" held a double meaning—it referred to both the act of barbecuing meat over glowing coals and the apparatus used for this purpose, such as a kettle braai or a permanent fixture. In my mom's case, it was a sturdy fixture resembling a fireplace, complete with a chimney. The walls were adorned with protruding spokes, offering various heights to rest the grill, depending on the intensity of the heat emanating from the coals.

Adjacent to the braai, a long tiled surface served as a preparation area, a slab where meat could be seasoned and spices could be arranged. It was also a spot to keep an eye on your beer while tending to the braai with the other. Our braai events often had a mysterious air surrounding the disappearance of beers, as if they had a mind of their own.

With the wine orders completed, I ventured into the kitchen to retrieve the meat and give it a thorough wash. The kitchen window provided a glimpse of the braai area, where I noticed L sitting alone on the slab, her presence catching my attention. Our eyes briefly met, and I couldn't help but notice a subtle twitch at the corners of her lips, hinting at some unspoken amusement.

And then, the familiar aroma of sizzling coals filled the air, signaling that braai time was near. The warmth radiating from the coals reminded me that they were still too hot to cook on. Behind me, the sound of glasses clinking and wine being poured resonated, confirming that the wine was hitting its mark. Engaged in a passionate debate about the existence of mankind, the individuals' voices grew louder, but I dared not turn to look in L's direction. Yet, I couldn't ignore the sensation of her eyes on me, teasing my skin with a tingling sensation that was eerie, yet strangely welcoming.

Sitting all by herself, isolated from the others, L exuded an air of elegance and grace. Her movements were deliberate and calculated, revealing that she belonged to a different class than the rest. When she spoke, her words were carefully chosen and articulated with precision. She carried herself like a princess, but I remained cautious, aware that creatures like her could be fragile, with claws hidden beneath their beauty, like thorns on a rose. Their tongues could lash out like whips, leaving lasting bruises. So, I kept my distance, my tongue yearning for the refreshing touch of an ice-cold beer.

As if she could read my thoughts, L gracefully hopped off the slab and sashayed into the kitchen. Before disappearing from sight, she whispered something to me, but the heated debate behind me drowned out her words. The wine worked its magic, and suddenly, I understood why L had been biding her time. Moments later, L reappeared, holding out a cold beer with a smile on her face. Astonishment washed over me as I accepted the beer with a grateful smile, muttering my thanks. With a gentle nod, she continued on her enchanting path, finding her place on the slab once more. Eagerly, I took a sip of the beer, feeling its coolness quench my thirst, and raised my bottle in a gesture of appreciation towards L. She reciprocated, raising her glass with a mischievous smile. Whoever or whatever force had presented me with this angelic being, L, I could never thank them enough. But was she truly an angel? Only time would reveal the truth.

As the wine continued to work its magic, the animated conversations around me grew more passionate. Finally, after arriving at this gathering, I felt a sense of relaxation wash over me, allowing me to fully embrace and enjoy the moment. L, perched on her slab like a contented kitty cat, observed my every move. I must admit, I relished in the attention she bestowed upon me. Her behavior hinted at a privileged upbringing, making me feel a sense of importance. At that particular point in my life, plagued by low self-esteem, this attention was a balm for my soul.

I had a neat braai trick. I carefully clamped and arranged the "boerewors," a deliciously spiced braai sausage, onto the braai grid. With a leap, I landed on the slab beside the enclosure, placing the grid on top of the chimney. The heat from the glowing coals and the wafting aroma of smoked meat cooked the sausage to sizzling perfection. This was my go-to trick to impress those who hadn't seen it before, including L. As I descended, our eyes briefly locked, and I caught a subtle wink and playful pout from her. It sent a wave of fluttering butterflies through my stomach.

From that moment on, I strutted around the braai like a proud rooster, putting on a captivating show. But only L seemed to notice. The others were engrossed in a debate about a financial issue, a topic close to my mother's heart.

It was then that something peculiar happened, causing my mind to wander. L joined me, her glossy green eyes reflecting the flickering light from the fireplace, casting an enchanting spell over her flawless face. She exuded an angelic scent, and I couldn't help but yearn to stand close to her. It was an unfamiliar sensation. Simply being in her presence was enough, without the need for physical contact or conversation. And then she uttered those words, "Kan ek jou help met iets, Uiltjie?" I couldn't believe my ears. In English, it meant, "Can I help you with something, Uiltjie?"

Uiltjie was a nickname coined by my mother's boyfriend, a term of endearment for me. It referred to my wide, observant eyes, resembling those of an owl. Personally, I attributed it to my anxiety disorder, but it had become a part of who I am. Among my mother's various boyfriends, he was the one who stood out the most, not just because of his wealth but also because of his genuine kindness.

What struck me as strange about L calling me Uiltjie was where she had heard it. None of the other girls present recognized me; I was a complete stranger to them. They had no idea I existed until this moment. Did she simply make it up? This is why I believe that life presents miracles at the right time. And there have been numerous occasions where similar peculiar things have happened to me.

And it was the first and only time she ever called me by that name. I could hear the playfulness in her voice, like she was teasing me, testing my reaction.

In any case, I left it there and declined her offer, saying I was fine. But as we stood together, I noticed the warmth of her presence, and because I am a good listener, she shared many a happy, and sad, story with me. The sound of her voice, so angelic and soothing, filled the air around us, creating a melody that resonated in my heart. And as I stood there, I couldn't help but inhale deeply, savoring her intoxicating scent that lingered in the air.

Even now, when I close my eyes and concentrate hard, I can still recall that scent, a mix of floral notes and warmth. But I quickly shake myself out of it, because when I do, I see her smile, the sparkle in her eyes, and hear the contagious melody of her laughter.

Don't we all have someone we left behind, a lingering presence in our thoughts? We might have had a compelling motive behind our decision.

To uncover the truth, be sure to accompany me on the forthcoming chapter of my tale. Until then, thank you for reading, and I hope to see you again soon.

Chapter Five

Once again, the universe was on my side, albeit briefly. I soon landed a job at a leading insurance company. Unlike today, IT skills were high in demand during the early 1990s. Just like my time in the government, my job was to convert the manual systems, field representative's used, into a computerized system.

However, my jubilation was quickly cut short when I showed up for work on my first day. To my surprise, it turned out that my manager was none other than a familiar face from my days in the commune in my previous town. There was something about him that sent a shiver down my spine. You know those detail-oriented people who go the extra mile to iron every single item in their wardrobe, including their socks.

That kind of guy, with his perma-neat hairstyle. They somehow always look like they have just stepped out of the shower. And smell like it took. It seems my intuition served me well. His dad turned out to be a director at the firm we worked for. Little did we know, he slyly hid his wedding ring, hoping to entice unsuspecting mistresses who were eager to advance their careers. Karma eventually caught up with him, but I will spare you the details.

And so, my days were filled with the never-ending cycle of work, from morning till night. Yet, for some strange reason, I always felt rejuvenated when I returned home. To my mother's house, where I still lived, for now. You see, L was one of the boarders, and she keenly awaited my arrival. Every night.

To test her *devotion*, I devised a cunning plan. A detour. One night, instead of going back home after work, I made a spontaneous decision to visit the renowned pub in this unique Boer Maffia town. The place was filled with men, some immersed in intense conversations about divorce, while others wore the weariness of recent separation.

As I entered the pub, the dim lighting cast a gloomy atmosphere, revealing worn-out wooden tables and chairs that creaked with every movement. The air was heavy with the smell of stale beer and cigarette smoke, mingling together to create an unpleasant scent that clung to my clothes. The low murmur of conversation filled the room, occasionally interrupted by bursts of laughter or the clinking of glasses.

All eyes turned towards me as I crossed the threshold, a sudden silence descending upon the patrons. I felt their gazes like a weight upon my shoulders, making me feel like an intruder in this close-knit community. Determined not to back down, I made my way to the bar and ordered a beer, the bartender's worn hands expertly grabbing a frosted glass from the fridge.

Seeking solace from the prying eyes, I retreated to a secluded corner, the worn leather of the seat creaking as I settled in. From this hidden vantage point, I could overhear the conversations of the older men, their voices filled with bitterness and resentment towards their wives. They swapped stories of failed marriages and discussed cunning strategies for divorce, their words laced with frustration and anger.

In this shithole of a pub, I couldn't help but feel a sense of unease. The sights, sounds, and conversations around me only reinforced my decision to test L's loyalty.

Without a second thought, I gulped down the cold beer, feeling its refreshing bitterness slide down my throat. Urgency propelled me out of the pub, my feet pounding against the pavement, carrying me as swiftly as they could. In Afrikaans culture, there's a saying that rings true: "Slim vang sy baas." It's a simple phrase, yet it carries a powerful punch. In simple terms, it warns that if you devise a cunning or sneaky plan, it will inevitably come back to bite you in the arse. Needless to say, I never set foot in that pub again.

However, my plan had worked surprisingly. As I returned home, the sight of an empty house greeted me, except for L. She had taken the initiative to order takeout, the tantalizing aroma wafting through the air enticing my senses. To my surprise, she had ordered two portions, ensuring that we each had our own.

Yet, her act of kindness came at a small price. Unlike the other boarders residing in my mother's house, L was the only one pursuing a career in teaching. This meant she had to spend long hours in front of her sleek computer, diligently working on her assignments. She was completely clueless when it came to operating the device without assistance. And so, that night, I became her chosen guide.

As I settled into the chair before the computer, I could feel its cool surface against my palms. L sat snug by my side, her gentle touch providing a comforting warmth. With every movement of the mouse, she would playfully utter suggestive phrases like "hey, be careful with my mouse" or "You can play with my mouse." And, with a mischievous twinkle in her eye, she would whisper, "Yes, please, touch my mouse." The warning signs were undeniable, yet I foolishly chose to ignore them. Little did I know, I was becoming putty in her hands, a puppet she was molding according to her desires.

In my defense, the work I aided her with yielded exceptional grades. In turn, she began testing my devotion towards her, playing games to gauge my commitment. Some evenings, I would return home to find her absent, only to hear her familiar footsteps in the early hours of the morning. I shamelessly admit I would stay awake, eagerly anticipating her return. It was her intoxicating scent and magnetic presence that had me hooked, unable to resist her allure.

Things were getting serious between us. We often found clever ways to spend time alone, escaping the prying, piercing gazes of the other boarders. Now, let me explain in more detail why I held negative views towards Christians or devout believers. To this day, I have never chosen to convert, and this is the reason why.

When I was young, my mother went through various religious phases, exploring different spiritual beliefs. As a young child, I had to endure long hours inside a church. And I am talking about these churches that exude charisma and charm.

In these charismatic churches, people embraced each other tightly, their arms squeezing and their lips pressing against cheeks in an overwhelming display of affection. I playfully nicknamed these individuals "Happy Clappies," as their constant, forced smiles never seemed to fade. As an introvert, I felt suffocated by their touch, longing for solitude and space to breathe.

But amidst the seemingly devout gatherings, I couldn't help but notice the ulterior motives behind my mother's religious fervor. With each new church she joined, she found herself entangled with a new man or receiving a financial windfall. The men would arrive at our doorstep, their footsteps echoing in the hallway as they disappeared into my mother's bedroom. And soon enough, their attention turned towards me.

During my bath times, one of these men would perch on the edge of the tub. His eyes fixated on me as he directed me into awkward and uncomfortable poses. Another took pleasure in scrubbing my body vigorously, claiming that he was cleansing me of the stains of sin. It was a disturbing experience, their eyes gleaming with a twisted desire as they invaded my privacy.

Throughout these brief encounters, I couldn't help but wonder where my mother was. Did she turn a blind eye to their actions, choosing to ignore the violation of her own child? The thoughts that swirl in my mind are too dark to share.

I truly hope that you now understood my reluctance to convert or "give my heart to Jesus," as so many had urged me to do. The reason behind it was simple—L and I couldn't progress further in our physical intimacy. We had reached a point where we engaged in fondling and shared passionate kisses, but it never went beyond that. The barrier between us was my lack of faith in Christianity.

However, L always had a plan, as she often did. One night, I returned home with anticipation, eager to see her. I entered the house carrying a six-pack of beer, whistling a cheerful tune. The sight of L always stirred a flurry of butterflies in my stomach. As I crossed the threshold, I felt like luck was on my side. The house was enveloped in darkness, except for the flickering candlelights emanating from the living room. Soft, blissful music floated through the air, filling the entire space. The enchanting atmosphere almost compelled me to shed all my clothes in that very moment. Luckily, I resisted the impulse.

L, the heavenly creature, emerged before me, her ethereal beauty enhanced by the glow of a white robe that draped gracefully around her. Her feet, adorned only by the touch of cool air, glided effortlessly across the room, accompanied by the soft jingle of a golden ankle bracelet. The familiar sight sent a shiver of anticipation down my spine.

As she delicately took hold of my hand, I could almost feel her touch resonating through my veins, my heart pounding so loudly that I was certain she could hear its rhythmic beats against my ribcage. I couldn't help but notice the way my pants clung tightly to my waist, betraying the excitement that pulsed within me.

But alas, my eagerness would prove to be my downfall once again. Standing at the center of the room were the other boarders, their eyes gleaming with an unsettling intensity fixed upon me. L guided me towards them, her presence guiding my every step, and requested that I kneel before them.

It was in that moment that they revealed the news they had received from the one they prayed to. The time had come for me to convert, to "give my heart to Jesus," as they reminded me with a curt tone. However, before I obliged, I quickly darted into the kitchen, snatching a cold beer in haste. I knew all too well where this was headed. L had cleverly devised this plan, using her Christian faith as a pretext to create intimate moments between us. But there was a catch —I had to become a Christian first.

Returning to the living room with the chilled bottle in my hand, my anticipation grew exponentially. I kneeled down, bowing my head, as their hands ventured beyond the boundaries of a simple blessing. I could feel their touch exploring more than just my shoulders and head, their prayers murmuring softly, seeking redemption for my tainted soul. The air filled with the mysterious chorus of glossolalia, unintelligible sounds that held an air of mystique. Yet, all I longed for was to hear the simple word, "Amen." And finally, it came, as if on cue.

My eyes snapped open, and I forced a wide grin upon my face, pretending to be overcome with emotion. It seemed my act had succeeded, as their hands met their cheeks in unison, their expressions resembling the awe of a child encountering a playful puppy.

And thus, dear reader, the tale of the significant moment that brought about my conversion comes to a close. As I stood amidst the hallowed halls of the living room, the soft glow of candlelight danced upon the intricately painted walls, casting vibrant hues across the sacred space. The hushed whispers filled the air, their melodic strains creating a solemn beauty that seemed to echo through my being. In that moment, I questioned the purity of my intentions, wondering if perhaps there were hidden motives guiding my path. But fear not, for the next chapter shall reveal the truth, as my beloved L and I embark on the blissful honeymoon phase of our newfound Christian relationship.

Chapter Six

Even though L and I were now both Christians, we kept our relationship a secret from the other boarders in my mother's home. The tension between us was palpable, and I could sense her yearning for my affections. I longed to reach out and touch her, to feel the warmth of her skin against mine, and to taste the sweetness of her lips. But societal norms forbade it, as we were not married. Despite her clever plan to create more intimate moments between us, I refused to succumb to her trap and marry her solely for my own desires. However, fate seemed to be on my side.

As the long summer varsity break approached, all the other boarders left to return to their faraway homes. Only L had told her parents that she needed some time for herself. With my job, I could only join her for a long weekend. But it turned out to be worth it.

Early in the morning, we gathered our meager belongings and set off. The keys to her car were pressed into my hand, a symbol of her affection and trust. I settled into the plush driving seat, feeling the soft leather against my skin like a warm hug, and our passionate kiss conveyed the depth of our longing.

Her rebellious nature revealed itself as we parked in the driveway of their lavish beach house, nestled in a town synonymous with opulence and whale watching. It was at that moment that I pondered why someone like her, raised in wealth, would choose to become a teacher. The puzzle of her decision perplexed me. The world was her oyster, and yet she sought fulfillment in guiding young minds.

The thought of being alone with her in such a grandiose home ignited desires within me I had never experienced before. Needless to say, we did not waste much time on meals during the long weekend.

The memories of those moments linger vividly in my mind, like a permanent imprint. We sat on the balcony overlooking the vast expanse of the azure ocean, while the gentle sea breeze tousled our hair and the salty air tickled our tongues. Our tongues, stained with the lingering taste of red wine, yearned for more fervent kisses.

As the full moon ascended into the night sky, one thing led to another, and the moment I had been longing for finally arrived. My reward lay before me, naked on the expanse of the king-sized bed. Under the soft glow of the moon, her skin shimmered like silk, casting a mesmerizing aura.

Oh, the anticipation overwhelmed me, causing my hands to tremble and my legs to feel like cooked spaghetti. My heart raced so fast that it threatened to burst from my chest. Sensing my overwhelming surprise, she offered me a delicate smile and beckoned me closer.

As I approached her, the intensity of my emotions manifested in every fiber of my being. The adrenaline coursing through my veins heightened my senses, making the soft touch of her fingertips against my skin electrifying. My breath became shallow, as if each inhalation was a desperate attempt to capture the essence of this moment and etch it into my memory forever.

Her eyes, filled with desire and vulnerability, held me captive. The weight of her trust weighed upon me, making my palms moist with anticipation. The trembling of my hands intensified, a physical manifestation of the overwhelming emotions swirling within me.

With a mix of nervousness and excitement, I reached out to caress her cheek, tracing the contours of her face with trembling fingers. The touch of her skin against mine sent shivers down my spine, igniting a fire that consumed my every thought. I could feel the warmth of her body radiating, drawing me closer, urging me to surrender to the raw passion that enveloped us.

As our bodies intertwined, the sensation of her soft curves against mine sent waves of pleasure cascading through me. The intensity of our connection transcended the physical realm, and in that moment, time ceased to exist. Every touch, every kiss, was an affirmation of our shared longing, a testament to the depth of our connection.

Lost in a whirlwind of desire, we surrendered ourselves to the intoxicating dance of passion. The room became a sanctuary where only our shared ecstasy mattered. In that moment, the world outside ceased to exist, and all that mattered was the symphony of our bodies moving in perfect harmony.

Under the moonlit glow, our souls intertwined, enveloped in a symphony of pleasure and vulnerability. The night became a canvas upon which our desires painted an indelible masterpiece, forever etched in the depths of our souls.

As we basked in the afterglow, our bodies entangled and our hearts intertwined, a sense of profound contentment washed over me. In that moment, I realized that love, passion, and connection could transform even the grandest of homes into a sanctuary of bliss.

It was a significant moment for me—the first time I looked into a girl's eyes during an intimate moment and didn't see the haunting image of my traumatizing family member. My sexuality posed no internal conflicts for me; I was entirely at peace with it.

It could be that because it was her first time, she had a sense of uncertainty, not knowing what to expect. But, I had nailed it. I could feel the burdens of my childhood traumatic experience slowly dissipating, allowing me to finally feel free. Despite the odds, we managed to make it work flawlessly.

Our exposed bodies became our playground, an exploration of our shared desires. The soft glow of candlelight danced on our bare skin, casting flickering shadows on the walls. The scent of expensive wine filled the air, mingling with the musky aroma of our passion. We hardly ate, too consumed by our hunger for each other.

As our bodies intertwined, a symphony of moans and whispers filled the room, a symphony only we could compose. Our fingertips traced delicate patterns across each other's flesh, igniting a fire that burned deep within. The touch of her lips against my neck sent shivers down my spine, electrifying every nerve ending.

If my memory serves me correctly, the only sounds that filled the air over that weekend were the soft whispers of intimate confirmations. The silence spoke volumes, as our bodies communicated in a language only lovers understand.

There are no words that can describe what it was like, but I can tell you this: it was pure bliss. I was her man, and she was my lady, bound together in a love that knew no bounds. I treated her with utmost respect, as if she were a princess, and in return, she transformed into a daring and adventurous spirit. If the chandeliers were lower, we would have swung from them like Tarzan and Jane, playfully exploring every nook and cranny.

However, as the saying goes, all good things must come to a close. The blissful long weekend, which seemed to pass by in a blink of an eye, suddenly came to a jarring halt. With a heavy heart, I gathered my belongings and dragged my feet towards the car, each step filled with a sense of reluctance. There was an inexplicable sense of finality hanging in the air, as if it marked the end between L and me. The faint scent of uncertainty lingered, mingling with the bittersweet taste of our farewell kiss. It was a moment filled with anguish and sorrow. The bus ride back home felt like a hazy dream as my mind wrestled with unanswered questions. And then, amidst the turmoil, a realization struck me—she had used me as a means to fulfill her desires. She had cunningly manipulated me into converting to Christianity, absolving herself of any guilt for our intimate moments. I had always made it clear that marriage was not on my immediate agenda, but the abruptness of our parting left me stunned. It became painfully clear that I was nothing more than her conquest, her challenge. The pain seared through me, leaving me utterly wounded.

As I sat on the bus, staring out the window at the passing scenery, my body felt weak and drained. Fatigue washed over me, as if every ounce of energy had been sapped from my being. My limbs felt heavy and sluggish, as if they were encased in lead, making even the smallest movements a struggle.

The pain I felt was not just emotional, but physical as well. It was as if my heart had been torn apart, leaving behind jagged edges that cut with every beat. Waves of anguish coursed through my veins, causing my body to tremble involuntarily. Tears welled up in my eyes, blurring my vision and leaving a constant burning sensation behind. I was no stranger to the pain of rejection.

As the bus carried me closer to home, the rumbling engine filled the air with a steady hum. I clung to the hope that by the time I see her again, things would have changed. But my shock intensified as I stepped off the bus. Everyone beside me knew that L had moved out and left. Bathed in the golden glow of the setting sun, her empty room echoed with emptiness, awaiting its next tenant.

I packed my belongings, feeling the weight of them digging into my shoulders, and set off on my journey. Eventually, I found a small room in a commune in a different town. Like all the times before, I could not face my demons head on. It seemed like I was not the only one with scars left by the intimate weekend. When my strength returned, I went on a search for L.

I learned that she had given up her studies, rejected her faith, and strayed from the comfortable path of Christianity. However, I was not about to give up on the one I loved or had once loved. I traced the breadcrumbs she had left, each step filled with anticipation and apprehension, and walked through the doors of a notorious club in Cape Town, called "Playground" for good reasons.

The pounding bass reverberated through the walls, vibrating in my chest, as the dim lighting cast shadows that danced across the faces of the patrons. I searched every nook and cranny until the early hours of the morning, determined to be sober when we reunited. Reluctantly, I sank into a corner, defeated. Just moments later, I felt a light tap on my shoulder, sending a shiver down my spine. Annoyed, I waved my hand to dismiss the girl. But then I looked and looked again, trying to make sense of what I was seeing.

L's transformation into a goth was evident in her all-black attire and the skull pendant hanging from her neck. The innocent L I had known, always dressed in brilliant white, was now decked out in entirely black, matching her hair, eyeshadow, and lip color. A mix of emotions welled up within me as conflicting scents of lavender and leather wafted through the air. I leaped up and embraced her, feeling the warmth of her body against mine. And then everything became clear.

She introduced me to her new lover, a gothic girl with dark, dramatic makeup and an aura of mystery. The sound of their laughter, filled with joy and affection, mingled with the pulsating beat of the music. They seemed to be madly in love. I pleaded with her, desperately longing for some solitude, but she assured me that she had no intentions of hiding anything from her new partner. We found a quiet corner inside the club, the plush bean bags molding to our bodies, and settled in.

I begged her for answers, my voice filled with a mixture of desperation and confusion. And she decided it was time to confess her secret. It came to light that my own mother was the mastermind behind everything L and I had shared. I felt utterly helpless and rejected. The taste of bitterness filled my mouth as I struggled to comprehend her betrayal. L, being a Christian at the time, knew of my mother's expertise in the field of psychology. Seeking guidance, she turned to my mother, hoping for advice on navigating her doubts about her own sexuality. And then she followed through with my mother's advice, and I became the unfortunate target of her actions.

Suddenly, my mind lit up like a switch had been flipped, illuminating the hidden truth lurking in the shadows. It finally clicked in my mind why she had called me "Uiltjie" earlier—a nickname that only my mother's boyfriend at the time used for me. My mother now despised the man with an intense, burning hatred. The weight of betrayal settled upon my shoulders, the room suddenly feeling smaller, suffocating.

It was a crushing pain, throbbing and searing through my chest, as I discovered that I had been nothing more than a pawn in a twisted game orchestrated by two heartless individuals. But what cut even deeper was the realization that I had allowed myself to lower my defenses. I had grown well-acquainted with my mother's deceptive tactics, and yet I had foolishly let my guard slip. The extent to which she would go to inflict harm upon me was nothing short of shocking.

Seeking revenge was not a principle I held dear, so I chose to release the anger and resentment that brewed within me. Confronting my mother was an impossibility, as she would vehemently deny any accusations thrown her way, even in the face of solid evidence.

Though I have a vague understanding of why my mother harbors such deep animosity towards me, that revelation must wait for another time. For now, my weary fingers crave respite, and I yearn for the refreshing touch of an ice-cold beer. Thank you once again for lending an ear to my story. Until our paths cross again, farewell, but only for now.

Chapter Seven

Just like the sharp pain that shoots through your tongue when you accidentally bite it while eating, life can deliver similar blows. In the midst of my work, I sought solace by drowning my sorrows in empty bars at night. It was my way of avoiding the cruel demon of rejection, refusing to confront it head-on. At this point, it felt like this demon followed me everywhere, silently targeting someone who never seemed to learn from his mistakes. And the weight of my other baggage grew heavier with each negative experience.

Desperation has a way of clinging to you like a contagious disease. It seeps into your pores, emanating a scent that others can detect, an experience that they can sense. Just like the desperation that arises when you lose your job and desperately search for a new one, the same desperation arises after a breakup, as you frantically seek a companion to numb the pain. But acts of desperation come with their own consequences, their own punishments. They lead us to make terrible decisions, and I was on the verge of repeating that pattern once again.

Part of my job involved visiting general practitioners to gather their data, which insurance companies used for their own gain. However, the doctors were always too preoccupied with their patients, barely sparing a moment to input the information. This left me at the mercy of their helpless assistants, who simply pointed at the files.

On this particular day, however, I found myself in the waiting room of a respected family practitioner in the small town where my mother still resided.

As it turned out, the regular secretary was on maternity leave, and a temporary substitute had taken her place. It was a clear case of nepotism. The petite blondie, with her sparkling blue eyes, surprisingly proved to be helpful. Little did I know, she had an ulterior motive. With my desperation lingering in the air, I became an easy target for her. She used her close proximity to her advantage, intoxicating me with her presence. I was amazed when she swiftly provided me with all the data I needed, her infectious giggle filling the air, and her subtle gestures conveying her eagerness to assist. To avoid confusion, we'll use the name D to refer to her in this story.

As I hurried back to the bustling office, the receptionist lady handed me a folded note. My eyes widened with surprise as I unfolded it, revealing the hastily scrawled name of D.

My heart skipped a beat as I realized I must have forgotten something important at their office. In those days, before cellphones became commonplace, we relied on handwritten notes and landlines. I picked up the old-fashioned handset and dialed the number written on the note. As the dial tone hummed in my ear, I anxiously waited for a response. Finally, her voice, soft and melodious, echoed through the receiver, causing a flutter of excitement and nervousness in my stomach.

It so happened that she still lived with her mother, and she extended a kind invitation for me to join them for dinner that very evening. Memories of past encounters with girlfriends' mothers flooded my mind as I recalled my unfortunate ability to unintentionally mess things up. I had an uncanny talent for creating awkward situations, leaving a trail of unfortunate mishaps in my wake. Let me briefly digress to explain, as this is where my analogy of biting your tongue comes into play.

Being a teenager in the vibrant eighties meant that masculinity was celebrated and emulated. It was the era of John Travolta, "Footloose," and countless shows featuring men with slicked-back hairstyles. At that stage in my life, I was fortunate enough to have a super-cool girlfriend named Y. She was the epitome of cuteness, and she enjoyed when I surprised her with gestures of affection. But let's leave it at that for now. One fateful afternoon, my friend asked me to accompany him to the local clinic to purchase a pack of condoms, as he had plans for an unforgettable night. In those days, there were no convenient vending machines; one had to visit the family health clinic.

We parked our bikes on the crowded sidewalk. With combs in hand, we meticulously styled our hair, striving for the perfect slicked-back look. Nervously, I opted to let my friend do the talking, as I was a bit shy in such situations. Unfazed by our mission, he boldly boasted about his exciting plans to the nurse-like lady behind the counter, her maroon epaulettes adding a touch of authority to her appearance. She scribbled down our details and proceeded to give us a thorough lecture on sex education. In our youthful pride, we pretended to know everything there was to know about the topic, emphasizing that we had only come for the condoms. Satisfied with our transaction, we bid the nurse farewell and went our separate ways.

Fast forward to the following Friday, when my girlfriend invited me to her house for a special dinner. And who should walk through the door? You guessed it, the very same nurse-like lady with the maroon epaulettes. She recognized me instantly and shooed me away, her disapproval evident in her stern gaze. From that moment on, I was forbidden from seeing her daughter again. It was a stroke of pure bad luck, but such is life. Little did she know that her daughter and I continued to meet secretly at a hidden spot in school, where we shared stolen moments and kissed until our lips turned blue.

Back to the present. As I was lost in my thoughts, D had to call out my name, snapping me back to reality. Reluctantly, I agreed to her dinner invitation, my anticipation building for her mother's reaction. Being a stray bachelor, I looked forward to a home-cooked meal, something my own mother had never treated me to.

I meticulously shaved and put on my most respectable attire, omitting a tie. Arriving early, I aimed to make a lasting impression. In one hand, I cradled a vibrant bouquet of wildflowers, avoiding the cliché of roses, and in the other, an expensive bottle of red wine.

Just in time, D rushed to the door, swinging it open with excitement, and greeted me with a mischievous smile. "Hello, D," I said, causing her to respond with a mischievous giggle. But to my surprise, she exclaimed, "No, I am C." Utter confusion furrowed my brow until it hit me. They were identical twins. My smile widened, and I instinctively hid the bouquet behind my back.

"Come in," C said. "D is taking a shower." It made sense since I had arrived early, and I felt flattered that such a fine lady was putting effort into looking her best for me. C led me to the living room, where I met their mother and their mischievous, ill-mannered brother.

My plan worked. I presented the bottle of wine and bouquet to the lady of the house, who was taken aback at the sight. She quickly extinguished her cigarette, snatched the gifts from my hands, and hurried to the kitchen. What surprised me even more was that everyone already knew my name before I even had a chance to introduce myself. It was hard to believe that someone as beautiful as D had taken a liking to me so quickly. And as if realizing I was parched, she kindly handed me a cold beer before dinner. Just like the sting of biting your tongue, I couldn't help but feel a strange sense of relief in that moment, knowing that the timing had gone awry, even if only temporarily.

As the dinner progressed, my gaze frequently wandered, captivated by the striking resemblance between C and D. If D's short blonde hair wasn't slightly darker from being wet after her shower, I wouldn't have been able to distinguish between them. Before they sneezed from the pepper, even their noses twitched in unison, reacting to the pungent aroma. With their ice-blue eyes locked in concentration, they even chewed their food in the same synchronized rhythm. I couldn't help but wonder why the person responsible for styling their hair hadn't chosen a unique look for one of them. It was like witnessing a mirrored image, a duplicate soul living in two separate bodies. My brain struggled to comprehend this uncanny duplication, yearning for the distinctiveness it craved.

I won't divulge the naughty thoughts that crossed my mind, but I can admit to feeling perplexed. It was nearly impossible to tell them apart. According to their mother, the secret lay in the tones of their voices. However, for me, it was a completely new experience that would take time to comprehend. I sat in silence, captivated by the symphony of their voices and analyzing the subtle nuances in their tones.

But soon enough, I realized that winning over their protective brother was my realistic goal. At that point, I believed he was merely protective, but little did I know, he guarded a long-kept secret that I will delve into later.

And to my surprise, they turned out to enjoy my company too. Since I was a newcomer in town, there was little they could use against me. The air was filled with a sense of anticipation and curiosity. It was truly astonishing to me that a family as kind and loving as theirs had so few friends.

Back in the living room, their mom quickly shared the secret. Despite being married, she had an affair that eventually became public knowledge, tarnishing their reputation within the tight-knit Boer Maffia community. The silence in the room was deafening as their story unfolded, and I could feel the weight of their pain. The scent of freshly brewed coffee lingered in the air, providing a comforting backdrop to their vulnerability.

It comforted me to know that her kids chose to side with her, affirming their loyalty to their mother rather than their father, who was the apparent victim of the scandal. The tension in the room was palpable, like a tightly wound coil ready to spring. I listened to their stories intently, choosing to share as few details about myself as possible. Little did I know that this loving family would become an integral part of my life, filling my heart with warmth. However, once again, I made a grave error, a decision that continues to haunt me today.

But I will save the details about that for my next installment. Right now, my exhausted fingers crave the sensation of an ice-cold beer against their tips. The sound of a bottle cap popping open would be a welcome distraction. Until then, goodbye, but only for now.

Chapter Eight

C and D's mother worked as a successful real estate agent, her expertise evident in their opulent home. The sprawling residence boasted an enclosed swimming pool, surrounded by vibrant greenery. An inviting outdoor Lapa beckoned for barbecues, the sizzling sound of meat filling the air. A charming cottage, where D resided, stood as a testament to her independence, a haven amidst the turmoil of the Boer Maffia-infested town. Both twins diligently pursued their studies, while D ambitiously took on part-time secretarial jobs, determined to gain valuable experience. Their brother K, though lacking self-motivation, tirelessly strived to complete high school, defying the odds stacked against him.

I quickly grew enamored with this extraordinary family. Had I crossed paths with them in a public setting, their remarkable circumstances would have remained hidden. But life is about seizing opportunities, and I was grateful that I took a chance on them, allowing our bond to deepen. And the same held true for them. Unexpectedly, it transpired that the same blood coursing through their veins flowed within me as well. A strong Scottish heritage intertwined with a deep fondness for English people, a peculiar sight in this Boer Maffia-infested town.

What endeared me further was that my newfound friends kept me away from the raucous pubs, at least for one evening each week. I became a familiar face at their dinner table, always arriving with offerings of wine, beer, and eventually a box of rich, velvety dark chocolate for D. However, I found myself in a precarious position. My heart fluttered whenever my gaze met D's, but her sister also elicited the same sensation, for they were mirror images of each other. I had yet to discern the subtle nuances that set them apart, such as the distinctive tones in their voices. Then, I realized. It was in their laughter. C possessed a deeper, resonant chuckle, akin to a Contralto, while D's laughter floated like a crystalline soprano. It was a breakthrough, albeit a peculiar one. If it meant making them laugh to distinguish between them, so be it.

As time passed, I made a deliberate effort to drive by their exquisite home during my work obligations. With a gentle knock on the door, C would graciously greet me, allowing me to leave a small token of affection for D. Whether it was a decadent piece of chocolate, a delicate flower, or a refreshing cold drink, I wanted to provide her with sustenance for her devoted studies. Though I always believed I had left the gift with C, it could have easily been D who opened the door. Yet, their infectious giggles, though not as distinctive as their laughter, echoed with joy and mirth, solidifying the bond we shared.

I was overjoyed that the force had brought us together, though uncertainty lingered in my mind. Was it the dark force or the light force? Based on my past encounters, I assumed it to be the dark force, as the light force had never made itself known to me. It was during this time that the pranks began, starting off harmless but with the potential to turn deadly.

The town we found ourselves in was infested with the Boer Maffia, and the scorching summer heat was unlike anything I had experienced before. Whenever I knocked on the door to leave a gift, D would graciously invite me inside for a refreshing cool drink and a quick swim. Stripping down to only my boxers, I would dive into the invigorating water, relishing its rejuvenating touch. And I must admit, D looked absolutely stunning in her swimsuit, accentuating her curves in all the right places. She was the personification of beauty, turning heads wherever she went.

We would playfully splash around in the water, our laughter filling the air. In those moments, D would let out a mischievous giggle, inadvertently giving herself away. "C!" I would exclaim, laughing wholeheartedly. "You sneaky little troublemaker. You fooled me once again." It turned out that all along, it was C that I was having fun with, laughing and joking together.

With her signature disarming smile, she would wipe the water from her eyes and gather her hair into a ponytail, exuding an irresistible charm. "It's just innocent fun," she would remark, climbing out of the pool with deliberate movements, granting me a captivating view of her alluring backside. During these times, their mother would be at work, her brother at school, and D herself working as a temp.

I later made a point to ask D to inform me when she wouldn't be at home. C, on the other hand, was the mischievous one, driven by her own motives, though I couldn't help but speculate about them.

As a young man, I possessed the skill of barbecuing. Over the weekends, their mother would purchase the meat and beers for me, while also preparing the most heavenly potato salad imaginable. I would take charge of grilling the meat over the blazing hot coals. And all the while, my eyes would feast upon D and C, frolicking in the swimming pool, radiating pure hotness.

During those fleeting moments, I couldn't help but notice a recurring sequence of events. As they emerged from the glistening pool, droplets cascading off their bodies, they lured me into their world of merriment. With mischievous grins, they beckoned me to join their playful escapades. D had a peculiar fondness for perching atop my shoulders, her weight pressing against me as I propelled myself upward, launching her into the ethereal expanse, her body pirouetting through the air with effortless grace.

Captivated by our frolics, C eagerly yearned to partake in the joviality. And then, it struck me like a bolt of lightning. Each time I exhibited the slightest hint of affection towards C, innocent gestures, really. Their brother's face contorted with an envious flush, his rage coiling within him like a venomous serpent.

His aggression sent shivers down my spine, instilling a genuine fear within me. Now, dear mortal reader, whatever conclusions you may have drawn, I can assure you, you are undoubtedly correct. Bravo for perceiving the truth concealed within these lines. Much, much later in my life, I unearthed the unsettling reality, and even now, it churns my stomach with a sickening dread. But please, stay with me a little longer, if you can bear it.

Before I eventually made a dreadful mistake, let me introduce yet another poor decision I made. For the first time after my breakup with

L, I felt like the universe was rewarding my pain with something good. And of course, the well always dried up. The upcoming Monday loomed ahead, reminding me of the business trip I had to take to a remote location. The company handed me the keys to a sleek BMW, its polished exterior shimmering in the sunlight. They were not concerned about my safety, but rather about impressing their clients, the doctors.

And so, I had in my position a fancy car and a striking girlfriend with a radiant personality. It was clear that my lack of knowledge made me appear ignorant.

I decided to proudly display them, as if they were my prized possessions, to none other than my mother. Besides, it had been over two years since I had last seen her.

With my stunning companion by my side, the drive seemed to fly by in an instant. I parked where I found an available space and slowly climbed out. You see, with my mother's house in a cul-de-sac, it meant that everyone visiting thought they could park anywhere they pleased, causing chaos. My keen eyes darted around and landed on the adjacent neighbor's kitchen blinds lifting with the nosy lady peering through the windows. And from the opposite side of the road, the elderly neighbor decided it was time to work in the garden, at four o'clock on a Sunday afternoon. Sneaky pervert.

At that stage, I was not sure what it was that made my mother emerge. Perhaps driven by curiosity, she caught sight of the extravagant car and imagined a wealthy man arriving with a bouquet of flowers and a suitcase filled with money. I have never witnessed a man graciously handing her a bouquet of flowers. In addition to other things, they gave her a sly wink.

Beside my girlfriend, I stood, basking in the smoldering glare of my mother's envy. Using her characteristic wrist flick, she invited us to enter her home. You know, that subtle gesture that silently signals, "hurry inside before the Boer Maffia catches sight of you."

With a smile and a nod, I took the lead, guiding D into the belly of the beast. The corridor stretched out before us, its walls lined with family portraits, a constant reminder of my absence from the collection.

The sunroom was bathed in warm, golden light streaming through the sheer curtains. As we entered the sunroom, the plush carpet cushioned our steps, muffling any sound. My mother's armchair stood tall and regal, its soft cushions inviting but also commanding respect.

My mother sank into her armchair with a sense of comfort and self-assurance. I always referred to the armchair as her shrine, a place where she would recline and demand adoration, her signature smirk never leaving her face. With a graceful flick of her wrists, she gestured towards the array of coffee, milk, sugar, and honey, as if conducting a symphony. This gesture was all too familiar to me—it signaled that I had to assume the role of her servant as punishment for abandoning her. My brother, too, exhibited the same habits. D stood there frozen, her eyes filled with an overwhelming sense of disbelief.

"Once again, the Prodigal Son returns," my mom exclaimed, her tone laced with venom. "And who do we have here?" she asked, swiftly shifting the conversation, catching D off guard. Her gaze fixed on D with a cold intensity, her eyes sharp and penetrating like those of a venomous serpent.

Standing her ground, D simply stated her name, her voice firm and unwavering. The room was filled with the sound of my mother's sharp intake of breath, the silence that followed thick with tension.

I busied myself with the task at hand, the clinking of cups and saucers as I prepared her majesty's coffee. Each movement felt heavy, as if carrying the weight of her expectations. She helped herself to the steaming brew, a small gesture that held a sense of entitlement. With a graceful wave of her hand, she gestured for me to return to my post, to standby.

Her highness, my mother, introduced herself to D, adopting a new Jewish variant of her name that added a touch of theatricality. D gave me a quizzical look, her eyes searching for answers. I simply shrugged, a wordless admission of my confusion.

"Isn't he just like his father, who loved pretty girls and fast cars?" My mother's voice carried a hint of playfulness, her words dripping with innuendo as she sipped her brew.

D's response was nonchalant, her tone betraying a hint of amusement. In that moment, I felt an overwhelming desire to embrace her, to kiss away the tension that hung in the air.

Apologies for interrupting, but this was one thing I could never understand about my mother. On one hand, she held a deep dislike for me, a constant reminder of my father and his genes. And on the other hand, she despised anyone I introduced as my other half, as if threatened by the happiness they brought into my life. It later became clear that she harbored a deep hatred towards people in happy relationships, a desire to "destroy" them, as she put it. This was not just speculation, but a cold, hard fact. Her targets were always those close to me, couples who were flourishing. She would stop at nothing to break them apart. A relentless pursuit.

Was it a case of "hell has no fury like a woman scorned?" It seemed unlikely, considering she was the one who cheated on my father, causing him to leave. I don't blame him for his decision. As an Englishman in a country plagued by the Boer Maffia, he had limited options. There must have been something in my mother's past, something unknown to me, that fueled this deep-seated animosity.

In any case, there we stood, on the plush carpet before her majesty, facing the brunt of her wrath. In the midst of a testing silence, the air hung heavy with tension, only broken by the sharp barking of a dog outside. Undeterred, D stood her ground, unaffected by the surrounding chaos.

Finally, D relented, her voice cutting through the silence like a knife. "I can't comprehend how such a beautiful son could have a mother as cruel as you." As she spoke, she reached out and took my hand, our fingers intertwining in a silent plea to escape this toxic environment as swiftly as possible.

My mother nearly choked on her coffee, her eyes briefly revealing a hidden admiration before she regained composure. Her reactions were always predictable, following one of two patterns. If it involved anyone other than me, she would scoff and dismiss it with a sinister laugh. When it concerned me, she would dramatically clutch her chest, feigning a deep wound, as if an arrow had struck her heart.

"Just wait until you witness his dark side," my mother retorted, her tone dripping with icy coldness.

"Well, I just have," D replied casually, shrugging her shoulders. "And it's you."

The scene unfolded before me like a grand spectacle. My mother's eyes darted back and forth between D and me, clearly taken aback. With determination, D held my hand firmly and guided me out of that house, away from the malevolence that lurked in every corner. The echoes of my mother's wicked laughter lingered in my ears as I started the car and drove away.

Never had I held such profound respect for any of my girlfriends before. D was the first who fearlessly confronted the beast, staring it down with unwavering wisdom.

In that moment, I should have married her right then and there, but alas, I was foolish. But that is a tale for another time. For now, I shall let my weary fingers rest as I embrace a warm cup of coffee. Outside, the rain pours relentlessly, its rhythmic patter creating a soothing melody. Two sunseekers find solace on the windowsill, seeking the warmth of my cozy cottage. Until our paths cross again, farewell, but only for now.

Chapter Nine

Life is not a smooth journey, but rather a treacherous path filled with unexpected obstacles. It's not as simple as hopping on and enjoying the ride, especially for those who are unfortunate. If you blindly navigate through the winding road of life, rest assured, you will inevitably collide with an unyielding force.

During my time in high school, I often found solace in escaping from home. The constant torment and my mother's hostility towards me became unbearable. She always favored my brother, regardless of how cruelly he treated me. Whenever I pleaded for her support, all she would say was that I needed to stand up for myself. I tried, believe me, I tried, but I stood no chance against him. He was faster, stronger, and more ruthless. To make matters worse, he was a psychopath who took pleasure in inflicting pain upon me.

Even as I sat at the dining table, my face bruised, lips scarred, eye blackened, nose twisted, and eyes filled with tears, my mother remained indifferent. Positioned at the far end of the elongated table, she allowed my brother, Jay, to steal the spotlight with his impeccably styled hair and smug grin. For this memoir, let's refer to my brother as Jay.

Driven by desperation, I meticulously planned my next escape from home, hoping that this time I would succeed. In all my previous attempts, I was apprehended and forcefully returned home to face my mother's wrath and Jay's assaults.

However, this time, I had a close friend who was caught in the midst of his parents' messy divorce. He tried everything in his power to gain their attention, from contemplating suicide to indulging in smoking and drugs. He even adopted a goth persona and pretended to be gay, but his pleas fell on deaf ears.

One early morning, we silently slipped away with our backpacks and embarked on our journey. Little did I know, the car we used was stolen, and my friend had taken money from a relative to sustain us during our extended absence from home. I had saved up my own money from odd jobs, such as gardening and cleaning swimming pools in our neighborhood.

Through cunning tactics, we managed to stay one step ahead, eluding capture. However, our funds eventually depleted, and our youth prevented us from finding employment. Once again, desperation clouded my judgment. The police apprehended my friend for his theft, but I managed to escape as I was unaware of his actions. The school agreed to readmit me, but my friend was immediately expelled. Little did I know that this reckless endeavor would catapult my social status to unforeseen heights.

But my mother would have nothing of my new stardom. And I even graced the cover of the city's newspaper.

She sent me to an agricultural boarding school, the smell of hay and manure permeating the air, to keep me tamed and prevent any daring escape. The unfamiliar task of castrating pigs and shaving sheep overwhelmed me. The sharp, pungent scent of the animals filled my nostrils, making me crinkle my nose in distaste.

But there I was. Low and behold, my brother was also at the same school, his presence casting a shadow of trouble over me. The sound of his laughter echoed through the halls as he regaled his friends with tales of his mischievous exploits.

He had been expelled for beating up a teacher, the sound of the altercation still ringing in my ears. The teacher's pleas for mercy fell on deaf ears as my brother's rage consumed him.

He ended up stealing a different teacher's car, the engine roaring to life as he sped away to attend a rugby game in a different city.

During the game, a teacher spotted Jay on camera, the click of the shutter freezing the moment in time. The sharpness of the image revealed my brother's identity, a damning proof of his actions. The pointing finger of the teacher cut through the air, directing the police toward him. The harsh sound of handcuffs clicking shut sealed his fate. My mother's miraculous rescue of Jay from his predicament has always haunted me. However, I could only speculate, and now I am certain that my initial guess was correct.

And there I was in boarding school, surrounded by whispers and wary glances. The weight of my brother's actions hung heavy in the air, suffocating me. The tense silence was broken only by the occasional hushed conversation, the words dripping with fear and curiosity.

He had wreaked havoc, leaving a trail of shattered trust and broken spirits. I was about to face the wrath of those he had harmed. The accusing stares of teachers, the frightened gazes of young girls, and the wary looks of fellow students. The weight of their judgment pressed down on me, threatening to crush my spirit.

Need I say more? I lasted a single day at my new school. The oppressive atmosphere suffocated me, making it hard to breathe. The walls seemed to close in on me, squeezing the air out of the room.

One of my brother's victims, a tall and imposing figure, identified me as his target. He towered over me, his presence overwhelming. He asked me what his nickname was, his voice dripping with menace. The sound of his deep, menacing growl sent a chill down my spine.

Foolish me, I remembered my brother talking about this guy, his funny nickname ringing a bell, and how he too was a bully. And so, I quoted the name my brother mentioned; the words tasting bitter on my tongue.

All I can say is that the world around me turned pitch black. The antiseptic scent of the hospital room invaded my senses, mingling with the faint aroma of disinfectant. A young doctor, his hands cold against my skin, sat next to my bed. His smile appeared genuine, but his eyes betrayed his true, impure intentions. The sharp prick of fear ran down my spine as his gaze lingered on me.

Without hesitation, the doctor delivered his verdict, his words like a punch to the gut. "You can never foster children." The weight of his words settled heavily on my chest, making it hard to breathe. My eyes darted around, searching for my mother's comforting presence. But of course, she was not there. The aftermath of her wicked deeds overwhelmed me completely.

At first, I was happy with hearing the news, a fleeting sense of relief washing over me. But I later also regretted it. It meant that I could freely indulge in my reputation as the town's Casanova, with no concerns holding me back. An unmistakable marker of prestige and social standing. How wrong I was. Most of the rejections I faced resulted from this, as potential wives would leave me with disappointed sighs echoing in my ears, aware that I couldn't fulfill their longing for children.

In the end, my mother triumphed, just as she always did. She relentlessly pursued legal action against the school, resulting in a staggering sum of money. With her debts finally settled, she embarked on an extended voyage abroad, leaving behind a trail of envy. Meanwhile, I reveled in the splendor of my newfound fame, if only temporarily. However, the accident proved to be an apparition from the past, forever haunting my every step.

Most men I knew went about boasting about their sexual pursuits, their victims totally unaware. But I was always different. Due to the removal of my testicles, my sex drive did not match that of men in their early twenties. Or even men in their fifties who try to relive their youthful days.

Even amidst the chaos surrounding me, the presence of an enchanting young woman still held me captive. I cringed under the gaze she bestowed upon me, squirming and purring like a contented kitten. Helpless against her irresistible charm, my desire for female affection made me vulnerable. Growing up, my mother rarely expressed any affection towards me, so it was particularly captivating when a younger member of her species gazed at me seductively. It became my weakness, a weakness that plagued me for a very long time and led to many pitfalls in my life. The dark forces clearly exploited this vulnerability to their advantage.

One particular scenario stands out among the rest. Let us shift our focus back to C and D, the captivating twins. D, who was on her path to becoming a chartered accountant, found herself in a distant city, pursuing her career as an apprentice at a prestigious financial firm. I supported her decision wholeheartedly, as I always wanted what was best for her. And she yearned to distance herself from this town infested with the Boer Maffia. This marked the beginning of my first long-distance relationship.

And there I was, once again, engulfed in self-pity. I maintained a close bond with D's family, visiting them as often as I could. One evening, fate found me alone with C at home. Her mother was away on a business trip, and her brother had been sent to boarding school due to his misbehavior, an agreement reached by his parents for once.

C and I spent the evening watching a movie, sipping rum, and frolicking in the swimming pool under the warm midsummer sky. With her sister's absence, C now lived in the cottage. She gracefully stepped out of the pool before I did, sashaying back towards the cottage, casting a mischievous wink over her shoulder. My gaze lingered on the curves of her alluring, perfectly rounded backside, glistening with water droplets.

Eventually, I emerged from the pool, only to realize I had no towel to dry myself. In a rush, I entered the cottage. And there, to my astonishment, lay C sprawled across the bed, completely naked. The soft, flickering candlelight bathed her exposed skin, causing it to shimmer enticingly. Frozen in my tracks, I couldn't help but feel overwhelmed at the sight of D's identical twin sister, as if I was gazing upon the love of my life once more. Her gaze swiftly shifted towards the mounting exhilaration emanating from within me, a wordless testament to my yearning.

Can you predict what happened next? I implore you to remain engaged for my forthcoming installment. The fervor envelops me, causing a rush of heat to suffuse my cheeks, while my fingertips throb with a longing for respite. Until we reconvene, stay captivated. Farewell, if only for now.

Chapter Ten

As I stood there, transfixed by C's naked form, a surge of desire coursed through me. The temptation to give in to my longing for female affection overwhelmed any rational thought. Her seductive gaze, filled with mischief and desire, drew me in like a moth to a flame. For a moment, all my promises to D and the life we had built seemed distant echoes.

Just as I was about to surrender to the intoxicating magnetism between us, a voice of reason cut through the fog of desire. It was my own conscience, starkly reminding me of the betrayal that would follow. The love I had vowed to D, our long-distance relationship—it all flashed before me like a haunting specter.

C noticed my hesitation and beckoned me with a slow, inviting gesture. Her fingers traced patterns on her bare skin, igniting a fire deep within me. I was drawn closer, my heart pounding with each step. The air crackled with forbidden desire as our bodies moved together, a tempestuous dance of stolen passion.

Every touch sent electric shocks through me, each kiss a wildfire that consumed my thoughts. The boundaries between right and wrong seemed to dissolve as we lost ourselves in a whirlwind of ecstasy. Yet, even amidst the fervor, guilt began to creep in, a shadow on the edge of our passion.

As the night wore on, the weight of my actions grew heavier. Images of D's face flashed in my mind, a painful reminder of the trust I had betrayed. With a trembling breath, I pulled away; the room falling into a thick silence. C's eyes mirrored my turmoil, a silent acknowledgment of our shared regret.

I stumbled towards the door, desperate to escape the tangled web of desire that had ensnared us. The cool night air hit my face, the stars above seemingly mocking my weakness. The guilt washed over me like a tidal wave, leaving me to grapple with the consequences of my actions. The long-distance relationship that once held promise now teetered on the edge, and I was left to confront the shattered fragments of my own integrity.

Relentlessly, C closed in on me, her footsteps echoing through the air. With a firm grip, she snatched my hand, yanking me forcefully into the dimly lit cottage. The wavering candle flickered, its feeble light casting eerie shadows that danced on her exposed form. A rush of guilt washed over me as I succumbed to her insatiable desires, fully aware that I had already ventured beyond the boundaries of my moral compass, forever unable to retrace my steps.

In that dimly lit cottage, time seemed to stand still. Every touch, every caress, carried a bittersweet intensity. The lines between right and wrong blurred further as we lost ourselves in a frenzy of passion. But beneath the surface, the knowledge of my betrayal lingered, poisoning the air between us.

As the night wore on, a sense of dread settled deep within me. The consequences of my actions loomed large, threatening to unravel everything I held dear. I knew that this moment of weakness would forever stain my relationship with D.

Yet, as much as I longed to break free from the grip of desire, C's allure was irresistible. Her touch ignited a fire within me that I couldn't extinguish. With each stolen moment, I was pulled deeper into the abyss, my integrity crumbling with each passing breath.

With every ounce of strength left in me, I tried to resist, to break free from the web that had ensnared us. But C's allure was overpowering, her desire relentless. I was a moth, drawn helplessly to the flame, unable to escape the consequences of my own weakness.

In that moment, I knew that I had crossed a line from which there was no return. My moral compass had been shattered, leaving me adrift in a sea of regret. The long-distance relationship that had once held so much promise now teetered on the edge of destruction, and I had no one to blame but myself.

As C and I succumbed to our insatiable desires, I couldn't help but wonder if I would ever find redemption. The guilt weighed heavy on my shoulders, a burden that I would carry for the rest of my life. In the quiet moments that followed, I could only hope that D would find it in their heart to forgive me, even though I knew deep down that I didn't deserve it.

Trapped in her intricate web, I struggled fruitlessly to break free, the suffocating grip tightening with every attempt. C and I clandestinely pursued our forbidden romance, our secret world cloaked in shadows. The reason behind my actions became clear—she was the spitting image of D, her identical twin. The thought of D abandoning me to chase her dreams was too painful to bear. Being with C felt like reliving the blissful honeymoon phase with D, smoothing out the creases that had marred our relationship.

To my astonishment, C differed greatly from D. While D was gentle, patient, and handled me with delicate care, sex serving as a mere bonus, C possessed an insatiable appetite for it. She was rough, lacking the femininity that D exuded effortlessly. And, above all, she was an ardent slapper. Jupiter, I endured countless slaps, often warranted by her suspicions of my gaze wandering to other women. Sometimes, she would slap me without any rhyme or reason, using my guilt as a weapon to ensure my silence.

This slapping spilled over into the bedroom, becoming a twisted form of arousal for her. I recall one particular occasion at a wedding, where she repeatedly struck me, oblivious to the prying eyes of someone familiar. This acquaintance approached me silently, his eyes pleading for me to escape her clutches. Over a beer later, he unveiled shocking revelations about her, painting a horrifying portrait. Yet, despite it all, I couldn't help but feel a pang of sadness for her. And so, I have guarded these secrets within me, locked away until this very day.

And yet, here I remained, ensconced in the confines of the life I had constructed. Unwittingly, I had carried the burden of physical and emotional abuse from my brother and mother, allowing it to seep into my present. C epitomized my limited understanding of love, embodying both mental and physical cruelty. Strangely, her affection felt like love because it was all I had ever known. She became my shelter, my safe haven. Despite the turmoil, I found solace in the familiarity of our relationship, sheltered from the dreaded specter of rejection.

But deep down, I knew that this twisted version of love was suffocating me. I yearned for the tenderness and understanding that D had once provided. The more I allowed myself to be trapped in this toxic relationship, the further I drifted from the person I used to be.

Each day, I became more detached from reality, living in a constant state of fear and uncertainty. The weight of my guilt and the knowledge of my betrayal consumed me, leaving me feeling empty and lost. I desperately wanted to break free, to find redemption and rebuild the shattered pieces of my life.

I spent hours in solitude, gazing at each fragment of the puzzle that was my life. My own image stared back at me from the twisted shards. Even in the darkest of clouds, the sun pierced through, casting its golden rays. It was in that moment that I noticed a recurring pattern, sneaking into my existence like a cunning serpent.

Once again, I blamed my desperation. With an absent father and a mother who showed no care for me, I yearned for acceptance. And because I was raised by such a mother, I sought out similar individuals who treated me unkindly. I documented my strange encounters, meticulously labeling them. L was categorized as a "strange woman," while C fell into the group of the "broken wing." There were many others. Then, I stumbled upon D's name, realizing she did not fit into any category. This left me with a peculiar mix of elation, remorse, and astonishment.

I realized I had lost the one person I loved deeply, slipping away like sand through my fingers. The one who truly cared for me and showered me with genuine affection. The one I called "love at first sight."

This moment of clarity was life-altering, providing a brief respite. I understood that I needed to confront my actions and face the consequences. I could no longer continue down this destructive path, eroding not only my relationship with D, but also my own sense of self-worth.

Summoning every ounce of courage, I made the agonizing decision to end things with C, resign from my job, and relocate to Johannesburg to reunite with D. It was a tumultuous battle as C fought tooth and nail to maintain control over me. However, I knew I had to break free, for the sake of my sanity and the opportunity to rebuild my life.

Should I stay, or should I go? The question echoed in my mind. Join me in the next installment to discover the answer to this question and many more. But for now, my fingers yearn for the touch of a warm cup of coffee. Until then, farewell, but only for now.

Chapter Eleven

The drive to the golden city, Johannesburg, felt like an eternity. As I drove, the sight of endless rolling hills and vast, open plains filled my vision. The anticipation of being reunited with D overwhelmed me, causing my heart to race and my hands to tremble on the steering wheel.

Feeling a mix of excitement and recklessness, I decided to stop at a motel along the way. The scent of fresh rain lingered in the air as I stepped out of the car, the cool breeze brushing against my face. I couldn't shake the feeling that I was taking a risk by rushing to see D, so I took a moment to gather my thoughts.

The next morning, hunger gnawed at my stomach. The previous night's excitement had left me with little appetite. I rose early, the first rays of sunlight filtering through the curtains. The sound of birds chirping outside filled the air, adding a sense of tranquility to my restless mind.

D was still unaware of my surprise visit. When I ended things with C, I had lied and said I was moving to a small town to focus on work. C had threatened to tell D about our relationship, but I knew she wouldn't risk jeopardizing her bond with her twin sister.

The long road stretched out before me, seemingly endless. The sun beat down on the asphalt, causing shimmering waves of heat to rise. Eventually, the familiar landscape of Johannesburg came into view, with its towering buildings and mine heaps creating a mirage-like effect.

I did not know where D lived, but I had the name of the company she worked for. I drove straight to the headquarters, a glass facade that stood tall and imposing. As I entered the building, my footsteps echoed on the polished marble floors.

With a chocolate in my hand, I approached the receptionist, my voice filled with excitement. She looked at me skeptically, her eyes scanning the name I provided. Unfortunately, they had no records of D's name. However, the receptionist's smile, albeit forced, softened as she started dialing the company's branches throughout the city.

In the midst of waiting, I couldn't help but notice a man walking out of the building, his voice carrying through the air as he spoke on his bulky Motorola cellphone. The sight of this new technology left me in awe, as everyone around me paused to watch, captivated by this marvel.

As the seconds turned into agonizing hours, my stomach growled with hunger. But my determination to find D kept me going. Finally, the receptionist beckoned me closer, a piece of paper in her hand. She handed it to me with a smile and a subtle wink, providing me with a glimmer of hope.

I rushed out of the building; the bustling sounds of the city filling my ears. I navigated the streets, occasionally stopping at petrol stations to get my bearings.

After some time, I reached my destination, a sense of relief washing over me. However, my relief quickly turned to disappointment as I realized that it wasn't a residential address, but another branch of the company. Frustration gnawed at me, but I couldn't give up now.

I hurried into the building, the receptionist's unfriendly demeanor not deterring me. I stated my case, my voice filled with urgency. The air in the office felt tense, as if everyone was in a rush. The receptionist reluctantly provided me with the information I sought, scribbling an address on a note and handing it over, her gaze cautious and stern.

With the address tightly gripped in my hand, I briskly left the branch, my determination fueling each step, eager to surprise D before she arrived home. The sun bathed the streets in a warm golden glow as I made my way through the bustling city, the sound of car horns and distant chatter filling the air.

Thankfully, I swiftly located her address, a quaint studio apartment tucked away in a quiet corner, and decided to appease my growling stomach. The aroma of freshly brewed coffee and pastries permeated the small café nearby, beckoning me inside. I indulged in a pint of beer, its frothy head a bittersweet distraction as I anxiously awaited the passing minutes to transform into hours. A decision I would soon regret.

Taking note of the hour, I concluded that D should have arrived home already. Settling the bill, a sense of urgency propelled me towards the rows of studio apartments. My heart pounded in my chest, the anticipation of our reunion electrifying my every nerve. Slowly, I drove past the numbers adorning each unit, my gaze fixed upwards. And there it was, the number that perfectly matched the note in my hand. Parking in the visitor's bay, my hands trembled uncontrollably with excitement.

Ascending the stairs with a hurried gallop, the sound of laughter floated towards me from a distance, a symphony of joy and affection. The corridor stretched before me, its sterile walls devoid of personality. Finally, I reached the door, my racing heart demanding a moment of respite.

Summoning courage, I rapped on the door, and it swung open abruptly. A man with flowing golden locks stood before me, his brow mirroring my own confusion.

"S-sorry to interrupt," I stammered, my eyes darting to the number on the note in my hand. "But I was looking for D," I added, using her full name.

"Honey!" the young man exclaimed, his voice booming. "You have a visitor." He introduced himself as G, extending a warm welcome and assuming I was family. The shock on both D's and my face was palpable as we locked eyes, disbelief coursing through our veins.

My gaze involuntarily shifted to her hand, where a dazzling diamond ring adorned her finger. My complexion drained of color, as if a wintery frost had settled upon me. However, for her sake, I knew I had to regain control over my emotions. Swiftly, I introduced myself to her fiancé as an old school friend. The kind-hearted man graciously invited me to stay for dinner, but I quickly fabricated a lie, claiming other plans awaited me.

I hurriedly dashed out of the building, my footsteps echoing down the dimly lit corridor. The cold air hit me as I slid into my car, the engine roaring to life. In that moment, no words in any dictionary could capture the whirlwind of emotions that consumed me.

As I drove past D's unit, my heart sank as I noticed the closed door.

It was as if she had already forgotten about me, moving on so effortlessly. It was a bitter payback for my regretful mistake of sleeping with her sister, yet she remained unaware. I couldn't help but wonder if infidelity was ingrained in her very being.

Seeking solace, I found a secluded spot nearby to park. Tears streamed down my face as I unleashed the pain that had been building within me. I had sacrificed my dreams, my career, the life I had meticulously crafted, and it seemed all in vain. The weight of my despair was suffocating.

Hope had flickered within me, yearning for a chance to rekindle the love we once shared. Now, I sat in a car that had become my temporary shelter, devoid of a home, a job, or any prospects. It was a stark reminder of how I had allowed the love of my life to slip through my fingers.

Countless questions haunted my mind. What if I had stayed, and she had come home? Or if I had made the move to the bustling city earlier? But I firmly believed that everything happens for a reason, even if it meant enduring heartbreak.

Join me in my upcoming installment, where I unveil how I extricated myself from the predicament I found myself in, only to stumble upon a fresh mistake. Farewell, my dearest mortal reader, but only for now.

Chapter Twelve

At that stage, as I sat in my car, the acrid smell of thick smog engulfed the rolling mine hills of the city. It felt like the most devastating time of my life. Here I was, a damaged soul, feeling as downcast as a drenched cat. Phoning my mother and asking if I could come back home was out of the question. She would revel in my misery and dismiss me with her favorite saying, "What is in it for me?"

My mind raced with thoughts of how to escape this predicament. It wasn't the first time I had chased after a girl, only to be met with rejection and a painful surprise. The sun was setting, painting the sky in shades of fiery orange and crimson. If I wanted to make a move, I had to hasten, or risk spending the night in my car in one of the most dangerous cities in the world. I couldn't explain how I knew the city so well, but later I discovered it was a result of genetic memory, passed down from my father, who had once called this very city home.

Knowledge about my father was scarce. According to the lies my mother fed me, he was a single child who had immigrated from Scotland to South Africa. Raised by a lesbian couple, his opportunities in life were limited. Being an Englishman in a country ruled by the notorious Boer Mafia syndicate presented him with even fewer chances. Whether he had left the country or not remained a mystery, hanging over me like an unanswered question. Allow me to elaborate.

When I was a young boy, I vividly remember walking into my mother's bedroom one stormy night. The thunder rumbled outside, its reverberations shaking the very foundation of our home. Afraid and clutching my pillow, I timidly knocked on her bedroom door, as per her rule.

"Come in!" my mother's voice rang out, laced with annoyance. With my legs trembling, I entered her room. There she lay on the bed, dressed only in her panties, sipping wine and engrossed in a self-help book. It was the only kind of book she ever read, apart from the Bible. Oh, and later on, she developed an interest in the Torah, after changing her name and converting in an attempt to seduce a wealthy Jewish man.

As lightning illuminated my mother's expansive bedroom windows, the panoramic view of the ocean came into view, only to be followed by the deafening roar of thunder. Without hesitation, fear trembling in my voice, I asked my mother where my father was. With a smirk on her face, she casually informed me that he had drowned in the ocean.

As a young child, I believed her. After all, children tend to believe everything their parents tell them. Much later in my life, I overheard a hushed conversation she shared with one of her trusted confidants. From the soft whispers, I could sense the heaviness in her voice, indicating that my father had vanished without a trace. According to the narrative my mother shared, it was a serene Sunday evening.

He had casually mentioned that he was going to the nearby shops to purchase cigarettes, only to never return. Honestly, this is the version I believed, and still hold on to, because knowing her, I could understand why he might choose to disappear. However, in a later revelation, she disclosed to someone else that my father had betrayed my mother, engaging in an affair with a Jewish lady doctor who lived just down the road from us. I apologize for my bluntness, but one would have to be naïve to believe this fabricated tale of her deceit.

In our country, under the rule of the Boer Maffia, what chances did a female Jewish doctor have of finding employment? Even my father struggled to secure a decent job due to his English background. It was pure nonsense, an elaborate lie. If anything, it was my mother who had strayed, entangled in a relationship with a Jewish man, well aware of her affinity for their perceived wealth. The only concrete fact I possess is that I have never set eyes upon my father, aside from a faded photograph capturing their so-called wedding. In that image, neither my father nor my mother adorned a wedding ring, leaving me to question the authenticity of their union.

My dear mortal reader, let me paint a vivid picture for you. In that pivotal moment, as I found myself in a predicament, I yearned for a father figure to call upon, someone to rescue me from the tangled web I had woven. It was as if the air around me grew heavy with the scent of desperation, a palpable tension filling the car. The silence was deafening, broken only by the echo of my own racing heartbeat. Oh, how I wished for the safety net of a father's love, the knowledge that I had someone to catch me when I inevitably stumbled and fell from grace.

Back then, as a young and naïve individual, I lacked the ability to see the positive aspects of life. Unbeknownst to me, growing up without a father had its advantages, albeit very few. With trembling hands, I nervously started the car.

"Damn you, D," I muttered under my breath, navigating the intricate veins of the city. The towering mine heaps loomed over the landscape like the aftermath of a chaotic, apocalyptic event.

"And screw you, G, for stealing my girl," I added, speeding down the highway, disregarding my safety. I was so consumed with cursing those who had wronged me that I paid no attention to the blaring horns of other vehicles as I swiftly weaved between lanes at an alarming speed.

Surprisingly, even doctors are perplexed by my exceptional memory capacity, unable to provide any explanation. Yet, I can assure you, at that moment, it was the first time I had ever heard the song "Insomnia" by Faithless blaring through the speakers. It felt as if the song was crafted only for me. The pulsating rhythm and hypnotic melody filled the air, igniting a fire within me and pushing me forward with unstoppable force.

Despite the bleak portrayal of the city I found myself in, there was something about it that intrigued me. Initially, I believed it was the connection to my father, knowing he had grown up here. However, as I parked my dilapidated car in the shopping mall's parking bay, in an affluent neighborhood, I discovered the true reason. Unlike the town I had fled from, where the Afrikaans Boer Maffia reigned, no one paid any attention to me in this city. Everyone around me spoke English, a stark contrast to my previous environment.

It was in that moment that I realized what it was: anonymity. In this diverse city, nobody cared about anyone else. It was a relentless rat-race for survival. Right then and there, I fell in love with it. I hurriedly entered the colossal mall, my eyes absorbing the intricate details while my mind whispered, "Babylon!" Truly, it was a city of gold. I merged with the bustling crowd of shoppers, on the lookout for any signs of a real estate agency. I needed something affordable, within the limits of my meager savings.

My eyes grew wide with awe as I spotted the neon sign of the bustling restaurant that was on everyone's lips. Back then, the world was new to us, like the Berlin wall falling. The scent of sizzling international flavors wafted through the air, enticing passersby. A line of eager patrons snaked out from the entrance, their excited chatter blending with the clinking of cutlery and lively music playing inside.

As I walked by, the host, elegantly decked out in a tailored suit, caught my attention. His mischievous eyes sparkled as he playfully wiggled his eyebrows. In that moment, a sense of familiarity washed over me, as if I had found a place to call home. However, I couldn't ignore the fact that his gestures held ulterior motives, while I, a guy with a penchant for girls, had different intentions.

Determined to find a place within my budget, I embarked on a desperate search from agency to agency. Lady luck, a fickle companion in my life, finally made an appearance. Her radiant smile and the twinkle in her eyes engulfed me, filling me with hope. Just a stone's throw away, a bachelor flat had become available in a residential complex. Excitement surged through me as I quickly made my way to an ATM, withdrew the funds, and returned with a smile. With a feeling of satisfaction, I handed over the deposit and paid two months' rent upfront. With some spare cash, I made my way to a nearby camping shop and purchased a single bed mattress and a sleeping bag.

Lady luck seemed to be on my side as I returned to the restaurant where the host had made his strange pass at me. Like a vigilant sentinel, he stood guard at the entrance. As I approached, he gave me a cheeky wink. Returning the gesture, I placed my hand on his shoulder, a gesture of camaraderie. As a novice waiter, I desperately needed a job, and the poor guy was my ticket in. He introduced himself as I, sharing the same initial as my name.

"Hello I," I greeted him. "Do you, by any chance, have a vacancy for a skilled waiter?" I asked, biting my lip enticingly, trying to play up my charm.

"We certainly need more than one waiter," he replied, his eyes scanning me from head to toe. Seizing the opportunity, I pulled him into a warm, tight embrace, planting a kiss on his cheek. It worked like a charm. Without backing away, he asked, "When can you start?"

"Right away," I responded, my wide eyes reflecting my surprise and excitement.

I'm not sure who had the widest grin, but I think he might have beaten mine, just by a hair's breadth. "Go and grab yourself a pair of black pants, and come back," he instructed, giving a flick of his head.

Euphoria coursing through my veins, I hurried towards the cheapest clothing wholesaler I knew. Amidst the racks of clothes, I found only one pair of black pants, a size too small. Ignoring the discomfort, I purchased them with the small change in my pocket. Rushing back to the dressing cubicles, I swiftly removed the labels and squeezed into the tight-fitting pants, ready to embark on this new chapter of my life.

Within ten minutes of securing my new job, I was back at the restaurant, greeted by the familiar scent of sizzling food and the clatter of plates and cutlery. My host friend, I, guided me through the bustling dining area, the air filled with the hum of conversations and the occasional burst of laughter.

As we made our way to the back, I couldn't help but notice the vibrant colors of the waiters' uniforms, the crisp white shirts contrasting against the deep red of their aprons. With a warm smile, I was seamlessly introduced to my fellow waiters, their friendly faces reflecting a shared camaraderie. The sounds of their jovial banter blended harmoniously with the lively ambiance of the restaurant.

In my fitted pants, I felt a sense of confidence, as if they were a secret weapon in my new role. As I attended to the customers, their appreciative nods and satisfied smiles rewarded me with a surge of gratification. The clinking of coins and crinkling of bills in my pocket were a testament to the generosity of the patrons.

Unexpectedly, amidst the flurry of activity, a voice whispered sweetly in my ear, offering a marriage proposal. My heart skipped a beat, and I couldn't help but blush at the audacity of the gesture. And then, as I cleared a table, I noticed a serviette with a lipstick stain, a silent invitation that left me intrigued. Next to the lipstick stain, there was a handwritten name and hotel room number, beckoning me closer.

Did I succumb to the allure of the tempting invitation? Tune in next time to uncover the thrilling secrets. My fingers yearn for a temporary break, desperate for relief. Until we meet again in my next installment, I bid you farewell, for now.

Chapter Thirteen

My dearest mortal reader, it deeply saddens me to admit that I fell for the alluring invitation scribbled on the serviette. But before I delve into that, let me recount the events leading up to this exhilarating moment. One aspect I cherished about the restaurant I worked for was the post-shift ritual of receiving a complimentary drink. The only condition was that we had to remove our branded T-shirts. It provided a wonderful opportunity to socialize and connect with my fellow waiters on a personal level.

During one such occasion, I forged friendships with four new acquaintances who would play a significant role in my life. There was Skinny Phillip, as I affectionately called him, and eager Patrick. And then there were the jaw-dropping blonde girls, Meghan and Cathy. Now, you may wonder why, for the first time in my narrative, I am using their real names. It's because they were American exchange waiters overseeing training for the restaurant chain in our country. So, how many Phillips, Meghans, and the other two names do you think there are in America?

But I digress. Let me return to the present moment. I found myself huddled in a corner, relishing my beverage and forming connections with anyone brave enough to engage in conversation. Unlike the Boer Maffia-infested town I had recently arrived from, these people were easy to talk to and remarkably friendly. Every second was a delight.

To add to the enchantment of the evening, we had the privilege of meeting the restaurant owner, a Greek gentleman, with an inspiring story. He generously offered us all another drink, perhaps because his storytelling captivated everyone. And I must admit, it was truly inspirational. Hats off to you, Theo!

After finishing my beer, I carefully unfolded the napkin with the hotel room number and quietly navigated through the tranquil mall. Following the signs, I made my way to the entrance of the opulent six-star hotel, connected to the mall by a breathtaking sky bridge.

As I stepped into the foyer, my eyes were immediately drawn to the majestic Twin Towers, standing tall and proud. My jaw dropped, and my heart filled with awe. I was momentarily unsure of what to do, and the thought of turning back briefly crossed my mind. However, my curiosity and the promise of newfound pleasures propelled me forward.

Suddenly, my weary feet found a renewed vigor. Nervously, but with a newfound determination, I crossed the threshold and approached the express elevators. As I pressed the up button, a surge of excitement mixed with uncertainty coursed through me. It was at that very moment that I realized I had no clue which floor housed the hotel room I was seeking.

At that slightly late hour, there was no elevator operator present, and I decided to take my chances. Also, I was unsure if the person who invited me was still awake. Nonetheless, I quickly figured out that the floor numbers and the room numbers were connected. The elevator door chimed happily as I exited, and I strolled down the luxurious corridor, feeling the softness of the plush carpet beneath my feet.

I finally reached the hotel room, the brass number on the door gleaming in the dim hallway light, matching the one written on the crumpled serviette. Before I rapped on the door, a wave of uncertainty washed over me, causing my pulse to quicken. The weight of the question lingered in my mind as I walked through the hotel, unnoticed until now. It hit me then, like a sudden realization, that I had no knowledge of who awaited me behind that door. But I had a faint idea, a glimmer of hope.

Thoughts raced through my mind, colliding and intertwining as I contemplated my actions. It dawned on me that I was seeking retribution for the rejection that gnawed at my heart, my stomach, and my very soul. It was my feeble attempt at leveling the playing field. Some call it a rebound, a temporary distraction from the pain. Yet, despite my conviction, my heart still ached, and my mind grappled with the deceit inflicted upon me by D, who had callously abandoned me for someone else. The pain was unbearable, coursing through my veins like a relentless storm.

Convinced, despite my doubts, I mustered the courage to knock on the door, my hand trembling. A faint glow seeped through the slender gap at the bottom, casting ethereal shadows on the plush carpet. A silhouette materialized, gracefully dancing towards the entrance.

With a sudden burst of anticipation, the door flung open, revealing the very person I had expected. It was her, the captivating redheaded woman from the restaurant earlier that night. The more wine she and her friends consumed, the more her friendliness grew, ultimately leading to this invitation.

"Hey sexy," her voice, dripping with seduction, filled the air, mingling with the lingering scent of garlic. "Please, come inside." Clad in revealing nightwear, she stepped aside, extending her leg to showcase its length, a tantalizing display.

Without a moment's hesitation, I crossed the threshold, the adrenaline pumping through my veins. She exuded an undeniable allure, and as I entered, I knew there was no turning back.

The room was dimly lit, with soft music playing in the background. The air was thick with anticipation and desire. As I closed the door behind me, a blend of excitement and nervousness washed over me. This encounter was meant to be a distraction, a way to forget the pain of rejection, but deep down, I knew it was more than that.

We moved towards each other, the electricity between us palpable. "Hello, I'm Nina," she said with a smile, her voice as smooth as silk. As we exchanged introductions, I noticed the faint tan line on her ring finger—a subtle but telling sign. The missing ring whispered of untold stories and hidden truths behind her chosen name.

"You can call me Al," I teased, throwing in a playful wink. Her giggle was light, mischievous, and it only seemed to amplify her beauty. She took my hand, her touch sending a shiver down my spine, and led me further into the room. The bed, perfectly made, stood as a silent invitation, urging us to surrender to our desires.

As our bodies intertwined, the weight of the past seemed to fade away. In this moment, there was only the intoxicating sensation of touch and the raw passion that consumed us. We lost ourselves in each other, seeking solace and pleasure in the embrace of a stranger.

But even as our bodies moved in sync, a part of me couldn't help but wonder if this was truly what I needed. Was I merely using her as a means of revenge, a way to prove my worth? Or was there something more genuine hidden beneath the surface?

As the night wore on, the lines between lust and longing blurred. We shared secrets and whispered promises, our vulnerabilities laid bare. In those stolen moments, I saw glimpses of a connection that went beyond physical attraction.

Amidst the lively chatter of our conversation, the aroma of freshly brewed coffee filled the air. As the words spilled from her lips, Nina's eyes sparkled with a mix of determination and excitement. She was the proud owner of a renowned computer training company and had journeyed to our city to unveil a new branch.

I, a humble waiter, had unknowingly caught her attention with my dedicated service. Her intent was crystal clear—she wished to extend an offer, inviting me to join her team as a trainer. A sudden surge of guilt washed over me, accompanied by a peculiar sense of relief. It became apparent that our presence in this place was driven by our own self-interests.

Acknowledging this truth, a weight lifted from my shoulders, and the guilt that had plagued me lessened, if only slightly.

But as the sun began to rise, reality started to seep back in. The ache in my heart resurfaced, reminding me of the pain I was trying to escape. I realized that seeking revenge through someone else's embrace could never truly heal the wounds within me.

With a heavy heart, I untangled myself from her embrace, knowing that I had to face my own demons head-on. I thanked her for the night, for the temporary solace she provided, and quietly left the room.

Walking out into the morning light, I felt a mix of sadness and relief. I had sought retribution, but instead, I found a glimpse of hope amidst the chaos. Perhaps, in time, I would find a way to heal and move forward, leaving behind the pain and the desire for revenge.

As I walked away from that hotel room, I carried with me the lessons learned and the faint glimmer of hope that had sparked within me. It was time to focus on my own healing, to find strength within myself, and to let go of the need for revenge. The journey ahead would be difficult, but I knew that I had the power to find true happiness, even without the validation of another.

Memories of my intimate encounter with Nina flooded my mind, and I was struck by the extravagant measures wealthy individuals would take to satisfy their deepest desires, surrendering to their darkest fantasies alongside an unknown companion. The peculiar requests they made were equally astonishing. One particular act stood out, involving pain, and a mischievous smile crept onto my lips.

In an instant, the past surged back, as if a veil had been lifted. I found myself transported to that moment again, surrounded by the scent of an idyllic, timeless perfume, blending soft florals and citrus notes. The distant sound of children's laughter filled the air, blending harmoniously with their joyful giggles. Miss S, my English teacher, had asked me to stay behind, a familiar routine in our unconventional teacher-student relationship. As she closed the door, the click of the lock sent a shiver down my spine.

"Come sit here," she gently invited, tapping her lap. Her slender figure perched gracefully on the chair in front of her desk. With her olive complexion, short ebony hair, and amber-like eyes, I had never considered how she remained unmarried at such a young age—a topic whispered about among my classmates, fueling endless rumors.

Longing for affection from a woman, I willingly settled onto her lap, eagerly absorbing her whispered secrets that sent shivers down my arms and neck. Her delicate touch would roam, exploring the curves of my body. I studied her eyes intently, noticing the flicker of anticipation as she focused on my lap.

She would guide my hands to certain parts of her body, instructing me to stroke gently until I felt the warmth and moisture enveloping my fingertips. Her soft moans and groans echoed in my mind, lingering long after they had faded away. Her body would tense, followed by a series of contractions and soft whimpers of pleasure. And just like that, it would be over, and she would dismiss me to my next class, leaving the lingering curiosity of my wide-eyed classmates.

In school, my nickname was "wet pants" due to my tendency to wet myself when nervous. If only they knew.

To this day, whenever the scent of Lenthéric Panache reaches my nostrils, a knot forms in my stomach, stirring deep emotions within me. Similar to Nina, my teacher S also immersed herself in the captivating fragrance.

I found myself sitting in the worn-out seat of my car, feeling the familiar grooves beneath my fingertips. The soft hum of the engine filled my ears, creating a soothing background noise.

In that moment, I weighed the decision that lay before me. The training position Nina had generously offered me beckoned, promising hours upon hours spent in her company whenever she graced our city with her presence. The thought of being able to travel alongside her, exploring unknown places and experiencing fresh adventures, was undeniably alluring. It tugged at my heartstrings, making it difficult to resist.

As the internal battle raged on, I couldn't help but feel overwhelmed with a mix of emotions. The prospect of embarking on this new journey with Nina held the promise of excitement, of escaping the confines of my routine.

Until the next installment, where the truth will finally be unveiled, I bid you farewell with anticipation. But it is only temporary, for our paths will cross again soon.

Chapter Fourteen

My dearest mortal reader, once again, disappointment weighs heavily upon me. I must confess that I declined Nina's alluring offer to become a trainer at her new company. As a guest during the grand opening, I faced the difficult choice of turning her down.

There was a peculiar satisfaction in my role as a waiter amidst the bustling restaurant, where the elegant patrons and clinking cutlery created a symphony of refinement. I took pride in serving, basking in the radiant smiles of those I attended to. The weight of my tray, balanced delicately in my hands, brought a sense of purpose and fulfillment.

In our fine establishment, I served numerous sports stars and their secret companions. One cricketer, known for his generosity, would often leave a sizable tip but forget his wallet for parking. His fresh, alluring blonde companion was a testament to his deceitful nature.

Through serving others, I embraced humility, prioritizing their desires above my own. The mingling scents of cuisine and warmth of the restaurant created an atmosphere of comfort and familiarity.

My dedication caught the eye of the owner, who soon invited me to a luxurious penthouse to discuss a new role—teaching fellow waiters about the skills I had acquired. This opportunity led me to bond with American exchange waiters, open-minded individuals embracing liberal ideologies. I relished spending time with them, gradually embracing my true self.

Phillip and Patrick would often invite me on our lunch breaks, affectionately dubbed the graveyard shift. In the food court, we mingled with the alluring Meghan and Cathy. My gaze would linger, reveling in the mischievous glances exchanged with my fellow waiters, particularly the young men who struggled to catch the attention of the same girls I enjoyed effortlessly.

This group introduced me to smoking a joint. We'd retreat to a secluded mall section, inhaling the potent substance deeply. Soon, laughter and hunger consumed us, and the nights were filled with peculiar dreams. One night, I found myself in a celestial meadow surrounded by vibrant flowers and butterflies. A man with a kind face and captivating eyes approached, his voice echoing, "Do not smoke Cannabis. It destroys your will to win."

His words resonated as I awoke, and since then, I've refrained from the substance, playfully calling it "mountain cabbage," much to the amusement of others.

During one of my leisurely strolls with my American friends, an unexpected encounter unfolded. As I walked along, a familiar face caught my eye: D, accompanied by her new fiancé, G. The sight of them, hand in hand but lacking the spark that once defined their relationship, took me by surprise. The honeymoon phase had evidently fizzled, leaving behind a veneer of familiarity that bred contempt.

D seemed astonished to see me with my new found friends, her eyes betraying a flicker of lingering affection. However, her palpable nervousness was unsettling—an unfamiliar trait that clashed with the confident woman I once knew. I was wearing a branded T-shirt, inadvertently revealing details about my current workplace. In that moment, I realized I had moved on, and crossing paths with my past was the last thing I desired. Our encounter was brief, and I silently hoped our paths would never cross again. My past life was firmly behind me, and I longed for it to remain so, especially from the prying eyes of my old town and my mother.

As days turned into weeks and weeks into months, life settled into a predictable routine. My workdays were filled with purpose, and my evenings were spent with my American friends, embracing my new self—V2.1.

But life has a way of surprising us. One afternoon, a familiar face appeared at the restaurant, inquiring about my presence. Initially, I thought it was D, but the voice belonged to C, D's twin sister. The shock was palpable. I asked her to wait at the bar while I finished my shift.

C's unparalleled beauty was a subject of endless teasing among my fellow waiters. Meghan, in particular, had the most to say, and it was then I realized that Meghan and I shared a secret affection. However, neither of us dared to make a move, fearing it might jeopardize our special bond. At that moment, I knew I had to put my new life on hold and confront the complexities that lay ahead.

For the time being, C shared my cramped bachelor apartment with me. The musty scent of old furniture lingered in the air as we navigated the narrow space together. Although I did not see us as being together again, her presence held a certain benefit. My brother, the holiness's wedding, was looming on the horizon. And now I had a date. The anticipation of the upcoming event filled the room with a sense of excitement and nervous energy.

Although, C did not have the best reputation as a wedding guest. I had seen with my own eyes the wild antics and unpredictable behavior unfold before me. But I had an ulterior motive, and I was eager to see my plan through to the bitter end. The distant sound of laughter and music from previous celebrations echoed in my mind, reminding me of the chaos that awaited us.

When the time came, I handed in a week's leave. C and I packed our stuff and left early, embarking on the five-hour drive to my hometown, Kimberley.

The anticipation of seeing the kindhearted people filled the car. Memories of warm embraces and familiar faces danced in my mind. The wedding invitation, or rather a set of straightforward instructions, was minimalistic in design. Make sure to arrive by five o'clock sharp and gather at the specified location. The words on the paper seemed to come alive, creating a sense of urgency within us.

When we arrived, my mother, who I had not seen in years, greeted me with her signature coy smile that instantly brought back memories. Entrusting me with the camera, she proclaimed me the designated photographer and assessed my outfit with a discerning gaze.

The girls had the freedom to wear whatever they pleased. Vibrant colors and flowing fabrics filled the room as the women prepared for the festivities. The sound of laughter and excited chatter filled the air, creating a joyful ambiance that permeated the entire house.

When it came to approaches, my family never adhered to traditional norms. My brother had found himself a wife from the local town, who was both beautiful and desperately impoverished. This meant that my mother had taken care of all the expenses and was now in charge. Known for her expertise, she fully embraced her position, orchestrating the event with grace and precision.

C and I inquired about the whereabouts of the pre-wedding party, and bid our farewells until the next big day. Once we settled into our hotel room, we indulged in the intimate connection we had longed for during the extended drive. The soft touch of her skin against mine, the sound of our shared laughter, and the scent of passion that filled the room created a sense of contentment and fulfillment.

Decked out in our extravagant attire, we stepped into the vibrant party, greeted as self-proclaimed VIPs. The waiters, who I had meticulously trained alongside me in the same restaurant group, guided us up the staircase. As we ascended, the pulsating beats of psychedelic rock permeated the air, creating an electrifying atmosphere.

At the pinnacle of the stairs, we discovered the focal point of the room. My brother, regarded as a divine figure by his bachelor comrades, sat regally at the head of the table, completely oblivious to my presence. It stung deeply that he failed to recognize his own flesh and blood, separated for more than a decade.

In a swift motion, I pivoted on my heel and descended the stairs, accompanied closely by C. Familiar with the owner, we secured a secluded, romantic spot where we could relish in the culinary delights. The symphony of revelry from above serenaded our senses as we savored each delectable bite. The harmonious blend of cheers, the shattering of bottles, the creaking of chairs, and the tinkling of shattered glass filled the atmosphere. Fortunately, my mother had taken the initiative to reserve the entire restaurant for the evening, courtesy of the financial backing from my brother's wealthy friends, who possessed unparalleled expertise in the diamond industry.

I refused to dwell on how my mother had skillfully persuaded the restaurant owner and my brother's affluent companions. Deep down, I already knew the answer. The expression on C's face mirrored my own thoughts, confirming that she, too, was privy to the lingering question in my mind.

At four o'clock on the following day, a Saturday, we gathered in the grand church, its towering walls echoing with the haunting melody of the organ. The anticipation hung heavy in the air as we waited for the proceedings to begin. Seated at the front, alongside the family, C and I eagerly awaited the entrance of the bride and groom.

The weight of anticipation hung heavy in the air, causing a collective restlessness among the attendees. Nervous whispers fluttered through the congregation, mingling with the distant notes of the organ. My heart, already burdened with a mix of emotions, seemed to beat with an erratic rhythm, as if struggling to keep up with the turmoil within.

The sight of my brother's best man confidently standing on the stage hit me like a punch in the gut. It was as if a dagger had pierced through my heart, leaving a sharp ache that seemed to intensify with each passing moment. The unexpected choice left me feeling a mix of confusion, disappointment, and a tinge of resentment.

But the drama did not end there. On the stage, my mischievous ex-girlfriend, now playing the role of the bridesmaid, cast a playful wink in my direction. A surge of conflicting emotions rushed through me, a tumultuous blend of nostalgia, lingering affection, and the bitter taste of past hurts. I knew deep down that her playful smile was a mere facade, concealing a potential storm that awaited me in the not-so-distant future.

As I dared to glance sideways, my eyes met with C's gaze, burning with a mixture of anger and betrayal. Her piercing stare felt like daggers digging into my side, intensifying the discomfort I already felt. The expression on her face was a clear reflection of her mounting curiosity and the urgency she felt to uncover the truth, demanding answers that she needed right then and there.

The physical effects of these emotions were palpable. A knot tightened in my stomach, constricting my appetite and making it difficult to swallow. My palms grew clammy, leaving a slight dampness in my grasp. Each breath I took felt shallow, as if the air itself had grown heavy with the weight of unspoken tension. It was as if the emotions swirling within me had taken a physical form, weaving their way through my body and leaving their mark on every fiber of my being.

Suddenly, the familiar wedding tune blasted through the organ speakers, causing everyone to spring to their feet. Gasps of astonishment filled the air as all eyes turned towards the back, wide with awe. The aftermath of the previous night's celebration party was clear on my brother and his soon-to-be wife, their expressions weary and their eyes bloodshot.

This presented an opportunity for me. I swiftly grabbed the camera my mother had entrusted to me and hurried to the aisle, where I kneeled down, capturing the moment frozen in time. As I returned to my seat, I winced under the weight of my mother's disapproving glare. "Be careful what you wish for," I whispered as I settled in. C, impressed by my audacity, rewarded me with a high five.

Even from my vantage point a few steps back from the stage, I could detect the lingering scent of alcohol and marijuana emanating from my brother's clothes. The minister wrinkled his nose in disgust, but the best man and bridesmaid found humor in the situation, their bodies shaking with suppressed laughter.

Do I need to say more? They exchanged their vows in record time. Before we had a chance to catch our breath, my mother, clutching a note, hurried onto the stage. With a firm embrace and a peculiar peck on the cheek of the minister, she seized the microphone and delivered her "blessings," as she called them.

She praised my brother as if he were a deity himself. If the note held any truth, he had a prosperous future ahead, with the world at his feet, idolizing his very existence. She emphasized her financial support, covering all expenses, including their honeymoon and a sleek new car at their disposal. I couldn't bear to listen to the empty words any longer. I snatched the camera and made my way out, anticipating their exit with confetti raining down on them.

In my rush, the bridesmaid noticed me and hurried over, causing annoyance to C. I introduced them, but the tension between them was palpable. And then, amidst the falling confetti, the holy figure and his new deity emerged. I quickly captured the moment on film, the sound of the camera's flash irritating their sensitive eyes. I accompanied them to the photo shoot, feeling the excitement in the air.

However, my brother, accompanied by his divine wife, saw this as an opportunity to indulge in drugs and substances I was unfamiliar with. I silently prayed that she wouldn't become pregnant during their honeymoon. Yet, I couldn't bring myself to care, and I froze these moments in history, capturing their impish smiles. I felt a deep sense of embarrassment as C witnessed this side of my family.

To be honest, I had reached my limit. My brother hadn't spoken a word to me the entire time, despite my attempts. As we followed behind the wedding car, thick white smoke billowed out of the open windows, the pungent smell of marijuana filling the air. We finally arrived at the reception, and I approached my mother, her hands moving with the grace of a conductor.

"This is a disgrace," I said, forcefully thrusting the camera into her lap. I angrily ripped off the tailor-made waistcoat she had spent hours crafting, then flung it right at her face.

Her face flushed with a mix of shock and hurt, her eyes welling up with tears. The room fell silent, and I could feel the weight of my actions hanging heavily in the air. The once cheerful atmosphere had turned tense and uncomfortable. My heart raced, and I could feel the adrenaline coursing through my veins, fueling my anger. I could sense that she was putting on an elaborate performance for the guests, playing the role of a victim. It was evident that she had carefully plotted to provoke me, and unfortunately, her plan had succeeded. While the guests remained oblivious, I saw through her facade. Her tears were insincere, merely a charade, and her shock seemed rehearsed. What frustrated me even more was my brother's inclination to always side with her, feigning concern as if he truly cared.

He and his wife stood frozen, their impish smiles replaced by wide-eyed astonishment. The guests, frozen in their positions, watched the scene unfold with a mixture of confusion and concern. The confetti on the floor, once vibrant and colorful, now appeared dull and lifeless, reflecting the somber atmosphere that had settled in.

Feeling the weight of my actions and the disapproving gazes of the guests, I turned on my heels and walked out of the reception hall. The cool evening air hit me like a slap in the face, momentarily numbing the storm of emotions raging inside me.

With C by my side, we hurriedly made our way to my car and drove off. The moment we stepped into our hotel room, she shut down my ex's advances with a bold and intimate gesture, asserting her exclusive claim on me.

In that moment, the weight of the past seemed to fade away, replaced by a newfound sense of liberation and possibility. The room became a sanctuary, shielding us from the judgment and disapproval that had plagued the reception hall.

However, a tinge of discontent lingered within me. C stood as a steadfast bridge, seamlessly connecting the fragments of my past to the tapestry of my present. It is often advised never to burn bridges, for they hold the potential for unforeseen futures. Yet, the word 'never' carries an undeniable weight.

It was in this moment that my hidden agenda surfaced, like a whisper carried on a gentle breeze. With a renewed sense of purpose, I eagerly prepared to set my plan into motion, my heart pulsating with determination. The palpable anticipation compelled me to begin my preparations for the much-needed week-long break.

Stay tuned, for soon I shall unravel the intricate details. Until then, farewell—but only for a short while.

Chapter Fifteen

Dearest mortal reader. I beseech you, do not pass judgment on me for what I am about to disclose. I implore you to find compassion in your hearts to comprehend my actions. In that quaint hotel room, I awoke beside C, my heart heavy with the knowledge of what I was about to do to her.

Seeking to ease my guilt, I ventured out and ordered a tray laden with a lavish spread of breakfast. Balancing the weight of two full English breakfasts and a steaming pot of coffee, I returned to the room and gently roused her from slumber.

The sunlight filtered through the sheer curtains, casting a halo-like glow upon her short, blonde hair. Even in her sleepy state, she possessed an innate beauty, as if the universe had gifted her with a perpetual radiance. Only the lingering scent of alcohol on her breath, mirroring my own, marred the perfection.

As she stretched and hurried to the bathroom, I stole a fleeting moment to appreciate the contours of her toned, naked body, knowing it would be the last time I would see it if my plan succeeded.

"What a delightful surprise," she exclaimed, savoring a sip of her coffee and elegantly biting into her toast.

"Eat up," I urged. "We have a long journey ahead."

Her curiosity piqued, she sat up abruptly, brimming with anticipation. "Where are we going?" she inquired, her voice tinged with curiosity.

Aware that she would ask, I swiftly revised my words in my mind and presented the meticulously crafted lie. "We are embarking on a visit to your mother," I playfully pinched her nose to conceal my deceit.

She stared at me, her mouth filled with breakfast, and I decided to elaborate. "Well," I continued, "since I still have a few days of leave remaining, I thought it would be splendid to travel to the Whale Coast." The town was notorious for its historical and present-day association with the Boer Mafia, and it happened to be where her mother lived. She, too, had moved from a town infested with the same criminal influences, just as I had done before her. However, I managed to break free from those shackles and moved to a city untainted by their presence.

I scrutinized C's face intently, searching for any signs of joy or disapproval. It seemed that she embraced the idea as she chewed with greater enthusiasm.

"We must keep it a surprise," I cautioned, for her mother remained unaware of my plans. Both of us now possessed mobile phones, albeit rudimentary ones, and I did not want C to call ahead and alert her mother to our impending visit.

An hour later, I carefully loaded our bags into the trunk of my car, the weight of the guilt heavy on my shoulders. Opening the passenger door for C, I couldn't help but notice the warmth of her smile as she settled into the seat.

The engine hummed to life, and we drove away from Kimberley, leaving behind my mother and brother, who were busy with post-wedding preparations. As I drove, the events of the previous evening played in my mind, each scene vivid and haunting. I realized that I had been invited to the wedding as a pawn in her game of spite, a way for her to spoil my brother and flaunt her animosity towards my father.

I, with my uncanny resemblance to him, was her target, and she reveled in having an audience for her cruelty. Please bear with me as I explain a few moments from my past. You see, a mental health specialist, assigned by my high school, once revealed that my anxiety stemmed from my time in my mother's womb. It was during that vulnerable period that I sensed her rejection. A close family member once confided in me that the moment I was born, my mother exclaimed, "Take him away!" in a fit of anger, declaring that I resembled my father too much.

By then, my father had already realized his mistake in marrying her and had left. In those days, abortions were not an option in our conservative country, so my mother had no choice but to carry the pregnancy to term. As a social worker, she risked her career if she had chosen otherwise.

My first memory of my mother's voice will forever haunt me. I can still hear her sharp words as I entered the kitchen, my stomach growling with hunger. "Go away!" she would snap, her tone filled with disdain. "You're just like your father, and I am not your maid!"

I would retreat, my heart heavy with disappointment. Nights were filled with nightmares, and the sound of her anger echoed through the house whenever I wet the bed. Then, when I started school, the pattern continued. Whenever the teachers shouted at me, I found myself frequently wetting my pants in embarrassment. It became so frequent that they felt compelled to refer me to a school psychologist who would evaluate my mental well-being. The psychologist prescribed medication that not only cured my bedwetting, but also sparked a bitter war between my mother and me.

Brace yourself, dear reader, and be prepared. The chilling air in the school psychologist's office clung to my skin as I sat on the uncomfortable wooden chair. I could hear the distant chatter of students in the hallway, their footsteps echoing through the empty corridors.

In a desperate plea for help, I poured out my heart to her. The fluorescent lights flickered above, casting an eerie glow on her face as she listened intently. I recounted the constant torment from my brother, the relentless bullying that seemed to have no end. My voice trembled with each word, the weight of my pain becoming unbearable.

Her eyes, cold and calculating, betrayed a hint of satisfaction as I shared my darkest secrets. The room felt suffocating; the walls closing in on me. I could almost taste the bitterness in the air as I revealed how my mother always took my brother's side, leaving me defenseless.

And then, the moment of truth arrived. I recounted how my mother's expression transformed into a sadistic grin, her lips contorting with malice. She ordered me to retrieve a long twig, her voice dripping with menace. Fear gripped my heart as I hurriedly complied.

Locked in the bathroom, the stench of cleaning products mixed with the metallic tang of fear. I could hear my own rapid breaths, the sound of my heart pounding in my ears. The first lash struck my bare back, the searing pain radiating through my body. My mother's eyes gleamed with a sick pleasure, her every movement fueling her sadistic enjoyment.

Outside the bathroom door, our loyal dog growled and howled, a symphony of warning and sympathy. The sound mingled with my brother's cruel laughter, echoing through the house like a haunting melody. But amidst the agony, I refused to break. I stood tall, my eyes defiant, determined not to shed a tear.

Her anger grew with each stroke, each lash, leaving its mark on my vulnerable skin. The twig splintered, its pieces embedding themselves in my flesh. The pain intensified, but I refused to show weakness. It only seemed to fuel her rage, intensifying her assault.

Finally, satisfied with her torment, she left me locked in the bathroom for what felt like an eternity. The sound of their laughter drifted through the closed door, a painful reminder of their callous indifference. Hunger gnawed at my empty stomach as the aroma of their delicious dinner wafted into the small space, teasing my senses.

The psychologist, her pen scratching against the paper, showed no signs of sympathy, yet I pleaded to share another story with her. With a subtle nod of her head, she silently urged me to carry on.

I told her about what happened in my classroom, believing it was important for her to be aware. Scratching vigorously, I caught the attention of my observant teacher. She beckoned me forward, her eyes filled with concern. As I approached her desk, the scent of her perfume enveloped me, a comforting contrast to the suffocating atmosphere I had just escaped.

"Show me," she demanded, peering over the rim of her glasses. I hesitated, my fingers trembling as I revealed the marks on my arms and back. A gasp escaped her lips, a mixture of shock and compassion. Together, we made our way to the principal's office, the sound of our footsteps echoing through the empty hallways.

The principal's piercing gaze bore into me, his office filled with an air of authority. I shifted nervously, my gaze darting between my teacher and the principal, seeking solace in the worn-out carpet beneath my feet. "My mother's boyfriend burned me with a cigarette," I whispered, my voice barely audible, the strands of hair twirling nervously around my finger.

"Speak up, boy!" the principal's booming voice shattered the silence, causing both my teacher and me to jump. Summoning every ounce of courage, I shouted at him, spittle spraying from my lips. "My mother's boyfriend burned me with a cigarette!"

As the words tumbled out of my mouth, a cold shiver of fear raced down my spine, accompanied by a wave of uncertainty that engulfed me. The room felt heavy, suffocating, as if the air itself held its breath in anticipation. I couldn't decipher if what I said was a lie or a forgotten truth, for the memory of where the bruises came from eluded me.

The faint scent of a long-forgotten illness, Chickenpox, lingered in my mind, reminding me of the past. But it had been years since I had suffered from that childhood affliction. The remnants of Chickenpox could sometimes leave marks on the skin, resembling burns from a smoldering cigarette. I made sure to explain to the teachers that it wasn't Chickenpox.

Yet, a dark shadow loomed over my recollection. My mother's boyfriend was a smoker, his cigarette smoke permeating the air with its acrid odor. He was the same man who invaded my privacy, barging into the bathroom while I bathed, manipulating me with money to pose for him. The medication they prescribed me, with its bitter taste and drowsiness, left me in a state of oblivion, like a horse tranquilized into submission. During those moments of unconsciousness, who knew what could have transpired?

This particular man held a deep disdain for me. A pastor in our church, he frequently invaded our home, bringing with him an air of sanctimony and unease. It was during one of these visits that I stumbled upon a sight that forever etched itself into my mind. I burst through the closed door of a spare bedroom, startled by the sound of my mother's moans. To my astonishment, her cries were not of pain but of pleasure. Their bodies were intertwined in an unusual and unexpected way. Only later did I learn what this position was called.

Stunned and a strange mix of amusement and horror washing over me, I couldn't contain my laughter. It erupted from deep within me, reverberating off the walls. But my momentary astonishment was short-lived, as my brother pounced on me with brute force, inflicting a merciless beating. That's when I realized the depth of his grudge. From that day forward, during church ministries, I sat in the front pew wearing a knowing smirk, taunting the pastor with my silent understanding.

And it was from that moment onwards that he began to pay me off, compensating me with crisp bills for any good deed I fulfilled for him. It made me wonder if he had something to do with the mysterious bruises that adorned my arms, a physical manifestation of his resentment and cruel intentions.

And with that, my dearest mortal readers, I conclude the haunting memories that engulfed my thoughts. As C and I continued on our journey, I stole a fleeting glance at her. She lay reclined in her seat, peacefully slumbering, her serene expression etched on her face. The vibrations of the car hummed beneath us as we traversed the winding roads, finally arriving at our destination—the quaint town where her mother resided.

A palpable sense of joy radiated from her mother as she laid eyes on us. In her mind, her beloved daughter, C, had been living with her twin sister, D. However, her heart overflowed with genuine happiness upon witnessing our reunion. Eager to assist, I helped C unload her bags, feeling the weight of our past and uncertain future in my hands. The sound of their jubilant reunion echoed through the house as I hastened towards the sanctuary of the bathroom.

Passing by the kitchen, the clinking of glasses and the muffled laughter filled the air, their minds consumed by the intoxicating nectar of wine. I hurriedly returned to my car, sliding into the driver's seat, and accelerated away, the scenery blurring as I left them behind, forever lost from my sight.

Even now, as I pen down this tumultuous experience, tears cascade down my cheeks, mingling with the ink on the page. The decision to sever ties was agonizing, but necessary, for I was a vessel of turmoil, unfit to coexist with C. There were countless unresolved issues within me that demanded attention, issues that I could not impose on her. Though she, too, grappled with her own demons, our lives together would have been a volatile concoction destined for failure. Sometimes, the act of cruelty is the kindest path one can choose.

In time, I discovered that she dedicated herself to her studies, ultimately becoming a skilled veterinarian. And, as if to affirm the righteousness of my decision, she found love in the arms of a woman we both held dear. The universe, it seems, has a way of weaving its intricate tapestry.

Fatigue weighed heavily upon me, unsure of my destination, both physically and emotionally. To unravel the unfolding of this journey, stay tuned. Until our paths converge again, farewell for now.

Chapter Sixteen

My heart ached, a heavy burden within me, as I reluctantly left C behind. The toxicity of her presence was suffocating, and I had no space for another needy soul in my life. Overwhelmed by my own struggles, I couldn't bear the weight of someone else's.

As I drove through the town, the sight of L's opulent home caught my eye. Its grandeur juxtaposed against my own feelings of emptiness. For a moment, I contemplated stopping, knocking on the door, and seeking solace. But I knew deep down that I had to sever ties with the past. It clung to me like shackles, dragging me down with each weary step I took.

Fatigue settled in as I pushed on along the never-ending road to Johannesburg. It stretched out before me like a glimmering ribbon, illuminated by the soft glow of the full moon. Questions raced through my mind, while the incessant ringing of my phone served as a cruel reminder of the choices I had just made.

I dared not close my eyes, fearful of losing control, yet C's face haunted my imagination, contorted with pain. Guilt surged within me like a tidal wave, tempting me to reconsider my decision. But I pressed on, determined never to look back again.

Amidst the drive, I pondered my choice, wondering if I would ever discover true love. I believed deep within my soul that she was out there, waiting for me, just as I longed to stumble upon her. My dear mortal reader, please forgive this brief interruption in my journey, as I take you back to the reasons I believed I deserved to find true love.

Growing up in a home devoid of warmth, with an absent mother and

Growing Slowly Nowhere

no father, I began a lifelong search for love. The empty rooms echoed with silence, the walls adorned with faded photographs of a family I longed to know. My desperate need for acceptance surpassed all fears, and I ended up growing up in many homes. Some of these homes occupied grand mansions, while others were cramped apartments filled with the scent of stale cigarettes and desperation. It was during my innocent youth that I stumbled upon a profound truth: love cannot be sought in the shadows or the pursuit of material wealth. Young children see everything, and I knew then that money and wealth did not sit around the same table. Little did I know, I will make a choice that will haunt me for the rest of my life.

I embarked on my search for true love. Did I end up finding it? Read on dearest reader, for the truth will reward you.

My journey led me through many homes, towns, and cities, each one leaving me with a deeper understanding of the complexities of human nature. In these places, I witnessed heartbreak and acts of cruelty, far removed from the love I so desperately sought.

The bitter taste of disappointment lingered in the air, suffocating the hope that flickered within me. But to find something, you have to know what it is you are looking for. Due to my dysfunctional family, my perception of love became greatly distorted. However, I was aware of its existence, and it continued to evade me for many years.

The first thing I did was immerse myself in the pages of love stories, learning to decipher their hidden messages. I stole many books from the children's library because I had no money, and perused the pages, searching for love. The musty scent of old paper mingled with the sweet aroma of imagination, as I delved into the stories that promised love's embrace. What I learned from the pages was that love is a fantasy, a never-ending story, and a happily ever-after. It was far from the truth. My search continued.

I turned to those surrounding me, their disappointed faces etched with despair. The opulent homes exuded a cold emptiness devoid of love's warmth. Meanwhile, within the humble abodes of the impoverished, affection seemed to reign supreme. With a heavy heart, I abandoned my quest, seeking love among those nearby, fully aware it would only lead to certain disappointment. After all, behind their kind acts, most people concealed hidden motives.

My ignorance only deepened the haze, distorting my perception of love further. I yearned to understand love before embarking on my search. Seeking guidance, I turned to a trusted teacher who recommended poetry as a wellspring of wisdom, crafted by the true pioneers of love: Shakespeare, Burns, Poe, and their ilk.

Yet, even in the realm of poetry, disappointment awaited me. Most verses were penned by men, seemingly dedicated solely to their mistresses. Though their words conveyed emotions and the agony of affection, they failed to reveal the essence of love. Unless, of course, one believes love is merely a red rose or a tempestuous ocean.

Curiously, I felt a sense of worthiness and entitlement to love, a sentiment shared by all. I yearned to know, and it was during this time that I discovered religion, a profound discourse on love. Turning to the scriptures, be it the Bible, Torah, or Qur'an, I found a resounding emphasis on love as a central and divine principle.

It was then, in that profound moment, that a brilliant breakthrough illuminated my mind. As I delved into the scriptures, a keyword emerged, resonating deeply with the mention of true love. The word that shimmered before me was "sacrifice." In the essence of these sacred texts, I discovered a profound truth: true love often intertwines with sacrifice. The aroma of selflessness, devotion to God, and acts of kindness and charity wafted through the pages. Sacrifice became an indispensable thread in the tapestry of a loving and faithful life.

Although I had discovered what I had been searching for, I set it aside for the time being. In my tender years, the concept of sacrifice eluded me, and I lacked the knowledge to put it to the test. This revelation seemed to unlock a mystical door into my life and experiences, bestowing upon me a peculiar epiphany. Later in life, long after I had forgotten about my pursuit of love, I began to have recurring dreams.

In these dreams, I would find myself observing a solitary schoolgirl seated in a serene courtyard during her breaks. Despite her lack of companions, she would relish her lunch and hum a cheerful melody to herself. Unhesitatingly, I would approach her, taking in every detail of her innocent face, her gentle blue eyes radiating love, and her mischievous smile teasing me with its enigmatic secret. In the dream, my hand would reach out towards her, and just as our fingertips brushed, I would awaken, and she would vanish from my sight. Undoubtedly, she was the girl of my dreams, my dream soulmate. My mission was to find her, and every step I took was filled with determination.

This dream, devoid of any doubt, stayed with me. I now possessed two invaluable keys: a blueprint of my dream girl and a path to finding true love - sacrifice versus dreams. However, it is commonly believed that our brains cannot conjure faces or fabricate them, and that the individuals we encounter in our dreams are people we have met before. I dare to disagree.

Years slipped by, and I now refer to them as my dark ages—a time when hope seemed as distant as the love I longed for. The weight of countless failed relationships and the despair of almost giving up on true love had taken its toll. You see, there is a detail I failed to confess. I have already mentioned the mishap that prevents me from bearing children or impregnating a woman.

The bitter truth of my infertility had caused many girlfriends to abandon me, leaving a lingering taste of disappointment on my tongue. Their longing for a future filled with laughter and the pitter-patter of little feet was understandable. I couldn't fault them for desiring what I couldn't provide. It forced me to adopt a preemptive strategy - rejecting them before they could reject me. I had just returned from yet another heart-wrenching experience, the reality of my situation still fresh in my mind.

As I drove down the long road, the weight of my realization settled upon me. I knew deep down that I hadn't made a mistake. It was only a matter of time before C would have ended our relationship, seeking solace in the arms of another man. The thought sent a pang of both relief and determination coursing through me. I eagerly anticipated the enchantment of meeting my true love, a dream I desperately clung to. The yearning for a genuine companion burned within me, fueling my resolve.

Would fate grant me the chance to meet her, or did life have other plans in store? Only time would reveal the answer.

As my story continues to unfold, my weary mind longs for a moment of respite. Until next time, goodbye, but only for now.

Chapter Seventeen

Returning to the bustling city, my birthplace awakened a sense of familiarity within me. The vibrant streets and bustling crowds resonated with a deep connection to my father's past. Each encounter with new faces left me pondering if they had crossed paths with him. I knew he was an avid pilot, starting with small aircraft and eventually becoming a commercial pilot. This revelation came from his closest friend, who often shared stories of their adventures while my father stayed at the farm between his trips from Johannesburg to Durban.

As I listened, the woman recounted a vivid memory of a late Sunday afternoon. Sitting on their expansive verandah, the air was filled with the clinking of glasses and the faint rustling of leaves. Suddenly, her husband's attention was captured by a rapidly approaching dust cloud, accompanied by the growing roar of an engine. Intrigued, he sprang into action, all senses heightened.

A blue car skidded to a halt in the dusty courtyard before them, commanding their immediate attention. The Fiat Twin Turbo stood gleaming in the golden light of the setting sun, leaving her husband in awe. Meanwhile, her gaze fixated on the striking figure that emerged from the vehicle, drawn to his Scottish accent like a magnet to metal. Though they struggled with English, my father understood their Afrikaans and responded in kind, forging an instant connection.

From that moment on, an unbreakable bond formed between them and my charismatic father. Like me, they were left bewildered by his sudden disappearance, recounting the same story to me countless times during my childhood. It was through their heartfelt tales that I discovered my father's deep passion for flying. While I didn't have concrete knowledge of his commercial license, it seemed plausible given the many passengers he carried on his long journeys, including the couple.

Armed with this newfound understanding, I made the city my hunting ground. Utilizing the spare cash I had earned, I enlisted the help of private investigators to aid in my search. I explored the flats where they had once lived, immersing myself in the echoes of their shared memories. Additionally, I frequented the airfields, immersing myself in the sights and sounds of aviation, hoping to uncover further traces of my father's legacy.

But my search led me down a fruitless path, like a maze with no exit. He had vanished without leaving a single trace behind. The only results my relentless search produced were waves of unease crashing over me, growing stronger with each passing day. I found myself contemplating the very existence of my father, lost in a sea of uncertainty. To this day, I possess only one solitary piece of evidence that he ever walked this earth. It is a photograph frozen in time, capturing a moment during their wedding. As I mentioned previously, neither he nor my mother adorned their fingers with wedding rings, an unusual sight as confetti cascaded down upon them like a colorful rain. However, within the confines of that photograph, you can see the undeniable proof of his fatherhood—the way our features mirror each other.

Doubts started to plague my mind, questioning the validity of my mother's stories, yet the answers I sought remained elusive. It was a maddening pursuit, for everyone who had known my father chose to align themselves with her, leaving me stranded in a sea of doubt. I even began to question the authenticity of his name as my mother had recounted it. All my attempts to find him yielded no results, leaving me to wonder how a man could simply vanish without a trace. From that moment onward, I referred to my father as the man with no name, a phantom figure haunting the recesses of my mind.

Defeated and consumed by misery, I sought solace in my work, as I always had in times of despair. I resigned myself to the fact that the truth would forever remain concealed. It became painfully apparent that my mother's lies were deliberate, carefully crafted to divert my attention away from the truth.

In the evenings, I sought refuge in the company of my American friends, immersing myself in the allure of beer, attempting to fill the void left by my father and mend the tattered fabric of my mother's deceit.

With the lingering effects of indulgence weighing heavily on my every breath, I yearned for a much-needed respite. Seeking solace and closure, I resolved to pour my heart and soul into the act of writing, allowing raw emotions to spill onto the illuminated screen before me in my makeshift study.

The soft glow of the computer screen bathed the room in a gentle, ethereal light, creating an atmosphere of tranquility. But despite the serene ambiance, inspiration remained elusive, for my perception of my father was distorted. All I possessed were the fabrications spun by my mother, a faded photograph that barely captured his essence, and the whispers of his presence shared by the couple living on the farm where he once resided.

Suddenly, like an unexpected tidal wave crashing upon me, a realization struck. I fixated on his love for flying, transforming it into an enigmatic figure, a focal point for my reminiscences of a life that once intertwined with his, envisioning myself standing by his side in those cherished memories.

As I delved deeper into my imagination, the memories of my father's passion for flying became vivid. I could almost feel the wind rushing through my hair as we soared through the endless sky, the exhilaration of defying gravity pulsing through our veins. In my mind, I could see his eyes sparkling with joy and a sense of freedom that only the open sky could provide.

With each stroke of the keyboard, I poured my longing onto the screen, weaving a tapestry of emotions and stories. I painted a portrait of a man who was both larger than life and deeply human, a complex blend of strength and vulnerability. The words flowed effortlessly, as if guided by an unseen hand, bringing me closer to understanding the man who had shaped my existence, even in his absence.

But as the pages piled up, I began to question the accuracy of my memories. Was I romanticizing my father's love for flying, or was it truly the essence of who he was? I found myself grappling with the fragments of his life that I had, trying to piece them together into a coherent narrative. It was a delicate balance between truth and fiction, between honoring his memory and creating something meaningful.

In the quiet solitude of my makeshift study, I allowed myself to explore the depths of my emotions. The act of writing became a cathartic release, a way to confront my own insecurities and fears. Through the process, I began to realize that my father's love for flying was not just about the physical act itself, but a metaphor for his untamed spirit, his relentless pursuit of dreams.

With each word, I felt a weight being lifted off my chest. The lingering effects of indulgence and the distorted perception of my father started to fade away. In their place, a sense of clarity and acceptance emerged. I may never fully understand the complexities of his life, but through my writing, I could honor his legacy and find solace in the memories we shared.

As the soft glow of the computer screen continued to illuminate the room, I knew that I had found my respite. The act of pouring my heart and soul into my writing had given me the closure I yearned for. And as I stood by his side in my cherished memories, I realized that his love for flying would forever be a guiding light, propelling me forward on my own journey of self-discovery and fulfillment.

As I lay in bed, the rain tapping softly against the window; I immersed myself in the tale I had woven. My heart raced with anticipation, for a revelation awaited in the next chapter. But for now, I must leave you with the promise of discovery to come

Chapter Eighteen

As I delved into the pages of my narrative, a musty scent of old paper filled my nostrils. The dim light of my makeshift study cast long shadows on the worn wooden desk, creating an atmosphere of introspection.

My eyes scanned the words on the page, absorbing the weight of my emotions. A sense of discomfort gnawed at the edges of my consciousness, like a persistent itch that couldn't be scratched. It was as if there was something hidden, lurking beneath the surface of my writing.

And then, like a bolt of lightning, I found it. My words reverberated with anger, each sentence dripping with the bitterness that had consumed me. The anger that had consumed me for years was still there, an unwelcome companion churning in the depths of my belly.

As I mulled over the details, memories flooded my mind, transporting me back to the moments that had shaped my path. And then, a painful truth emerged. I realized that I, like a wounded animal, attracted a particular breed of humans whom I called vultures. They sensed my vulnerabilities, honing in on them like predators stalking their prey.

They devoured every ounce of my good-naturedness, leaving me hollow and depleted. I had unknowingly offered myself up to these people, willingly opening myself to their manipulations. And in return, they discarded me like a sack of rotten potatoes, moving on to their next unsuspecting victim. To them, I was nothing more than a means to an end, a source of temporary gratification.

It was these people, the broken nation, who fueled my anger.

Despite coming from stable backgrounds, they remained needy, driven by their own selfish desires. Whether it was heartbreak or financial burdens, they saw me, the broken soul, as their beacon of hope. In a bold experiment, I turned to those who had never spared me a second glance. In our bustling workplace, filled with twenty waiters attending to their patrons, only four were my loyal friends. Or so I had thought, because loyalty was a quality that belonged to me alone, not to them. A realization washed over me that I had unintentionally filled my life with people who didn't belong, and I had no idea why.

With newfound determination, I attempted to approach the healthier, more balanced individuals among my coworkers. But they could smell my desperation, my brokenness, and it repelled them. They sensed my weakness, avoiding me as if I were a contagious disease. During this period of my journey, I deemed it as "shaking the disease," a metaphorical shedding of the anger and toxicity that had consumed me.

To break free from the chains of my own anger, I knew I had to redefine my circle of friends. I had become the go-to person for anyone in need, the one they turned to with their burdens. I had unwittingly become their vomit bucket, a receptacle for their troubles. It was time to narrow my friendship circle, to distance myself from those who drained me of my own well-being.

And to achieve that, I subtly faded into the background, employing a sinister approach. Instead of joining them in a game of shooting pool, I would opt for a movie when they suggested going to the bar. If I did go to the bar, I ended up playing darts with unfamiliar faces. Rather than participating in nighttime quiz games at the pubs, where I found myself continuously buying rounds of drinks, I sought solace in the library.

During my countless hours in this contemporary, modern library, a shocking revelation unexpectedly crossed my path. In my quest for medical research, I accidentally stumbled upon a thought-provoking study centered around the use of anti-depressants.

My curiosity peaked, I carefully plucked the book from the towering shelf. As I scanned the index, my eyes fixated on the brand of medication that had been prescribed to me.

Like a veil being lifted, memories of the past flooded my mind. Once again, I found myself in that sterile environment, the faint hum of equipment and the scent of antiseptic enveloping me.

The staff gently covered my head with an icy gel and skillfully attached electrodes to my scalp. The Neurologist strolled into the room, his smile inscrutable. Perhaps he derived satisfaction from the financial gain. With a low hum emanating from the devices around me, the air became charged with static electricity. In the midst of this electrifying ambiance, a mesmerizing array of images flickered on the large white screen.

The neurologist's voice echoed in my mind as he presented me with a rapid-fire barrage of peculiar questions.

"Do I prefer boys or girls?" he inquired, accompanied by a chuckle.

Without hesitation, I responded, "Girls."

"Girls with either ample or modest bosoms," he persisted.

My gaze darting around, I anxiously searched for my mother. In a barely audible murmur, I replied, "Small."

For what felt like an eternity, he mercilessly probed my mind with an incessant barrage of questions. My eyes nervously glanced at the glowing amber screen, its waveform fluctuating with each response, occasionally punctuated by a jarring beep that sent shivers down my spine.

It seemed as though his focus was fixated on my sexuality, disregarding everything else. The questioning finally ceased, and he proceeded to subject me to a series of tests, evaluating my reflexes. Later, he directed a blinding beam of light into my eyes, emitting a dissatisfied grunt upon discovering a minor defect. Throughout this ordeal, the monotonous scratch of his pen against paper persisted, akin to a broken record.

Satisfied with his assessment, he tore a lengthy sheet of paper from a nearby machine. With intense scrutiny, he studied its contents and motioned for me to follow him. Eagerly, I hastily threw on my clothes, puzzled as to why I had been forced to undress. Yet understanding that he must have had a purpose.

Taking a seat across from the neurologist, I sat beside my mother, facing the worry etched on his face. He proceeded to unveil startling revelations about myself, unknown and incomprehensible to me.

"You will never excel in any athletic endeavors," he declared, causing my brow to furrow in confusion, while my mother's mischievous grin widened.

"Your coordination skills are severely lacking, and I strongly advise against pursuing a driver's license," he continued, causing my shoulders to slump in disappointment.

"I recommend enrolling in a special needs school," he coldly stated, "as I do not foresee you progressing beyond the tenth grade." My mouth went dry, while my mother's laughter filled the room, her triumph gleaming in her eyes.

"You suffer from a severe anxiety condition, for which I will prescribe medication," he pressed on, explaining that this medication would be a lifelong necessity.

As I held the book in my hand, the name of the prescribed medication stared back at me, jolting me back to reality. Filled with a mix of apprehension and determination, I eagerly flipped through its pages, desperate to uncover the truth.

I was stunned beyond belief, my jaw dropping to the floor as I discovered that the medication prescribed to me was actually meant for individuals battling bipolar mood disorder, schizophrenia, and other unrelated conditions. The sheer weight of this revelation had me questioning the legality of administering such potent dosages and even prescribing this drug to kids my age.

My curiosity was instantly sparked, urging me to delve deeper into my research. As I continued, a wave of realization washed over me, for I discovered that the dosage I had been taking as a teenager greatly surpassed the recommended allowance for my age group.

In a hushed tone, I mumbled to myself, "Did my mother intentionally drug me?" The sound of my words echoed in the tranquil library, drawing peculiar gazes from those around me. Undeterred, I made a firm decision to expand my research and seek guidance from a professional. The only question was, who would be the right person to consult?

The gripping reality of my situation began to unfold, sending shivers down my spine in anticipation of the next chapter of my journey. Until then, farewell for now.

Chapter Nineteen

My dearest mortal reader. Life has a way of surprising us with harsh realities, don't you think? Call me paranoid, or use whatever word you find fitting. But I couldn't bring myself to confide in anyone about my troubles. Instead, I trusted the soft voice in my head and made a drastic decision.

Without a second thought, I ceased taking my prescribed medication. The nights stretched on endlessly; the darkness enveloping me as sleep eluded my grasp. The weight of anxiety pressed upon my chest, threatening to suffocate me. Panic attacks were always looming closer, their presence a constant threat that couldn't be ignored. My appetite vanished, replaced by a desperate reliance on coffee, hoping it would grant me some respite. Little did I know that this choice would only worsen my sleeplessness and intensify my anxiety.

But like every endeavor I had embarked on before, I was determined to see it through, regardless of the toll it took on my well-being. I became convinced that my mother had somehow influenced the Neurologist to prescribe me these lethal doses. My research only deepened my confusion, as none of the conditions listed on the label applied to my own suffering.

And so, I forced myself to endure the torment. It was pure hell, my dear reader, as the days passed by in a blur of agony. The weight loss was undeniable, causing my coworkers to nickname me "twig," while others mockingly referred to me as "owl," a cruel reference to my perpetually wide eyes. The cruel wordplay caught on, spreading throughout my workplace until everyone knew me as "twig owl."

Yet, I remained steadfast in my decision, hoping for the positive signs that I desperately yearned for. I knew deep down that I had inflicted this torture upon myself and that I had to bear the consequences of my own actions.

During this time, I had the pleasure of meeting Nina, a young waitress, and my coworker, who would soon become a dear friend. As I reflect on those moments, I can still see the dimly lit restaurant where we worked together, the clinking of dishes and cutlery filling the air as we went about our tasks.

Nina, with her delicate frame and pale complexion, exuded a fragility that was hard to ignore. It was in this bustling environment that our friendship began to flourish, shielded from the outside world.

Nina's story unfolded before me, each word piercing my heart. She had been raised in an opulent home, her dreams of becoming a renowned ballet dancer nurtured by her supportive parents. However, the ballet teacher, a stern figure in her life, constantly reminded her of her weight, triggering a downward spiral. The taste of bitterness lingered in her mouth as she battled bulimia and ultimately succumbed to anorexia. Her parents, unable to understand her pain, turned their backs on her, leaving her to find solace in her own meager apartment and a job as a waitress.

Unbeknownst to me, as I carried on with my own struggles, Nina had been there all along. The world had turned a blind eye to my existence, but she chose to stand by my side. The flickering light of hope in that dark tunnel became brighter with each passing day.

As time went on, the fruits of my decision began to manifest. The vibrant colors of life slowly seeped back into my world. The taste of food, once dull and uninspiring, regained its allure. I would go for long runs, feeling the earth beneath my feet, the wind whispering through my hair. The sound of my heart pounding in my chest became a symphony of triumph. At night, I would sink into a deep slumber, comforted by dreams that danced vividly in my mind.

In the midst of my personal transformation, I discovered a newfound passion for cooking. The kitchen became our sanctuary, filled with the aroma of herbs and spices from around the world. Together, we would create culinary masterpieces, our laughter echoing through the room as we experimented with flavors and techniques.

During our precious lunch breaks, we would escape to the nearby food court, the vibrant sights and sounds of the bustling crowd providing a backdrop to our shared moments. We would indulge in nourishing meals, savoring each bite with gratitude.

As we sat side by side in the movie theater, the scent of buttered popcorn wafted through the air, intermingling with the effervescence of coca cola and the sweetness of wine gums. The silver screen would come to life before our eyes, transporting us to worlds of adventure and emotion.

In the warmth of my cramped apartment, I would read my written stories to Nina, her eyes sparkling with delight. The soft touch of her hand on my shoulder filled me with a sense of validation, igniting a fire within me to continue creating. Together, we reveled in the praises that flowed from her lips, knowing that our bond was unbreakable.

Those hours spent in the kitchen, stirring pots and pans, were a symphony of flavors and aromas. The sizzle of onions hitting the hot pan, the fragrant spices dancing in the air, the vibrant colors of the ingredients coming together in perfect harmony—it was pure bliss. We delighted in the fusion of international cuisines, our taste buds transported to distant lands with each mouthful.

In those moments, surrounded by the sensory delights of sights, sounds, smells, and feelings, our friendship blossomed. Through shared meals and culinary adventures, we found solace and strength in each other. And as we continued on this journey, navigating the twists and turns of life, our bond grew stronger, like the flavors melding together in a perfectly seasoned dish.

Over time, Nina underwent a remarkable transformation. She bloomed like a radiant flower, her once anorexic figure now filled out gracefully. I couldn't help but be captivated by her newfound beauty, with her flowing light brown hair gently cascading over her shoulders, her charming smile, and her captivating baby blue eyes. It was a sight that electrified me, making it nearly impossible to resist.

In my cramped apartment, she would entice me with her ballet moves, gracefully pirouetting while her short dress twirled around her shapely, toned legs. I would gaze at her every contour, my mouth going dry, as I took a long sip of wine.

Nina was truly a sight to behold, and I couldn't help but notice the way my male coworkers' attitudes drastically changed towards her. She had become an object of desire for everyone.

To celebrate my own accomplishment, I made the inevitable choice to interfere. It was a decision I would deeply regret. Despite knowing everything about Nina, I reached out to her parents and invited them to experience our exquisite restaurant.

As the evening grew late, a sense of anticipation filled the air, mingling with the aroma of delicious food wafting from the restaurant. Standing guard at the entrance, I scanned the crowd, my eyes darting from one face to another, searching for the couple who embodied everything I had come to know about Nina's parents.

Nina, in her usual restless manner, constantly hovered by my side, her energy palpable. Determined not to spoil the surprise, I cleverly kept her occupied, diverting her attention away from the entrance. And then, amidst the bustling crowd, my gaze fell upon a couple exuding an air of affluence as they gracefully approached.

There was something about the way they moved, the lady's refined manners, that made my heart skip a beat. Without hesitation, I stepped forward, introducing myself to their astonishment. With a warmth in my voice, I guided them to the table I had meticulously reserved, eager to see the joy on Nina's face.

Oh, how I wish you could have witnessed the sheer astonishment that washed over Nina as she hurried to attend to the table, oblivious to the fact that it was her own parents. Time seemed to freeze as her eyes widened, tears welling up, overwhelming her. In perfect synchrony, her parents leaped from their seats, their arms enveloping their long-lost daughter in a tearful embrace.

Overwhelmed with happiness, my own eyes welled up, and I discreetly made my way towards the bathrooms, allowing Nina to revel in this precious moment. Ahh, the lingering fragrance of forgiveness fills my mind, a gentle reminder of the power of letting go.

Their reunion was a joyous one, embracing their daughter and accepting her for who she had become—a charming waitress. They left her a generous tip, and I could see that they had taken a liking to me as well, conspiring to make me a part of their family by putting a ring on Nina's finger. But I knew deep down that a woman as extraordinary as her would never fall for someone like me, not in that way at least. We were meant to be friends, and friends alone.

Unexpectedly, everything changed. Nina stopped showing up for work, leaving me bewildered. Determined to find out the truth, I embarked on an investigation that revealed a heart-wrenching reality. Nina was no longer with us. She had tragically taken her own life, leaving me burdened with an overwhelming guilt that I couldn't bear. Each passing day felt heavier than the last, and the pain in my chest seemed to intensify with every beat of my heart.

Then, out of the blue, her father, a skilled surgeon, walked into the dimly lit restaurant. With a slight smile, he extended an invitation for me to join him for a cup of freshly brewed coffee. Hesitantly, I made my way across the room, the plush seat beckoning me, its velvety fabric caressing my skin as I sank into its comforting embrace.

Her father's face held an expression of raw honesty, his words startling in their candor. A man in need, he confessed to succumbing to the forbidden allure of an affair with his secretary. The weight of his guilt became clear as he revealed that his wife had discovered his betrayal, threatening him with divorce. Desperate and lost, she had turned to a dangerous blend of sleeping pills and wine, her intoxicated confessions inevitably reaching Nina's ears.

In a desperate plea for attention, Nina sought solace in the arms of narcotics, their seductive allure consuming her. Unfamiliar with their potency, she unknowingly took an excessive amount, her body found in a sewer pipe. The local newspaper seized upon the tragedy, publishing a photograph that made headlines. With her needle-filled arm and exposed form, Nina lay before my eyes, a haunting image that shattered my perception of the girl I once knew. Days turned into nights as I mourned her loss.

Forgive me, dearest reader, for this sudden transition to the present tense, but I hope you can appreciate the effort. "Hello Nina!" I whisper, the sound of my voice mingling with the gentle hum of the air conditioning. "It's me, Uiltjie, just as you used to call me." The ache of missing her tugs at my heart as my fingertips glide effortlessly over the keyboard, guided by the inspiration she continues to provide from above. "Until we meet again, know that I carry your absence with me, a weight upon my soul. Goodbye for now, sending hugs and kisses from me to you."

In the peaceful quiet of my solitude, I often find myself having heartfelt conversations with Nina. I imagine her presence so vividly.

Little did I know, the universe had a consequence in store for my act of kindness. Stay tuned for the next chapter, where everything will be revealed. For now, I say goodbye with tears in my eyes, longing for our upcoming reunion.

Chapter Twenty

If I had known then what I know now, the hair on the back of my neck would have prickled, urging me to flee out of that restaurant right then and there. But none of us can see the future. It lurks in the shadows, its watchful gaze piercing through the air like fiery embers.

My heart was heavy with the sorrow of losing my best friend, Nina. The weight of her absence was a constant ache, impossible to ignore. Although I swiftly formed new connections, they could never replace her. She was a beacon of beauty, kindness, and grace - my personal Snow White.

It was during this tumultuous time that I stumbled upon something extraordinary, seeking solace amidst the turmoil of my recent withdrawal from prescribed medication. I embarked on a journey of fasting, honoring Nina, who had once battled with anorexia. The effects were nothing short of magical; I could feel the positive transformation coursing through my body, revitalizing my sleep, mood, and overall well-being.

However, just as I sensed a breakthrough, the universe hurled a spinning boulder in my path. While diligently fulfilling my duties as a waiter, an unwelcome ghost from my past, D swaggered into the restaurant, a conspicuous black eye staining her face. As a reminder, D was my long-lost girlfriend, one half of an identical twin, who had forsaken me for a younger, seemingly more successful partner.

As it turned out, it was this very same younger partner who had inflicted the black eye upon her. Shockingly, she confessed that it wasn't the first time, finally summoning the courage to escape the toxic relationship, only to seek refuge in my arms once more. But I refused to be her sanctuary. Instead, I offered her temporary respite under my roof.

Oh, what a foolish decision it was. Men like him, G, were possessive, and he haunted me relentlessly, serenading his loss with drunken hiccups in the early hours of the morning. To make matters worse, it came to light that D had accumulated an astronomical amount of gambling debt, a vice she had eagerly shared with her now ex-lover. And now, Mister Blackjack wanted his money back.

I found myself hurtling down a treacherous path, and I knew I had to act swiftly. With her presence in my life, chaos seemed to reign. I began to notice money disappearing from my secret stash, leaving me bewildered and uncertain. I couldn't bear to cast her out onto the unforgiving streets. And then, as if the universe sensed my anguish and reveled in its own cruel humor, D's brother appeared out of nowhere, seeking information about his sister.

He was known for his cowardice, but now he seemed determined to confront D's abusive ex-fiancé, the one who had left her battered and bruised. Despite my reservations, I mustered the compassion to drive him to the ex's apartment, where they drowned their sorrows in aged whiskey, their laughter mingling with the scent of oak and camaraderie.

I had to act, and act quickly, feeling the weight of urgency in my bones. My life was on a good track, but they came like a train ready to derail me. Having depleted all my leave on Nina and her funeral, I pleaded with my boss for a few days off, the desperation in my voice palpable. With his typical sinister smile, he agreed, his nod sending shivers down my spine. I knew he was going to make me pay for it later.

I gathered D and K, and informed them I was taking them on a much-needed holiday for a short break. Without hesitation, they packed their meager belongings, the sound of zippers and rustling fabric filling the air, and loaded them into the trunk of my new car, a sleek BMW 318i that I took great pride in.

As the evening grew late, the world around us dipped into darkness. It was past seven o'clock when we finally embarked on our journey. D, seeking solace, swallowed a sleeping pill, the sound of a pill bottle rattling, before succumbing to a deep slumber in the backseat.

Meanwhile, K, always eager for a thrill, discovered my hidden stash of cheap whisky, the clinking of glass echoing through the car. I silenced him with a finger pressed against my lips, a deceptive act to mask my true intentions.

Yet, as K indulged in the forbidden drink, he eventually succumbed to its effects. He extended the bottle towards me, offering me a taste, but I declined, promising to buy a fresh bottle once we reached our destination. In no time, K drained the bottle, his grip on it tightening as he drifted into a snoring slumber beside me, his body sprawled across the passenger seat.

In the early hours of the morning, faced with a crucial decision, I weighed my options. Should I stop for fuel and risk waking D and K, their snores providing a symphony of obliviousness, or should I press on, risking running out of fuel? But of course, dear reader, I chose to stop for gas. As I pulled up beside the pump, I signaled the eager petrol attendant to keep quiet. His mischievous smile betrayed his amusement at the sight of my intoxicated passengers.

I hurriedly dashed into the shop, the scent of freshly brewed coffee mingling with the smell of gasoline in the air, and purchased an extra-large cup. After relieving myself, I rushed back to the car, the chill of the morning biting at my skin.

Once again, the open road stretched out before me like an endless ribbon, the promise of escape and secrecy. D and K continued their slumber, their dreams fueling a fiery debate in their sleep, a hint of a smile playing on my lips.

Yet, I pushed the limits, my foot heavy on the accelerator, disregarding the speed limit and the consequences. I had to reach our destination before the sun rose and they awoke, my determination fueling my reckless driving. The wind whipped through the open windows, the sound of the rushing air mixing with the occasional mumbled words from my sleeping companions, causing my muscles to tense. But for now, they were lost in their dreams, and I dared not think about what those murmurs might mean.

If only I had known then what awaited me at the end of this journey, I would have turned around, desperately seeking an alternative plan. Little did I know that I was going to encounter D's identical twin sister, C, and a shocking revelation. Their brother's animosity towards me was about to be revealed. During the early days of my relationship with D, I had noticed this trait.

But in that moment, gripping the steering wheel so tightly that my knuckles turned white, I continued to speed towards our destination, the adrenaline coursing through my veins.

As the fiery sun slowly peeked over the distant horizon, casting its warm golden glow upon the land, we finally arrived at our long-awaited destination. The gentle swaying and constant changing of direction stirred my slumbering passengers from their deep sleep, their weary eyes blinking open, adjusting to the new day.

Before they had a chance to voice any protest, I skillfully turned into the familiar driveway of their mother's house. The engine's smooth vibration was a reassuring sensation as I cautiously pulled the key from the ignition, remembering K's previous unauthorized joyride.

A sleek black Mercedes caught my eye briefly, but I dismissed it, focusing solely on completing our journey. Their mother burst from the house, arms wide, her fatigue mingling with the warmth of their reunion. The embrace, while heartfelt, bore the marks of weariness. D's gaze, however, held a silent warning that sent a shiver down my spine.

But as if the universe had conspired to reward my efforts with a twist of fate, I was met with a sight that defied expectation. Stepping into the house, I was jolted by the presence of C, my ex-girlfriend and twin sister to D and K, entangled in an intimate embrace with our mutual friend. The scene, while not entirely unexpected given our tangled past, still struck a discordant chord within me.

The scent of their grandmother, always intrusive and now unexpectedly present, added another layer to the chaotic tableau. Feeling the weight of the situation, their mother guided me to a spare bedroom for respite. As I prepared to rest, I discreetly hid my wallet and car keys, well aware of K's mischievous tendencies.

With a sigh of resignation, I surrendered to sleep, oblivious to the shocks that awaited me upon waking.

Dear reader, the next chapter promises revelations that will challenge everything you thought you knew. Until then, I bid you goodnight and eagerly await our next encounter.

Chapter Twenty-One

I felt a sudden shift in the weight on the bed, causing my eyes to snap open. The mattress creaked under the pressure of the grandmother, fondly known as "Granny," perched on the edge. Her mischievous smirk adorned her face as she spoke, her voice laced with anticipation, "Hey precious child, get dressed. I am taking everyone out for dinner." In her eyes, a glimmer of something sinister flickered, hinting at her hidden intentions. Startled by the late hour, I hastily leaped out of bed and slipped on my shoes.

We made our way out of the house, with C and her new lover intertwined, stealing glances in my direction. The family piled into Granny's sleek black Mercedes, while I chose to drive myself, hoping for a swift escape if the opportunity presented itself. And I had a feeling it would.

Luckily, the outdoor restaurant they had chosen was conveniently located on my planned route for departure after dinner. As we arrived, I parked my car with the front facing in the direction of my potential escape, just in case. A friendly host greeted us and guided us to a secluded table. It became clear to me that Granny had ulterior motives in mind.

We settled onto our benches, and I deliberately chose a seat as far away from the twins as possible. They sat in a row like obedient ducks, while K and I took our places facing Granny. The unease within me grew with each passing second. Granny boldly ordered a bottle of exquisite French Champagne and a platter of oysters. This extravagant choice was unlike her usual frugal nature.

As the others eagerly indulged in their drinks, I cautiously sipped on my sparkling beverage, fully aware of the long drive that awaited me. The oysters arrived, and without the customary table prayer, everyone eagerly dug in. While the rest remained oblivious, I became increasingly unsettled. Granny's expression and the way her knuckles turned white as she tightly gripped her glass made it clear that things were about to get real.

And, in a nutshell, things went completely haywire. The room was filled with tension as Granny's piercing gaze locked with mine, her words hanging in the air like a heavy fog.

"Son," she said, her voice rising, commanding everyone's attention, "Consider yourself lucky that you escaped the clutches of this family." Confusion wrinkled my brow as I urged her to continue. My mind screamed in alarm, the word 'danger' echoing incessantly.

"You see," she said, her finger pointing accusingly at C, then at K, "While these two hooligans lived on the farm with me, I caught them red-handed, their forbidden love exposed like a vibrant flame."

A gasp escaped everyone's lips, the sound hanging in the air, as the mother desperately tried to silence the chaos. "Mother!" she exclaimed, but Granny paid no heed to her pleas.

"Silence!" Granny's shrill voice shattered the tense atmosphere, her words forcefully cutting through, "I'm talking."

C, her mouth full of oyster, froze mid-chew, her eyes wide with shock. Meanwhile, K stared down at his shoes, a mix of shame and hostility written across his face. Suddenly, his animosity towards me became clear as day.

"And that's not all!" Granny continued, her voice piercing the room. "You!" she pointed her finger menacingly at her daughter. "I caught you in the bath with a man half your age, the splashing water betraying your secret indulgence. So much for paying for the garden services." I scoffed, struggling to suppress my uncontrollable laughter.

"And you!" she pointed at D, her voice filled with disappointment, "had the chance to marry this man," her finger now directed at me, "but your impatience got in the way."

Embarrassment flushed my cheeks, but beneath it, a sense of vindication washed over me. I could tell that Granny was far from finished.

She downed her champagne in one gulp and ordered another bottle. C's lover girl excused herself and slipped away unnoticed. The room grew warmer, the heat prickling against my skin, but I stayed captivated by the unfolding drama. The taste of the champagne danced on my tongue, the effervescence bringing a momentary respite.

"And now that I'm dying," Granny pressed on, her voice filled with defiance, "you all want a share of my fucking money." The room fell silent, the weight of her profanity hanging in the air. Our small audience gaped at the spectacle, but I remained unfazed.

Granny's revelation had brought the tension in the room to an unbearable level. The shock on everyone's faces was palpable, but I couldn't help but feel a sense of detachment from it all. Perhaps it was the knowledge that I had always been an outsider in this family, never truly belonging.

As Granny ranted on, her accusations flying like arrows, I couldn't help but marvel at the audacity with which she laid bare the family's secrets. It was as if she relished the chaos she had unleashed, reveling in the power she held over everyone.

The realization hit me then, like a bolt of lightning. Granny had orchestrated this entire dinner, carefully choosing the restaurant on my escape route, strategically exposing the family's darkest secrets. It was all part of her plan to assert her dominance, to remind us that she held the strings to our fates.

But what did it matter to me? I had long since severed my ties with this dysfunctional family. Their drama, their greed, their dirty secrets meant nothing to me. I had chosen my own path, away from their toxicity.

As Granny's tirade continued, I decided it was time for me to make my exit. I stood up abruptly, causing everyone to turn their gaze towards me. Ignoring their bewildered expressions, I calmly walked towards the exit, leaving behind the chaos and drama that had consumed this family.

I knew that the moment I stepped out of that restaurant, I would be free. Free from their manipulations, their expectations, and their deceit. And as I stepped into my car, ready to drive away into the night, I couldn't help but feel a sense of relief wash over me.

In that moment, I realized that I had made the right choice. I had escaped the clutches of this family, just as Granny had warned. And as I drove away, leaving behind the chaos and dysfunction, I knew that I was finally free to create my own destiny, away from the toxic web that had ensnared us all.

Chapter Twenty-Two

As I embarked on the long journey home, the universe seemed determined to prove a point to me. Leaving behind the toxic family had been the right decision, and the universe seemed to agree. To my utter astonishment, as I made my way, a reputable, Internationally Acclaimed IT company's recruitment department reached out to me. The phone call came unexpectedly, and I couldn't help but wonder where they had obtained my details. Perhaps Nina, from the computer training company, had played a role in it. Or maybe it was connected to an article I had posted about the abysmal state and service of call centers in our country.

Regardless of how it happened, I eagerly listened to the recruiter's voice, her words flowing like torrents. I couldn't believe my luck. It was the first time something like this had ever happened to me. And to top it off, the company was willing to relocate me. Little did they know, I had already made the move to the city where their head office was located.

The next day, they arranged for me to stay at a fancy hotel for my interview. I knew exactly where it was located, and after a brief mental calculation, I knew I had to press on. However, as I crossed the halfway mark to Johannesburg, fatigue weighed heavily on my eyes. It was a dangerous endeavor, and not even the excitement from the upcoming job could keep my eyes open.

In the distance, I spotted a quaint roadside motel and decided to take a chance. The year had gifted us with one of the coldest winters we had ever experienced, and the road was lined with snow as far as the eye could see. Carefully maneuvering my car, skidding in every direction, I finally managed to park.

Stepping out of the car, the cold air hit my face like daggers, sending a shiver down my spine. I hurried into the reception area, seeking warmth. They informed me that they had a small room available, but warned me that there was no water due to the pipes freezing over. Despite this inconvenience, I didn't mind. All I needed was a few hours of sleep, and hopefully, I would wake up to a warm cup of coffee. I knew I had to rise early to ensure I made it to the interview on time.

I gratefully accepted the small room, just thankful for a place to rest my weary body. The motel stood in complete stillness, with no one in sight, serving as a stark contrast to the lively city that awaited me. The room was basic, but it provided the solace I needed. I lay down on the creaky bed, enveloped in the warmth of the thick blankets.

As I closed my eyes, exhaustion took over, and I drifted into a deep sleep. Hours later, I woke up to the sound of my alarm, groggily rubbing my eyes. The room was still cold, but I had a sense of determination that pushed me forward. I gathered my belongings, preparing for the day ahead.

As I made my way to the reception area, hoping for that much-needed cup of coffee, I was met with disappointment. The motel's staff informed me that they were still unable to restore the water supply due to the frozen pipes. Disheartened but undeterred, I thanked them and set off on the final leg of my journey.

The drive to the company's head office was treacherous, with the icy roads posing a constant threat. But I persevered, my focus unwavering. I knew that this opportunity was worth every obstacle I faced.

Finally, I arrived at the impressive building that housed the IT company. The interview went well, and I left feeling a sense of accomplishment. The universe had indeed aligned in my favor, granting me a chance to escape the toxic environment I had once called home.

Days turned into weeks, and soon enough, I received the news I had been eagerly waiting for. The company offered me the job, and I gladly accepted. It was a fresh start, an opportunity to leave behind the negativity and embrace a brighter future.

As I settled into my new life, I couldn't help but reflect on the journey that led me here. The universe had sent me a sign, guiding me towards the path I was meant to take. Leaving behind the toxic family was the first step, and the unexpected call from the IT company was the validation I needed.

Now, as I looked out of the window of my new apartment, I marveled at the view of the bustling city below. I had come a long way, both physically and emotionally. The hardships I faced on that long journey home were merely stepping stones to a better life.

And as I sipped on a warm cup of coffee, I couldn't help but feel a sense of gratitude for the universe's intervention. It had proven its point, and I had emerged stronger and more determined than ever before.

Once again, a force came into play, enveloping me in its cosmic grasp. The universe, keenly aware of my vulnerability to rejection, threw a bone at me. And that bone took the form of Rebecca, a sultry British lass whose body was a work of art.

As soon as our eyes met, I sensed trouble, but her allure was impossible to resist. Her infectious giggle reverberates in my mind to this day, a symphony of joy. The vibrant aura of her personality captivated me, as did her impeccable updo, a masterpiece adorning her head. Her hazel eyes, soft and mesmerizing, complemented her gentle nature. She was a catch, no doubt, and I could sense the curiosity emanating from my fellow workers. I, too, was intrigued, but cautious of the sharp claws hidden beneath her kitten-like exterior.

Rebecca's role was to train me in my new position as a product specialist, responsible for keeping the service center agents updated with the latest technologies. Our one-on-one sessions were filled with distractions, my focus constantly drawn to her short, vibrant mini dress that accentuated her shapely legs.

She embodied the essence of a typical English rose. On Fridays, she would reward my progress with a drink at the company's VIP club, a privilege she possessed. The invitations extended beyond the workplace, to her opulent apartment, where we both fell in love, not with each other, but with the enchanting world of Harry Potter and his friends.

Nestled on the couch, with our drinks in hand, we indulged in the magical tales that transported us to another realm. In those moments, I would steal a kiss, intoxicated by her giggles. And she, in turn, would playfully strip off my shirt, adorning me with an apron, as she put me to work in the kitchen. As a newcomer to our country, I took it upon myself to introduce her to our local favorites, a pastime she wholeheartedly embraced. Together, we embarked on culinary adventures, exploring the diverse array of restaurants our city had to offer.

What truly touched my heart was when she handed me the keys to her sleek and modern BMW 320i cabriolet. The car, a powerhouse on wheels, injected a surge of adrenaline as we zipped through the city streets, our hair dancing in the wind. The sights and sounds of the bustling metropolis blended into a symphony of life as we embarked on our thrilling journey.

As I strolled into the opulent restaurant, Rebecca gracefully accompanying me, my eyes were immediately drawn to a cluster of figures gathered around a grand, elongated table. My jaw plummeted to the floor as I recognized them—renowned actors, revered for their roles in a wildly popular sitcom. The air buzzed with excitement, mingling with the tantalizing aroma of delectable cuisine wafting from the kitchen.

In the midst of the evening's festivities, I found myself engaged in conversation with one of the illustrious stars—a captivating and well-known actress. Her warm smile illuminated the room, filling me with a sense of awe and appreciation. With my troubled past and toxic family left behind, I felt as if I had ascended to a heavenly realm. This was undoubtedly the pinnacle of my existence, a time of utter perfection.

Little did I know, fate had other plans in store. Adhering to the right course of action, things began to unravel terribly. But for now, I lay my pen to rest, promising to divulge the full account in my next installment. Goodnight, cherished reader, and farewell, albeit temporarily.

Chapter Twenty-Three

It is difficult to say who I fell in love with faster: my job or Rebecca. When I was with her, I yearned to return to my office, the familiar scent of ink and paper engulfing me. As I worked, my thoughts would wander to her, like a gentle breeze caressing my mind. I would stealthily navigate through the corridors, the sound of my footsteps muffled by the plush carpet, until I reached her office. Closing the door behind me, I would steal a kiss, our lips brushing in secret harmony.

Our clandestine relationship danced in the shadows for months on end, a hidden symphony that no one knew of. Though we often appeared in public together, we mastered the art of deception. Yet, our stolen glances, filled with longing, could not be concealed. We were walking a perilous path, danger signs looming around us, but my own greed and desires blinded me.

The pattern was glaringly obvious, but my neediness clouded my vision. It was only in retrospect that I could see it, not in the heat of the moment. Rejection would send me running into the arms of another, a feeble attempt to numb the pain. Perhaps it stemmed from my mother, who knew not how to express affection. But if I were a crisp bill in her pocket, she would have showered me with love and tenderness.

Time flew by swiftly, as it always does during moments of bliss. Yet, within the depths of happiness, darkness lurked in the shadows, observing with an intense, fiery gaze. People like me are often labeled as magnets for misfortune, or vessels for others' troubles. And once again, I found myself hurtling down a treacherous slope at an alarming speed. Blinded by my newfound social status, I mingled with socialites, celebrities, and influential figures.

Rebecca, dear reader, was exactly that—a socialite. And with her came an array of indulgences, as is customary in her world. To intensify our intimacy, she introduced me to narcotics, the white powder that graced our nostrils. Its pungent scent stung my eyes, causing my nose to run, but its effects were unparalleled, igniting a fire within me like nothing else.

Once again, my overwhelming desire to impress another person led to my downfall, plunging me back into the unforgiving embrace of rejection. Narcotics were simply not suitable for someone like me. My feeble mind was ill-equipped to handle their potent effects. Imagine this: you inhale the white powder or consume another substance known for intensifying intimacy. Your mind ventures beyond its familiar boundaries as you desperately try to keep it in check. Your body suddenly takes on a life of its own. Inhibitions fade away, and you find yourself yearning to pounce on any captivating figure with two legs, unleashing your inner madman. To provide context, your body becomes Casanova, while your mind transforms into a fearless gunslinger, akin to Billy the Kid. Picture the loss of control, as you dart around like a headless rooster, careening off walls. Your girlfriend, the one who provided you with the substance, the same person you strive to impress with your masculinity, charm, and intellect, watches you with wide eyes, questioning if this is your true nature. By the time you regain your composure, it is too late. You have irreparably embarrassed yourself, leaving no opportunity to salvage your tarnished reputation.

In short, this recipe for self-destruction is a bitter concoction. I cannot blame her, for once again, I found myself alone. But it pained me to witness her in the embrace of another, swiftly moving on. It became clear, once more, that I was merely a plaything, a temporary pleasure for her. The anguish pierced my heart like a sharp dagger. Welcome to the cold embrace of the corporate world. And oh, what a cruel surprise it proved to be.

The corridors and offices of the corporate realm are teeming with ambitious young women, willing to do anything to ascend the ladder of success. Please forgive my frankness, dear reader, but at the time, this was an undeniable truth. Our rainbow nation had recently emerged from the clutches of Apartheid, yet white men still dominated the higher positions. Due to our weakening currency, many international companies had established their presence in our cities, erecting towering buildings and creating heavenly workspaces. They paid no attention to the Boer Maffia and instead imported their own staff, often favoring the fairer sex. I must confess, Rebecca was the finest manager I had ever encountered.

However, local women faced an arduous climb up the ladder, given their previous disadvantages. They managed to secure positions above white males of similar age, which, on the surface, seemed like progress. But it had its consequences. The corporate arena became a fierce battleground for success, with women joining the ranks and becoming fiercely competitive.

They were abundant, these ambitious women, most adorned in identical attire. Their short mini skirts swayed as they moved, elegant reading glasses perched atop their noses, and their tongues as sharp as double-edged swords. To mend my broken heart and move on from Rebecca, I had a plethora of options to choose from.

It was then that I met E, an ambitious young blonde who captivated more than just my attention. We had a monthly festivity called "Bums on the Seat," whenever we signed new agents to join our contact center. To celebrate their initiation and onboarding, the company transformed a parking basement into a vibrant party area. The scene was a sensory overload—the pulsating bass from the speakers reverberated through the air, mingling with the laughter and chatter of the crowd. The aroma of beer and excitement filled the space, creating an intoxicating atmosphere.

With my two newfound friends by my side, we stood on the sidelines, eagerly observing the festivities unfold. Suddenly, I sensed a shift in the energy around me. I turned my head to the side and realized both of my friends were gaping in awe. Intrigued, I followed their gaze and there she was—a stunning blonde, exuding confidence and allure. Her white shirt clung to her body, drenched in beer, leaving little to the imagination. The room fell into a hushed silence, as if the world had momentarily paused to admire her beauty. I scanned the room and noticed the envious glares from other women clinging possessively to their male partners.

But I couldn't care less about their envy or my own chances with her. The alcohol coursed through my veins, amplifying the thumping bass and intensifying the party atmosphere. As an introvert, I found solace in observing from the sidelines, my nerves building as I rehearsed my upcoming welcome speech in my mind.

With the formalities out of the way, it was finally time to let loose and have some fun. I couldn't believe my luck as I grabbed a beer, realizing now it wasn't just luck, but something far more sinister. The music lured everyone onto the dance floor, and a conga line quickly formed. It was a peculiar sight, as if the line had contorted itself to revolve around E, the center of attention. Her mischievous smile spoke volumes.

Suddenly, with a forceful tug on my shirt, I was pulled forward. I opened my eyes to see it was E, beckoning me to join the conga line. She positioned me in front of her, her hands firmly resting on my shoulders. As she whispered her intentions into my ear, a shiver ran down my spine, a mix of excitement and trepidation.

I fell into her snare, entangled in her web like a helpless fly. She affectionately called me her "cwazy little wabbit," playfully pinching my nose. In her embrace, I found both the nurturing warmth of a mother figure I had always yearned for and the allure of a stunning girlfriend with an insatiable hunger for intimacy. It was a dream come true, a man's ultimate desire.

The envy of my colleagues only fueled my satisfaction, especially when I caught the glimpse of jealousy on Rebecca's face as our paths crossed. It was the perfect rebound, a triumph over her failed game. Little did I know then that E's terms of endearment came with a heavy price tag. I was unknowingly diving headfirst into my own dangerous liaison, becoming the protagonist of a treacherous tale. The secrets that lay ahead were yet to be unveiled. Join me in my next installment to uncover the truth. Until then, happy reading. Buy now, for the journey begins.

Chapter Twenty-Four

A cosmic presence loomed over me, casting a dark shadow like the pull of a black hole. Once again, I impulsively dove into a relationship, desperately seeking refuge from the sting of rejection. Unbeknownst to me, it could potentially be my final venture if my partner had her sinister intentions fulfilled.

My loyalty was on the verge of being tested, not to my partner, but to my own self. The troubles in our relationship surfaced early on, during its nascent stage. Dear mortal reader, let me share my perspective that it is not wise for a Scorpio to date another Scorpio if you believe in such cosmic alignments. It becomes an unyielding battle of intellect and a relentless pursuit of dominance. While she wielded her intimacy as a weapon, I retaliated with calculated strikes, leveraging my senior position at our shared workplace.

E, with her above-average beauty, held the delusion that she was entitled to a managerial role. Quite an ambitious endeavor, considering she had only just joined our company. Despite my persistent questioning, her past remained enigmatic, a mystery I couldn't unravel. All I knew was that, like me, she had relocated for this job opportunity. And she had moved from a nearby city, where she told me she came from a house shrouded by poverty. Her father, once a mineworker, now struggled to find employment, while her mother tirelessly baked to support the family. To make matters worse, her parents had just welcomed twins into the world, despite their advanced age. She sent money home to support her family financially, a responsibility that fueled her ambitions. I understood why she was hired, but I must admit, E possessed cunning intelligence.

One evening, as I entered her apartment, the aroma of a perfume she reserved for special occasions wafted through the air.

"Hurry," she urged, "we're running late." She slipped into a revealing miniskirt that left little to the imagination. However, possessiveness was not a trait I possessed, so I let it slide. I couldn't help but notice the glimmering top she wore, offering a tantalizing view of her cleavage, adorned with a delicate black lace bra.

"Where are we headed?" I inquired, a mix of curiosity and amusement in my voice.

She shot me her signature intense gaze. "Don't tell me you forgot," she challenged, daring me to disagree.

"Oh, yes!" I exclaimed, the memory flooding back to me. Hastily, I changed into my evening attire and escorted her to my BMW 320i, the company car, and we sped out of the underground parking lot.

Rudi, a wealthy British executive who worked alongside us, lived in a lavish mansion atop a hill in an affluent suburb. We weaved our way up the winding road; the tires screeching as we approached the gated entrance.

With a low hum, the metal gates swung open, granting us access. Following the cobblestone driveway, we parked in the courtyard adorned with an elegant fountain.

We joined the other guests at the party, most of them already in a state of blissful euphoria, their eyes glazed over and their movements slow and languid. The scent of marijuana hung heavy in the air, mingling with the earthy aroma of sweat and the sweet, intoxicating notes of incense. It was not a typical house party, like the ones I had grown accustomed to. This was something else entirely—a pulsating, sensory overload of desire and indulgence. To put it bluntly, it was an orgy.

As I looked around, I couldn't help but feel a mixture of fascination and discomfort. Couples, entwined in passionate embraces, lay sprawled across the plush leather couches, their bodies tangled together in a symphony of limbs. The room reverberated with the sounds of moans, groans, and the thumping bass of house music, creating an electric atmosphere that seemed to vibrate through my very core.

E, seemingly unaffected by the debauchery unfolding around us, stood confidently amidst it all, her allure shining through the chaos.

Little did I know, she had more than just her looks up her sleeve. This was pushing the boundaries in a way I had never witnessed before.

In need of a reprieve, I decided to explore the rest of the dwelling. Stepping outside, I found myself confronted by two imposing Dobermans, their fierce growls and bared teeth serving as a warning to anyone who dared to approach. Sensing their territorial nature, I quickly retreated back inside, my heart pounding with a mixture of fear and relief.

Seeking solace, I made my way through the house, eventually finding myself in a secluded corner by the azure pool. The gentle caress of the sun's fading rays warmed my skin as I reclined on a comfortable lounger. Yet, even in this moment of tranquility, the distant sounds of intimate acts reached my ears, a constant reminder of the debauchery unfolding just beyond my line of sight. Determined to escape the sensory overload, I closed my eyes, trying to shut out the world around me.

After what felt like an eternity, I finished my beer and decided to venture back inside to fetch another. As I made my way through the house, I searched for any sign of E or our guest, assuming they were engaged in a conversation somewhere amidst the chaos. However, the hazy atmosphere made it difficult to distinguish one person from another, and the conversations I overheard were fragmented and nonsensical. It seemed that everyone was either as high as a kite or lost in a haze of intoxication.

In my wandering, I stumbled upon a dimly lit games room adorned with an impressive collection of hunting trophies. The eyes of a majestic blue wildebeest trophy seemed to follow my every move, its gaze both haunting and captivating. Seeking a moment of solitude, I decided to indulge in a solitary game of billiards, the click-clack of the balls providing a rhythmic soundtrack to my thoughts. Lost in the game, I found solace in the company of the silent, watchful wildebeest, its presence both comforting and eerie.

In the distance, a distant bell resonated, its melodic tone signaling the long-awaited dinner announcement. Famished, I carelessly tossed the billiards cue aside and hastened my steps back to where I found the guests gathered. The ornate, elongated dining table stood adorned with an assortment of pizza boxes, their enticing aroma wafting through the air, mingling with the flickering glow of the high chandeliers. As I approached, the muted whispers of the stoned diners reached my ears, their voices a hushed symphony that piqued my curiosity.

Turning my attention to the seated guests, I noticed their gazes fixed upon me, their knowing smiles reflecting a secret shared. It became clear that I had missed something, an occurrence that had unfolded in my absence. E and Rudi, our esteemed guest, stood side by side, their postures revealing a tale left untold. Rudi's eyes lowered, a subtle admission of guilt, while E feigned ignorance, her gaze pretending I did not exist.

However, my hunger outweighed my curiosity, and I succumbed to the allure of the awaiting seat. Settling into the plush cushion, I eagerly seized a slice of pizza, its warm cheese and tangy sauce tantalizing my taste buds. Amidst my indulgence, a particular word caught my attention, whispered in repetition. "Bathroom," it murmured, gaining volume as one person exclaimed, "bathroom floor!"

The surprise in her voice hung in the air, causing all eyes to shift towards Rudi and E. The guilt etched upon her face was undeniable, while his expression bore a hint of pride or accomplishment.

Lost in my world of flavors and textures, I failed to connect the dots, oblivious to the unfolding drama. It was only when the gazes of the guests darted towards me, their laughter and giggles filling the room, that my senses awakened.

A guest's lips parted, astonishment shining in her wide eyes, as she uttered the words that nearly choked me. "Rudi and E... on the bathroom floor?" Her hands came together in a thunderous applause, accompanied by the raucous laughter and praise of those around me.

As the realization dawned on me, my face flushed with a mix of embarrassment and disbelief. How could this be happening? The room seemed to spin as the guests reveled in their scandalous revelation. I felt like an unwanted guest, swallowed by a wave of laughter and applause that jeered at my lack of knowledge.

E's eyes met mine, a flicker of guilt and mischief dancing in their depths. I couldn't bear to look at Rudi, knowing what had transpired between them. The betrayal cut deep, slicing through the facade of our seemingly perfect life.

Stunned and overwhelmed, I pushed away from the table, abandoning my half-eaten slice of pizza. The taste turned bitter in my mouth, mirroring the sourness of my emotions. I stumbled towards the exit, desperately needing fresh air and space to clear my mind.

Outside, the night air hit me like a punch, momentarily stealing my breath. I stumbled towards the edge of the pool, its tranquil surface reflecting the moonlight. The serenity of the azure water called to me, offering solace in its stillness.

But even as I stood there, contemplating a plunge into the depths, I couldn't escape the echoes of laughter and the lingering image of Rudi and E entwined on the bathroom floor. The betrayal echoed through my veins, poisoning the very core of our once unbreakable bond.

In that moment, I made a decision. I couldn't stay in this toxic environment, surrounded by people who reveled in deceit and debauchery. I needed to find myself again, to rediscover the person I had lost in the chaos of this twisted reality.

With a heavy heart, I turned away from the pool and walked back into the house. The laughter and whispers followed me, but I shut them out, focusing on the path ahead. Despite the guests' taunts, I confidently walked through the house and reached the front door.

As I emerged, the full moon's gentle glow embraced me, bringing a glimmer of hope in the darkness. I didn't know where I was going or what lay ahead, but I knew it couldn't be worse than the pain and betrayal I had endured.

With each step, I left behind the clamor and recklessness, opting to embark on a voyage of exploration. The road stretched out before me, a blank canvas waiting to be painted with new experiences and possibilities.

As I walked away from that house, a surge of emotions washed over me. The betrayal still stung, but amidst the pain, I could feel a glimmer of something else - a determination to change. I realized that I had lost myself in the midst of this toxic environment, allowing the deceit and debauchery to cloud my own sense of identity.

But no more.

* * *

I refused to let this betrayal define me. I refused to let it consume me. It was time to take back control of my life, to rediscover the person I once was before the darkness of this twisted reality took hold.

With each step I took, the weight of the past began to lift. The laughter and whispers of the guests faded into the background, replaced by a newfound sense of purpose. The moon's gentle glow illuminated my path, guiding me towards a future filled with hope and possibility.

As I walked into the unknown, I carried with me the lessons learned and the scars that would forever remind me of the dangers that lie beneath seemingly perfect lives. But I also carried a flicker of hope, a belief that I could find my way back to happiness and peace.

The road ahead was uncertain, but I was ready to face whatever challenges and adventures awaited me. It was time to rebuild my reality, one based on trust, love, and authenticity. It was time to surround myself with people who valued those qualities, who would lift me up instead of tearing me down.

So, dear reader, as I embark on this voyage of self-discovery, I invite you to join me. Let us explore the mesmerizing pursuits that await, as I strive to find my own happiness and purpose. Until then, farewell.

Chapter Twenty-Five

Time moves on, relentless in its passage, refusing to wait for any wound to heal. A wise man once shared a story with me, a tale that has remained etched in my memory. He spoke of the profound truth that everything we do, every action we take, occurs in the past tense. At such a young age, I struggled to fully comprehend the depth of his wisdom, yet his words echoed in my mind.

He urged me to ponder on it, to reflect on the profound nature of our existence. Every word we speak, every sound we hear, is already in the past. As the vibrations reach our ears, even milliseconds have passed, and by the time our brains process the information, it has already slipped away into the vast realm of the past. This concept mirrored the very nature of our perception of the world. When we gaze upon the moon, what we see is a reflection of the past. The light that reaches our eyes has traveled immense distances, traversing the vastness of space and time. Everything we lay our eyes upon is a testament to what has already occurred.

He further expounded on this notion, emphasizing the importance of cherishing those who matter most and distancing ourselves from those we wish to forget. Just as the further a planet is from us, the longer it takes for its light to reach our sight, so too must we create distance between ourselves and those who bring us pain and heartache.

He continued his teachings, reminding me that the world we inhabit lacks the ability to pause, to come to a screeching halt like a car, tractor, or speeding truck in an emergency. It spins on, its speed incomprehensible. Therefore, he implored me to release the grip of the past, to let go of what has already transpired, and instead, fix my gaze upon the horizon. I still remember the way he would turn the rearview mirror inside the car to face in the opposite direction, a physical manifestation of his philosophy. "The first rule of driving," he would say with a smile, "is to look ahead, not back."

These lessons have served me well in life, guiding me through the intricacies of existence. However, simplicity eludes us in matters of the heart. E would often saunter by my office on her way to the contact center, her presence a visual trigger for a tumult of emotions within me.

In the depths of my love for her, she betrayed my trust. And to my dismay, she ended up securing the coveted management role. Rumors swirled, whispers of discontent from others who were not pleased with the outcome. Yet, I found myself helpless, a mere spectator in the face of her manipulations. People like her have a tendency to push boundaries too far, ultimately leading to a bitter downfall in the corporate world.

As the aroma of freshly brewed coffee filled the air, I moved about the kitchen, my actions silent but purposeful. Meanwhile, she would steal furtive glances in my direction, her eyes darting over her shoulder. I couldn't decipher her intentions—was she trying to taunt me or flirt with me subtly, testing my response?

Grabbing my cup of coffee, I leisurely made my way to the balcony, relishing the gentle breeze caressing my face. The coolness brought a sense of tranquility amidst the chaos. Unsurprisingly, she joined me, puffing on a cigarette, her silence speaking volumes as she seemed to revel in my misery. But I refused to be intimidated. I couldn't help but wonder if her actions were driven by a desire to snatch my coveted job, fully aware of her willingness to do whatever it takes to climb the corporate ladder.

During one of my lunch breaks, I ventured to the nearby mall to restock on essentials. On my way back, I found myself drawn to the bustling food court, longing for a small indulgence. And there, by sheer chance, I encountered Rudi. A wicked smirk adorned his face as he recounted every sordid detail of what had transpired between him and E on the bathroom floor. The sound of his voice grated on my nerves, testing my composure. My mind screamed for retribution, while my conscience urged me to simply avoid him.

The more I pondered their actions, the more I suspected a conspiracy against me. It felt as though their presence loomed ominously wherever I went. The torment they inflicted upon me became unbearable. And in a moment of weakness, I too stooped to their level, engaging in childish behavior that was entirely out of character for me. However, I decided—if they could play their games, then I could too.

I began to strategize, determined to outmaneuver E and Rudi. I knew I had to be smart and calculated, not succumbing to their petty tactics. In contrast to them, my coworkers cherished me and were well aware of my diligent nature. Their smiles and warm greetings filled my senses, boosting my confidence. I centered my entire strategy around this key, the one object that held all the power.

During lunch breaks, instead of sauntering to the cafeteria alone, I asked others to join me. The people I invited all had some connection to Rudi and E., whether through work or friendship. I would subtly prod them for information, leaning in to catch every whispered detail.

The food trick failed to produce the desired outcome, so I decided to change my approach. I noticed a change in Rudi and E, avoiding the same people I had mingled with.

The centerpiece of my fresh approach was the VIP area, where I had the privilege of experiencing the exclusive ambiance. When my workday came to an end, I would frequently arrange a casual get-together with a friend or two, where we could relax and enjoy some wine and cheese. Despite their unfamiliarity with fine dining, this group always preferred a cold beer, their casual conversations contributing to the overall atmosphere.

Over time, I noticed something peculiar. I would catch glimpses of the shy girl in the contact center watching me intently as I strolled around, her fascination evident in her eyes. Every time I looked at her, her eyes would quickly dart towards the screen. With her raven hair, dark eyes, olive complexion, and shy smile, she was a vision of beauty. The faint scent of her floral perfume lingered in the air, drawing me closer. My apologies, dear reader, but the mere thought of her in a bikini made my knees weak. Upon discreet questions, I discovered her name was Monique, a delicate English rose.

With a watchful eye, I observed her closely, fully aware of E's presence, and took note of the few male counterparts that accompanied her. Right then, I noticed a lone figure standing out from the crowd with his shimmering golden hair. He was my target, so I lured him into the VIP lounge with the promise of a drink. While discreetly prodding him, I felt a surge of excitement as I stumbled upon a crucial piece of information, forcing me to keep my composure intact. Rudi was hopelessly in love with Monique, and he had exhausted every effort to capture her affections.

"You cunning devil!" my mind screamed, while my lips remained silent.

I had devised a challenge that was perfectly tailored to achieve the desired outcome. On the upcoming Friday, I lounged on a comfortable couch, keeping a close eye on the entrance to the VIP lounge while pretending to be engrossed in a flight magazine. Rudi and E's laughter echoed in the air as they confidently entered the lounge, stealing a glance at me.

With quiet anticipation, I waited, knowing that the wine would soon cast its spell. Before long, their laughter reached my ears, prompting me to leap up and hurry to the contact center. As I entered, Monique's eyes locked with mine, conveying a silent understanding. She too leaped up and hurried towards me, our fingers intertwining. Together, we burst into the VIP lounge, our laughter filling the room and our arms wrapped tightly around each other. Monique, with her British finesse and class, effortlessly embodied the role with impeccable manners.

Seizing a bottle of wine, I poured two glasses, causing a hushed silence to fall over the room. Though I dared not look, I could feel the penetrating gaze of Rud and E fixed upon me. With wineglasses in hand, I took Monique to a nearby couch, where we flawlessly executed our act.

As the tension in the room grew thicker, I could practically taste the bitterness of Rudi's envy and the simmering challenge emanating from E. It was as if the air itself crackled with their emotions, electrifying the atmosphere.

My heart raced with a mixture of excitement and satisfaction, pumping adrenaline through my veins. The rush of blood to my cheeks left them flushed, betraying the thrill that coursed through me. A mischievous sparkle danced in my eyes, mirroring the sly satisfaction that filled my mind.

Monique, beside me, carried herself with a regal grace that belied the chaos within. Her fingers intertwined with mine, offering a sense of solidarity and strength. The touch of her skin against mine sent a shiver down my spine, intensifying the emotions that swirled within me.

Our conversation brimmed with energy, words intertwining effortlessly as we wove a tapestry of intrigue and deception. With each passing moment, the charade grew more immersive, captivating the unsuspecting audience of Rudi and E.

But amidst the facade, I couldn't help but steal glances at my nemesis. Rudi's jaw clenched, his eyes narrowing with a mix of anger and envy. It was a gratifying sight, fueling my desire to outwit him even more. E, on the other hand, wore a mask of shock and disbelief, yet her eyes gleamed with a fiery determination, silently vowing to retaliate.

In this moment, I reveled in the power of manipulation, relishing the taste of victory. But I knew that the challenge had only just begun. The glimmer in E's eyes served as a reminder that she was not one to be underestimated. As the wine continued to flow, I braced myself for the battle that lay ahead, ready to navigate the treacherous waters of this game we played.

Chapter Twenty-Six

Dearest mortal reader. It seemed that with every clever plan I made, life retaliated, tightening its grip on me. I loved my job and everything I did, but I couldn't help but wonder if I was trapped in the clutches of a universal beast called the "comfort zone."

I was on the verge of discovering that as I sank deeper into my comfort zone, life would shake me out of it with increasing force. At some point, we all reach a stage in life where there is no possibility of turning back—the Point of No Return. We can only reflect upon that time, unable to return to it.

One late afternoon, as I drove up my driveway, my eyes caught sight of a sleek silver Audi Coupe parked ahead. Little did I know what surprise awaited me. Retrieving my belongings from the car, I made my way towards the comforting embrace of my house, the taste of whisky lingering on my tongue.

Approaching the front door, I noticed it standing wide open. Concern furrowed my brow, and a wave of caution washed over me. After all, I was in Johannesburg, a city notorious for crime.

Frozen in my tracks, hesitant, I cautiously approached the entrance. Yet, in the air, a cloud of intoxicating perfume hung, drawing me in. Compelled by its familiar scent, I ventured inside.

And there, seated at the dining table, was E, a glass of wine in hand and a neatly poured whisky waiting for me. It dawned on me that during our time together; I had given her a set of keys to my house, and she still had belongings scattered about. Now, she had gathered them, packed neatly in bags beside her.

I was about to inquire about her presence, but deep down, I already knew. The memories of her deceit had left a bitter taste in my mouth, and my heart pounded against my ribcage. All I wanted was to get her out of there.

"I miss you terribly," she said, her voice filled with remorse, "and I am so sorry for hurting you."

As a sucker for female affection, a result of my deprived upbringing, her smile and kind words weakened my knees. Yet, I maintained a facade of strength. My fragile ego had often failed me, but I was not willing to let her off the hook that easily.

Little did I know this was a clever coup, targeted towards me. Dear reader, you know what is written about a scorned woman. I was about to be ensnared in a black widow's web, and she used my vulnerability against me in a masterful act of deception.

Love and affection made me blind to people's faults. I sank into a chair and nursed my whisky, the rich aroma wafting up to my nostrils. She subtly shifted her hand over the polished wooden table and caressed my fingers. Her move was irresistibly seductive, and I could feel myself becoming more and more ensnared by her tantalizing actions.

"Why did you do it?" I asked, my voice trembling, tears welling up in my eyes.

Oh, she played me like a finely tuned instrument. Her grip tightened around my hand, her touch sending a shiver down my spine, and she continued to caress my fingers. She guided my hand, placing it on her heart, just above her supple breasts, which she gave me a teasing glimpse of as she leaned in close, the scent of her perfume enveloping me.

"I made a terrible mistake," she said, her voice laced with a hint of regret, biting her lip to tease me. "I was weak, and I had too much to drink. The next thing I knew, we were in the bathroom and —"

"No!" I interjected, my voice barely a whisper, placing my finger over her sensual lips, "spare me the details."

She opened her mouth and sensually sucked on my finger, the warmth and wetness sending a surge of desire through me, her tongue twirling around it. A spark ignited deep within me, quickly transforming into an intense flame of desire.

Pretending to be strong, and showing that I had the strength to resist her, I reluctantly withdrew my finger. But we both knew she had the upper hand, and she used her allure to seduce me. She moved closer, the fabric of her skirt rustling as she adjusted it, and crossed her legs, the smoothness of her skin brushing against mine. With her hands on my thighs, her thumbs moved in a soothing rhythm, amplifying the heat building within me, transforming it into an uncontrollable inferno.

Again, she leaned in close, her warm breath grazing my ear, teasing my senses. "Please forgive me," she whispered seductively, her voice like silk, "we can start over, and take things slow."

Her words lingered, tempting me with a fresh start. But I knew giving in would bring more heartache. The memories of her betrayal were still raw. I couldn't ignore the feeling that this was just another manipulation. Plus, there was a chance to pursue things with Monique. Deep down, I sensed that was why E was here. I wasn't sure if she came on her own or if Rudi influenced her. But somehow, I eventually found out.

Summoning what little strength I had left, I pushed myself away from the table, breaking free from her enticing grasp. "No," I said firmly, my voice filled with determination. "I can't forget what you did. I can't trust you again."

Her eyes flashed with a mix of disappointment and frustration, but I knew I couldn't let her sway me. It was time to reclaim my power and protect myself from further pain. "You need to leave," I stated, my voice unwavering. "I can't have you in my life anymore."

She pleaded with me, her voice now tinged with desperation. "Please, just give me another chance. I promise I'll do everything to make it right."

But I had heard those words before, and they had proven empty. I had been blinded by love once, and I refused to make the same mistake again. With a heavy heart, I stood my ground. "No," I repeated, my voice filled with finality. "It's over."

Her face contorted with a mix of anger and hurt, but I couldn't let her manipulate me any longer. I turned away, my heart aching, and made my way towards the door. As I stepped out into the cool evening air, I took a deep breath, determined to move forward and heal from the wounds she had inflicted.

Little did I realize that this choice would have haunting

consequences.

"I'll be back to collect my other things," E said, her eyes welling up with tears, desperately pleading one last time. The room fell silent, except for the faint sound of a ticking clock echoing in the dimly lit space. The scent of nostalgia hung in the air, as if it were a melancholic melody. With a heavy heart, E turned and walked away, leaving behind a sense of longing that lingered in the room.

With a heavy heart, I closed the door behind me, its weight echoing in the silence of the room. The soft click of the latch reverberated through the air as I left behind the allure of her seduction, stepping into a future where my strength and resilience would be tested. As I turned the key in the lock, the metallic jingle filled the hallway, a final reminder of the home we once shared.

My eyes darted through the room, taking in the details that still belonged to her. The faint scent of her perfume lingered in the air, intertwining with the musty smell of forgotten memories. There were remnants of her presence scattered about, tokens of a connection that refused to be severed. I felt the weight of her absence, the emptiness of a space once filled with passion and desire.

A sense of unease settled upon me as I noticed the small details, the subtle signs that she would return. It was her way, a lingering shadow that refused to be cast aside. She had a hold on me, a grip that kept me from permanently shutting the door on her. I toyed with the idea of sending her a message, a cruel act of revenge, claiming that her belongings were discarded without a second thought. But as I searched my heart, I found no malice, only a sense of triumph over her deceit.

Seeking solace, I sank into the comforting embrace of a worn chair. I reached for the glass of whisky, the clink of ice against the crystal resonating through the silence. The rich aroma filled my senses, mingling with the faint scent of her perfume that still clung to my clothes. With each sip, a wave of nostalgia washed over me, memories and regrets swirling in a bittersweet dance.

Deciding to wash away the remnants of the past, I immersed myself in a long bath. For a moment, I allowed myself to believe that I could wash away the memories as easily as I washed away the soap from my skin.

But as the water drained away, the start of my troubles emerged.

My gaze landed on a small crevice above the row of wardrobes as I stepped into my bedroom, a hidden nook that held the promise of untold stories. Intrigued, I couldn't help but notice a tightly wedged, large box in the narrow space, with E's initials elegantly etched into its side. My brow furrowed in deep thought, and a surge of determination propelled me forward. In one smooth motion, I swiftly brought a chair to my side, stood on it, and effortlessly freed the box.

The weight of the box surprised me, defying logic. There was no way E could have managed it alone. E was petite, delicate, unable to lift such a burden without assistance. Panic gripped me as I rushed outside, my footsteps echoing in the night's stillness. When the caretaker's cottage finally came into view, I wasted no time and urgently rapped on the door.

With a tired sigh, he pulled open the door, adorned in his worn nightgown. I inquired if he had come to my place today and if he had done anything to assist E. His response sent shockwaves through me. While I was toiling away at work, a man had arrived, disappearing into my house. Desperation fueled my inquiry as I pressed for a description, and with each word, the realization dawned upon me. It was a perfect match for Rudi, a man intertwined in her web of deceit.

Regret washed over me, a bitter taste in my mouth. I should have summoned a locksmith, changed the locks to protect myself. But in my naivety, I had been ensnared by her seduction. The pieces of her puzzle were falling into place, revealing a sinister truth that I had been blind to. As the shadows lengthened, I knew that this was only the beginning, a prelude to a tale that would unravel with each passing moment.

To uncover the twists and turns of this gripping story, I invite you to join me in my next installment. Until then, farewell, but only for now.

Chapter Twenty-Seven

News of Rudi's sudden resignation spread like wildfire through the bustling office building, igniting a wave of whispers and murmurs that echoed down the corridors. The air was thick with anticipation, and I couldn't help but wonder if E, the object of Rudi's affection, had played a role in his departure. Their once-secret romance had become common knowledge, but the rumors of Rudi's grand plans to pursue an acting career in the USA failed to resonate with me.

Then, like a breath of fresh air, the news of E's resignation reached my ears, and relief washed over me like a cool summer breeze. My heart soared with joy, but a nagging curiosity crept in. What were they up to? The answer would reveal itself soon, though I had no inkling at the time.

As the days dwindled, E and Rudi strutted about the office like proud roosters, their presence commanding attention. E, particularly, took every opportunity to captivate me and others, openly displaying her affection for Rudi. However, I saw through her facade. In the past, her actions might have unsettled me, but I had moved on. Their embraces held no sway over me anymore. But then, they took it a step too far.

On Friday afternoons, my close circle of friends and I had a cherished tradition. We would escape to a nearby pub, seeking solace in the comforting ambiance as we waited for the chaotic rush hour to subside. The tantalizing aroma of savory platters danced around our senses, teasing our hungry stomachs. We relished in the shared experience, savoring the anticipation of reconvening at our favorite spot later.

If I had known what awaited me, I would have never left. Nevertheless, we must face our destiny head-on, without hesitation.

One by one, we dispersed, our laughter fading into the distance as we embarked on our homeward journeys. Eager not to miss out, I hurried home, my anticipation heightening with each passing minute. Though I often felt like the center of attention, deep down, I knew it was because of my ability to treat my friends to rounds of free drinks. It was my way of contributing, a product of my upbringing as a fatherless individual with an absent mother.

As I pulled my car into the driveway, a shiver of unease raced down my spine, reflected in the caretaker's troubled expression. Ignoring his wary demeanor, I hurriedly passed through the imposing gates and stepped into the courtyard. My dear reader, what transpired next can only be described as a cruel twist of fate—a cosmic joke that turned my world upside down.

Let me paint you a vivid picture. The sliding door on the side was my usual point of entry into the house. Enclosed by a towering wall, the courtyard welcomed me through an iron gate. Though modest, it served as a gathering space where I often hosted barbecues for my guests. The small table and kettle grill were the only adornments, a testament to my bachelor lifestyle.

Without wasting a moment, I made a beeline for the sliding door, my work laptop and refreshing drink cradled in my hands. As I fumbled for the key, hidden deep within a pocket, I placed my belongings on the patio table, including my cellphone. With a gentle nudge, the sliding door effortlessly slid open, unveiling the softly illuminated scene within.

The faint, acrid scent of gas hung in the air, a chilling omen I foolishly ignored in my eagerness to answer the incoming call. With a sense of dread creeping in, I spun around, snatched my phone, and pressed it to my ear.

The voice of my friend boomed through the speaker, urging me to hurry and join them at our usual hangout spot. Anticipating his long-winded tales, I pulled out a cigarette and carefully placed it between my lips, fumbling for my lighter.

I brought the silver lighter closer to the tip of the cigarette. With a quick flick of my thumb, the flint sparked, creating a blinding flash of light that momentarily seared my vision. The sudden heat from the flame washed over my face, sending an unwelcome chill down my spine.

As the flame danced to life, I instinctively recoiled, taking a step back from the house. With the sliding door left partially ajar, the gas seeped out into the darkness, a silent but deadly intruder. But before I could fully comprehend the looming danger, a thunderous explosion tore through the quiet night.

The force of the blast slammed into me with the ferocity of a hurricane. I was thrown backward, my body slamming against the wall with a bone-jarring impact. The shockwave reverberated through me, my head snapping back with a sharp, disorienting thud. Darkness engulfed my senses as I succumbed to the overwhelming blow, spiraling into unconsciousness.

As I slowly regained consciousness two days later, my eyes fluttered open, struggling to adjust to the blinding glare of the fluorescent hospital lights. The sterile scent of antiseptic and disinfectant filled the air, mingling into a sharp, clinical aroma. Confusion washed over me as I realized I was in an unfamiliar hospital, far from the comfort of my home city. They had expertise in dealing with my specific condition, I was told later.

Suddenly, my memory surged back, flooding my mind with vivid images of the devastating explosion. The beeping of the monitors filled the room, a relentless reminder of my precarious state. Panic began to rise within me, but a compassionate nurse quickly arrived, her soothing voice easing my distress. Soon after, a doctor administered a tranquilizer, calming my frayed nerves.

Despite the sedatives taking effect, two police officers entered my room. Their crisp blue uniforms and polished badges caught the overhead light, their presence both reassuring and authoritative. They informed me that an investigation into the explosion had been opened. "The incident reeks of foul play," they admitted, concern etched into their brows. It became chillingly clear—the gas pipe had been deliberately severed, cleverly anticipating my arrival. If I had been indoors, the explosion would have been fatal. The news sent a shiver down my spine.

The names E and Rudi flashed through my mind, and suddenly the caretaker's troubled look made sense. The officers exchanged glances, their pocket notebooks filled with details I had provided. Their firm handshakes and warm smiles conveyed gratitude, though I could sense the weight of their concern.

As I recovered, the hospital room became a flurry of activity. My true friends emerged—not the ones I often treated to beers, but those I had met through the library and book clubs. They arrived in pairs, their footsteps muffled on the linoleum floor, bringing flowers and gift cards, their voices filled with genuine concern.

Surrounded by the familiar faces of my friends from the library and book clubs, the sterile hospital room seemed even colder, and I felt a pang of loneliness. The thought was impossible to ignore—despite the seriousness of my condition, my mother hadn't once called to check on me. Her absence felt like a void, a stark contrast to the concern and kindness shown by those who had come to visit.

I could hear the gentle rustle of flowers and the soft murmur of voices in the room, but the lack of a familiar voice from my own mother was a bitter reminder of her absence. Each missed call, each unanswered message, seemed to echo in the empty space she had left. The realization stung, adding a layer of hurt to my already fraught emotions.

As I tried to focus on the present, on the kindness of those around me, I couldn't shake the feeling of disappointment. The contrast between the support from unexpected sources and the silence from my own family was a harsh reminder of the complexities in my life.

To my surprise, one late afternoon, the caretaker from my residential complex entered my room. His face was twisted with nervousness, his hands fidgeting with the hem of his jacket. He glanced over his shoulder, ensuring no one else was around, before perching on the side of my bed. With a quick, cautious movement, he produced a half jack of whisky and two packets of cigarettes, their crisp packaging crackling softly. He carefully concealed them in my bedside drawer, a secret offering of comfort. Although I had no need for these items, I thanked him with a warm embrace, feeling the roughness of his coat against my cheek.

He stayed by my side until I finished my early dinner. His eyes revealed a mixture of worry and urgency, hinting at something important on his mind. I waited patiently, the sound of departing visitors and the closing bell signaling the end of visiting hours.

What crucial insights does the caretaker have? Join me in the upcoming episode to uncover the answers. In the meantime, take care, stay protected, and anticipate our reunion with eager senses.

Chapter Twenty-Eight

I anxiously awaited as the caretaker held back, ready to spill the juicy details. Suddenly, a stern-faced nurse sauntered in and chased out all the visitors. I let out a sigh of defeat as my shoulders drooped. Memories of the explosion flashed in my mind, the deafening boom still ringing in my ears, and I was eager to learn if E and Rudi had something to do with it. But deep down, I already knew the answer, and I yearned to hear the confirmation from someone other than my own conclusions.

Many people from work visited me during my hospital stay. Among them was the beautiful rose Monique, her vibrant presence always managing to brighten up my pale face. And as you might have guessed, everyone except E and Rudi paid their respects. From the bits of news I had gathered, they were eagerly preparing their exit from the company, with a farewell party looming on the horizon. Thankfully, I was confined to the hospital bed, unsure if I even made it onto the guest list. But deep down, I knew I was, because E always wanted to deliver the final blow.

An assessor from the insurance company paid me a visit. He shared another shocking revelation, his voice filled with disbelief. "My apartment was filled with gas because someone intentionally cut the pipe to my gas stove," he said, sending a shiver down my spine.

From his detailed explanation, I learned that a knife had been used, not a screwdriver, adding to my suspicions. However, he sympathetically understood that no one would do something like that to themselves, and assured me that my claim would be processed once the police concluded their investigations.

Talk of the devil. They showed up not long after the assessor left, their footsteps heavy and authoritative. What they told me brought a mischievous grin to my face. Both Rudi and E had been brought in for questioning, their voices filled with vehement denial.

But the police treated them as the main suspects in an attempted murder investigation, their words falling on deaf ears. The thought of their distress brought a sly grin to my face, my lips curving with satisfaction. And on top of it all, this news would surely spread like wildfire, casting a shadow over their farewell party. I couldn't help but revel in their failed attempts.

Yet, miraculously, I bore only a few scars and bruises, a dull ache throbbing in my head and a deep sense of wounded pride.

Great was my surprise when the caretaker returned, his footsteps soft and cautious. With a sneaky gesture, he surreptitiously stashed a bottle of whisky and a pack of cigarettes in my bedside table drawer. I asked him to go to the teller machine and withdraw some money. When he returned, I slipped a pile of crisp bills into his pocket. His weathered smile said it all, a silent understanding passing between us. I knew then that he would become a frequent visitor, his presence bringing a sense of comfort and companionship in the sterile hospital room.

Careful not to startle my favorite visitor, I subtly pressed him for details about that fateful day when I nearly lost my life. With the crisp bills now in his pocket, he recounted the events with a content smile on his face.

While I was at work, E had arrived and gathered her belongings, carefully transporting them to the sunlit courtyard. She had even asked the caretaker to keep an eye out for me, her whispered exchange followed by the jingle of money. With a shy smile, he admitted that he had agreed to their cunning plan.

Not long after, Rudi arrived with a rented pickup truck. Together, they loaded her meager possessions onto the back, the clatter of boxes and the thud of furniture echoing through the air. But they didn't leave immediately. Instead, they disappeared into my house, their footsteps fading into silence.

"You see," said the caretaker in his distinct African accent, "they looked like mischievous monkeys who had stolen bananas." I smiled at his description, knowing all too well the mischief they were capable of.

"I could smell the lingering scent of their passion," he said, "like a lioness enticing her mate."

I sat upright, my ears perked, hanging on to his every word. I felt an odd sense of relief as I envisioned the flames consuming my bedding, creating a fiery inferno.

The visitor bell wailed in the distance, piercing the stillness of the air, and the caretaker leaped up, his eyes darting to his worn-out watch. I did not know it then, but I held him in high regard for what he had told me. It took him over two long hours to reach the hospital, enduring countless train rides and a hectic taxi journey. Finding words to express my immense gratitude for his visits seemed impossible.

Soon after, a striking female figure entered my room. Her curly red hair cascaded down her shoulders, and a faint scent of lavender followed her every move. She introduced herself as a psychologist with a gentle smile and a kind demeanor.

"To help you cope with your trauma," she began, brushing a strand of hair away from her piercing amber eyes, "we have arranged for you to be transferred to a specialized mental health clinic." Her voice was calm and reassuring, though the gravity of her words lingered in the air, mixing with the aroma of freshly squeezed orange juice I sipped.

I observed her closely, my emotions a mix of apprehension and hope. "Your medical insurance has approved this transfer," she continued, "and your employer supports this decision as well." Her words offered a sense of relief, particularly as I was still reeling from the recent destruction of my home.

In that moment, as I sat there, captivated by the psychologist's words and the emotions they evoked, I allowed myself to believe that this upcoming stay at the specialized mental health clinic could be the turning point I desperately needed. The psychologist's presence and the hope she instilled in me became a beacon of light, guiding me towards healing and recovery.

She went on to describe the facility's excellent reputation and the comprehensive mental health services they offered. Her enthusiasm for the clinic was palpable, and as she spoke, I felt a tentative sense of optimism about my upcoming stay.

When I inquired about the duration of my recovery, she explained that it would depend on my progress. This insight provided comfort, knowing the clinic would offer not just treatment but a temporary refuge from the devastation I had endured.

As I listened to the psychologist's words, a wave of relief washed over me, causing the tension in my body to slowly dissolve. The weight of my trauma seemed to lift, as if a burden had been taken off my shoulders. My racing heartbeat began to steady, and the knots in my stomach started to loosen. It was as if her gentle demeanor and encouraging words were working their magic, soothing not just my mind but also my physical being.

I didn't realize it at the time, but as I looked into her compassionate eyes, I sensed a genuine concern for my wellbeing. The soft lines on her face and the gentle curve of her smile conveyed a warmth that enveloped me. Her kind words, like a soothing melody, wrapped around me, easing the tension that had been gripping my body. In that moment, I couldn't ignore the weight of the bad experience anymore; I understood that I needed help to overcome it. As tears welled up in my eyes, a sense of relief washed over me, knowing that someone was there, ready to support me. With each passing moment, the tightness in my frayed nerves began to loosen, gradually dissipating. It hadn't crossed my mind that I would require help, but in that profound moment, an overwhelming gratitude swelled within me for the care that awaited me.

As night approached, I discreetly handed a bribe to the nurses, requesting them to inform my visitors of my new location. The thought of seeing the caretaker again, his comforting presence amidst the chaos, was a source of solace.

The following morning, I was transported to the facility in an ambulance. The smell of disinfectant greeted me as I was shown to my room. The expansive dining hall, filled with the sounds of cutlery and murmured conversations, was a stark contrast to the quiet of my previous environment.

Later, I met with a dedicated psychologist and psychiatrist. Each introduction stirred a mix of trepidation and hope within me as I prepared for my journey toward healing.

As evening fell, the once tranquil atmosphere transformed into a lively, almost carnival-like energy. Visitors arrived, their voices blending into a vibrant hum. The air was now filled with a heady mix of perfumes and lively conversation, creating a scene that, in its own way, felt both overwhelming and oddly familiar.

Dear reader, join me in my next installment to uncover the secrets hiding in the depths of this mental health clinic. Until then, take care and goodbye for now.

Chapter Twenty-Nine

Although I lived within the safe walls of a mental health clinic, recovering from the torment of trauma, I felt a constant disconnect. The sterile environment seemed to amplify my meager existence, unraveling in unforeseen ways. Dear reader, the first challenge I encountered was the surplus of time for contemplation. My mind, devoid of the usual distractions of work, technology, and companionship, became a whirlwind of thoughts and emotions.

Imagine, if you will, two serpents coiling within the recesses of your mind, their venomous whispers hissing ceaselessly. Your thoughts transform into a battlefield where the forces of good and evil wage a relentless war for dominance.

One serpent persistently chastises, while the other exalts the choices that have shaped your life. The outcome remains uncertain. And, to intensify this internal conflict, the one source of temporary relief from this mental anguish is taken away—alcohol.

I yearned for the respite of beer and the comforting presence of friends to hush the cacophony within my mind. Yet I dared not expose my hidden stash of two whiskey bottles concealed amidst my meager possessions. The warning came down sternly—any possession of substances meant immediate expulsion from the clinic, and I couldn't afford the exorbitant expenses without medical insurance coverage.

The time had come to confront my inner demons, a daunting task from which I could not shy away. My thoughts delved into the deepest recesses of my memory, unearthing echoes of bygone times. As I connected the dots, my understanding grew, and I could no longer evade the truth that I alone was responsible for the predicament in which I now found myself.

I have always valued my unwavering honesty. Sitting in the psychologist's office, I couldn't help but notice her raven hair flowing over her shoulders, brushing against her straight bangs. Her gilded jewelry jingled with every movement, creating an aura of mystery and power. She reminded me of Cleopatra, a symbol of strength and wisdom.

I shared my bone-chilling encounters and true discoveries with her, holding nothing back. Her icy fingers tightened around mine, reminding me of the importance of my journey towards recovery. Before me, she revealed my program in its entirety—a detailed roadmap to healing. I eagerly anticipated the upcoming exercises, group discussions, and creative activities that would help silence the venomous echoes of the snakes in my head.

However, each of these activities held their own allure, tempting me to stray from my path. But the psychologist sternly warned me, her words etched into my memory. She reminded me that I was not there to be anyone's "vomit bucket," a receptacle for their problems. I was there to heal, to focus on myself.

Soon enough, I realized the truth concealed behind her words. I couldn't hide from my fellow patients, who were like hound dogs, always seeking a sympathetic ear. They sniffed out my listening skills, making me their prey. It became increasingly difficult to find solace, as they would crawl through my bedroom window or whisper through the cracks at the bottom of the bathroom door.

The younger girls, just emerging from their teenage years, were particularly persistent. They all had their own reasons for being there, most of which were self-inflicted due to heartbreaks or a lack of love from affluent parents. Desperate for attention, they would offer me anything in exchange for my time—from intimacy to concealed liquor and narcotics.

As I watched the younger girls, their seductive eyes and enticing offers, a small voice inside me whispered, "Stay strong, focus on your recovery." Their beauty was undeniable, their allure a dangerous temptation. But I couldn't afford to be swayed by their charms.

I knew that giving in to their advances would only lead to more pain and setbacks. I had come to this place to heal, to find solace and strength within myself. I couldn't let their desperate cries for attention distract me from my own journey.

So, I hardened my resolve, reminding myself of the battles I had fought and the progress I had made. I closed my eyes for a moment, taking a deep breath, and whispered silently, "I won't let their allure weaken me. I am here to recover, to rebuild my life. Nothing will stand in my way."

It was then that I met Mel, an international model, seeking solace in our country. Picture this: as a newcomer, the yoga instructor placed me at the back of the class. It was my first encounter with yoga, so imagine the view I had of the perfect, slender female bodies contorting into mesmerizing poses. The scent of incense and sweat filled the air, mingling with the sound of soft music playing in the background.

I remember little of the instructor's voice, but the sequence of events remains vivid in my mind. The younger girls whispered their intentions and secrets in my ears, drawing closer to me. As I moved away, I noticed the men doing the same to Mel. Twisted into strange poses; they swarmed around her like persistent flies. The redness in her face did not stem from exertion, for it was evident that she was fit. No, it was anger that fueled her gaze as her eyes darted around the room, until they landed on me. In no time, I found myself with a silent partner, deflecting the girls' advances while Mel repelled the men. Our strategy proved effective, as it discouraged those who targeted us.

As it turned out, Mel, like me, was on a path of healing, referring to this time as her "post-rehab" period. She had chosen our country as her sanctuary, shielding herself from the allure of narcotics that lurked in the streets of the outside world. To my surprise, we shared the same healing program, attending group discussions and creativity classes together. The younger girls, and guys in her case, soon abandoned their pursuit of us and formed light-hearted bonds amongst themselves, filling the room with laughter. In the midst of the madness, I had found a friend and a sense of purpose. It was a great relief.

Late at night, as the world around us quieted, Mel would sneak into my room through the concealed window. The taste of my secret whisky lingered on our tongues as we savored each sip, knowing we had to make the bottle last. Just before the bell signaled lights-out and medication time, she would plant a gentle peck on my cheek and hurriedly return to the female dormitory.

I was filled with gratitude for my newfound friendship. The aroma of sizzling bacon filled the air as Mel, a vegan, willingly traded her crispy strips for my savory hash browns. She would willingly exchange her steaming cup of coffee for a glass of my tangy, freshly squeezed orange juice. It was as if the universe possessed a wry sense of humor, aligning our paths as I healed from my trauma.

Amidst the serenity of the shaded tree, I marveled at the universe's matchmaking skills. Mel, an international model, intrigued me with her captivating presence. With her flowing dark brown hair, captivating green eyes, and tall slender body, she was a vision of enchantment. As she delicately sucked on a dandelion stem, a gentle breeze carried away the fluffy seeds, creating a whimsical dance. Suddenly, she turned onto her stomach, her sensuous lips framed by strands of hair, and posed a question that caught me off guard.

In her heavy foreign accent, she asked, "What do you think of being friends with benefits?"

My heart raced as I considered Mel's proposition. Friends with benefits? It was a concept I had heard of before, but had never personally experienced. The idea of a casual, physical relationship with no strings attached was both enticing and nerve-wracking.

I looked into Mel's captivating green eyes, searching for any hint of what she truly desired. Was she looking for a distraction from her own demons? Or did she genuinely want to explore a deeper connection with me?

As I hesitated, unsure of how to respond, Mel leaned in closer, her breath warm against my skin. "Think about it," she whispered, her voice filled with a mix of seduction and vulnerability. "No expectations, no commitments. Just two friends enjoying each other's company, in every way."

Her words hung in the air, tempting me to surrender to the allure of pleasure without consequences. To discover if I had succumbed to the allure of her enticing invitation, come with me on my next adventure. Until then, bid adieu amidst the gentle whispers of the wind and the scent of blooming flowers, and indulge in blissful contemplation.

Chapter Thirty

Mel completed her healing program a week before me. It was a bittersweet farewell, the air heavy with a mix of sadness and relief. The warmth of the sun kissed our cheeks as we stood there, exchanging numbers, promising to stay in touch. I felt a sense of vulnerability, a knot in my stomach, knowing that she would no longer be by my side.

But true to her word, every night she called me, her voice like a soothing melody amidst the quiet stillness of the night. As I lay beneath the shade of our favorite tree, the scent of dandelions filled my nostrils. We spoke for hours, sharing our thoughts, our fears, and our dreams.

To my surprise, amidst our conversations, Mel's offer for a friends with benefits arrangement remained. It lingered in the air, a tempting yet complicated proposition. I wrestled with my feelings, unsure of what was real and what was just a figment of my imagination.

As I continued my program alone, the absence of Mel became more evident. The activities seemed dull and lifeless without her by my side. The female presence, with their stories of sorrow and heartache, flooded my mind, leaving me feeling overwhelmed. I fought to stay focused, to block out their voices, as I desperately tried to heal.

In a creativity class, a flicker of hope emerged. We were taught the power of visualization, a tool to shape our future selves. Closing my eyes, I immersed myself in the exercise, envisioning the person I longed to become. And there, in the depths of my mind, I saw her — Mel. Standing beside me, on the shores of a tranquil ocean. The azure waters stretched out before us, a mesmerizing sight. Was it just a vision, or had I fallen for her? The answer eluded me, leaving me with a mix of confusion and curiosity as I embarked on a journey to rediscover my purpose.

Breakfast, lunch, and dinner time were the worst. The cold, sterile room echoed with my solitary presence as the unappetizing aroma of the food lingered in the air. Shortly after, a nurse strolled into my room, her footsteps barely making a sound, and beckoned me to the psychologist's office. As I entered, her smile transformed into a penetrating stare, locking onto me with an unwavering intensity. Swiftly, she recounted my progress, her voice devoid of any emotion, as if reciting a rehearsed script. It became apparent that this was merely a formality, as her true purpose lay elsewhere.

Without hesitation, she interrogated me about my detachment, probing into the depths of my psyche. With urgency, she expressed her grave concern regarding my antisocial behavior, and promptly referred me to the psychiatrist. I was taken aback, struggling to comprehend the idea of being forced to socialize with a group of mentally unstable individuals. Pardon my bluntness, dear reader, but that was precisely how I felt. It was disconcerting, considering that this was the same psychologist who had previously warned me to steer clear of such individuals.

However, if I had any hopes of escaping this place, I knew I had to comply with the prescribed program. To my astonishment, she extended the program by a week, pending her review. It became clear to me then that someone had reported my behavior and my friendship with Mel.

Just before the early dinner, I casually made my way into the psychiatrist's office. He appeared to suffer from a condition of sorts, his head constantly trembling like a fragile leaf caught in a gust of wind. His thick glasses teetered precariously on the edge of his nose, causing him to constantly readjust them. He seemed to be in constant motion, alternately standing and sitting, creating a sense of unease within me. It felt as though I was aboard a turbulent ship, battling waves of nausea.

I couldn't fathom how he managed to read, but he swiftly delivered his verdict, using medical terminology to label my antisocial behavior.

"Oh no, here we go again," I whispered to myself, my eyes widening in disbelief as I watched him.

He diagnosed me with "avoidant personality disorder," a term that sent a chill down my spine. It felt like a stamp of permanent abnormality, branding me as someone who would forever struggle with social interactions. The psychiatrist recommended therapy sessions and prescribed medication to help manage my symptoms.

Feeling defeated and overwhelmed, I reluctantly agreed to follow the treatment plan. The days blurred together as I attended therapy sessions, participating in group activities with the other patients. It was a strange mix of individuals, each battling their own demons in this sterile environment.

As time passed, I began to notice a change within myself. The therapy sessions provided a safe space for me to express my thoughts and fears. The group activities forced me to confront my social anxieties head-on, slowly chipping away at my walls of isolation. I discovered that there were others who understood my struggles, and their support became a lifeline in this suffocating place.

While the cold, sterile room continued to haunt me during mealtimes, I found solace in the company of my fellow patients. We formed a bond, united by our shared experiences and determination to overcome our mental health challenges.

Gradually, the penetrating stares and rehearsed scripts of the nurse and psychologist faded into the background. Their initial skepticism transformed into genuine encouragement as they witnessed my progress. It was as if they had seen the spark of resilience flicker within me and were determined to fan it into a flame.

With each passing day, I felt a glimmer of hope ignite within me. The program, initially seen as a prison sentence, became a catalyst for personal growth and self-discovery. While the tremors of the psychiatrist still unnerved me, I recognized his expertise in guiding me towards a path of healing.

As my time in the clinic drew to a close, I realized that this place, with all its coldness and sterility, had become a crucible for transformation. It had forced me to confront my fears, challenge my assumptions, and ultimately find strength within myself.

But an overwhelming concern ate away at my mind like a persistent hunger. The thought of my charred house, reduced to ashes, left me with nowhere to seek solace once they set me free. Despite the hardships I faced during my time here, it provided a temporary sanctuary amidst my state of homelessness. I could only yearn for guidance from the vast cosmic forces that governed our destinies. To unveil the secrets that lay ahead, accompany me on this journey through my forthcoming installment.

Chapter Thirty-One

Leaving the clinic, I carried with me not only the weight of my diagnosis but also the resilience and newfound understanding of my own capabilities. The sun began to set, casting a warm golden glow across the city streets as I made my way to Mel's opulent duplex apartment in an affluent suburb. As I entered, the scent of expensive perfume filled the air. The enormous windows offered a breathtaking view of the bustling city below, its lights flickering like stars in the distance.

Sitting together on her plush sofa, the sound of laughter and conversation filled the room, intermingling with the soft music playing in the background. Mel, her foreign accent dripping with seduction, leaned in closer, her voice laced with the sweetness of expensive champagne. "So," she said, her eyes sparkling mischievously, "are you ready to become friends with benefits?" Her words hung in the air, accompanied by the enticing sound of her giggles.

Earlier in the day, we had been splashing around in her pool, the cool water caressing our skin as we laughed and played. Now, as she sat before me in her swimsuit, her perfect curves accentuated by the soft glow of the evening, I couldn't help but feel a mixture of excitement and vulnerability. My heart raced, my knees weak, as I realized the tantalizing possibilities that lay before me.

"Yes," I said, a hint of anticipation in my voice, "but I also have a proposition for you."

Her radiant smile widened, illuminating the room with its brilliance as she leaned in close. A soft floral scent wafted from her, enveloping me in an intoxicating embrace of her divinity.

"Pray tell," she purred, her voice a seductive melody sending a shiver of excitement down my spine.

I, too, knew how to play the game. Leaning in closer, our breaths mingling, our lips barely grazing, I whispered, "Once a week, you must partake in a social group discussion."

In response, she inched even closer, our lips meeting in a tantalizing touch, as she whispered, "You have a deal."

The crack of lightning illuminated our desires in a dazzling burst of light. Suddenly, the room was engulfed in darkness as the power cut out, leaving us in a state of exhilarating uncertainty. Our hearts pounded in sync, the sound reverberating through the air like thunder. Without hesitation, I pulled Mel close, the heat of our bodies mingling in the darkness.

Our hands traced each other's curves, fueled by the sudden flashes of lightning that illuminated our passionate connection. The soft touch of her fingertips sent electric shocks through my veins, igniting a primal desire within me.

As the storm raged outside, its thunderous roars matching the rhythm of our passionate embrace, we surrendered to the irresistible pull of the moment. Clothes were shed, discarded like the remnants of our inhibitions, as we melted into a frenzy of desire, lost in a world where only pleasure existed.

Every touch, every kiss, became a symphony of ecstasy, a dance of raw desire that consumed us both. The room became a playground of pleasure, our bodies entwined in a dance of sensuality, fueled by the intoxicating combination of lust and longing.

Time ceased to exist as we surrendered ourselves to the intoxicating whirlwind of passion, our moans and whispers blending with the symphony of raindrops against the windowpane. In that moment, we were free from the constraints of society, lost in a world where pleasure reigned supreme.

As the storm finally subsided, we lay entangled in each other's arms, basking in the afterglow of our forbidden liaison. The air crackled with a newfound connection, a bond forged through desire and vulnerability.

With a soft, contented sigh, Mel turned to me, her eyes filled with a newfound depth of affection. "I never expected this," she whispered, her voice a gentle caress. "But I'm glad we took the leap."

I smiled, my heart filled with a mix of satisfaction and anticipation for the next chapter in our thrilling journey. Little did we know, this night was just the beginning of a passionate and unpredictable adventure that would forever alter the course of our lives.

As our connection deepened, I couldn't help but marvel at the electricity that seemed to flow between us. With each passing day, our connection evolved into something more profound. Beyond the physical attraction, we discovered a genuine friendship rooted in mutual respect and understanding. Our encounters became moments of solace in a chaotic world, a sanctuary where we could be vulnerable and free.

Amidst the whirlwind of emotions, I remained committed to my proposition. Each week, we eagerly took part in a group where stimulating discussions challenged our perspectives and opened our minds to new ideas. These conversations, often accompanied by glasses of fine wine, allowed us to connect on a deeper level, transcending the boundaries of mere physical intimacy.

Through these discussions, we uncovered layers of ourselves that we hadn't even realized existed. We shared our dreams, fears, and aspirations, opening up parts of our souls that had long been hidden away. In this space of intellectual and emotional exchange, we found solace and growth, nurturing a connection that went beyond the realms of physical pleasure.

As time passed, our bond continued to flourish, defying societal expectations and stereotypes. We defied the notion that a friends-with-benefits arrangement had to be shallow or temporary. Instead, we crafted a unique dynamic that combined passion with intellectual stimulation, nurturing a relationship that was both fulfilling and meaningful.

In the end, our journey taught me that love and connection can be found in the most unexpected places. It taught me to embrace the complexities of human relationships, to let go of preconceived notions, and to cherish the moments of genuine connection that come our way.

Leaving the clinic that day, little did I know that what awaited me was not only a diagnosis but also a transformative experience that would forever shape my understanding of love, resilience, and the power of human connection.

Chapter Thirty-Two

"I had the time of my life," in the proverbial sense. The memories of my past and the haunting presence of my father had disappeared. Even the absence of contact from my mother didn't bother me during that time. Mel, my angelic companion, brought me a sense of peace I had never experienced before. Rudi and E's attempt to destroy my life had given me an unexpected power. But now, my adventure with Mel was coming to an end, although our agreement remained intact.

Returning to work was a horrifying thought, but Mel and I had a plan to make it bearable. As the morning sun rose, we shared our usual early morning kiss, but this time, there was a hint of sadness. Driving on the highway felt like traversing a barren wasteland after months of reveling in an oasis. The open road stretched out before me, and my thoughts wandered back to the incredible moments we had shared, from scuba diving in warm, azure oceans to our time in Mozambique. The memories brought a constant smile to my face.

Yet, the thought of Mel returning to her country loomed on the horizon, a fate I couldn't bear to think about. With a heavy heart, I arrived at work and parked my car. Little did I know that a surprise awaited me inside. As I walked towards the office, the sight of vibrant balloons, colorful runners, and joyful placards greeted my eyes. The air was filled with excitement, and the sound of laughter and chatter echoed through the corridors.

With newfound confidence from my time with Mel, I stepped into the elevator, ready to face the surprise. The doors opened, and my colleagues shouted, "Surprise!" Their exclamation filled my ears, and I couldn't believe what I saw. Overwhelmed with emotions, I dropped my belongings and covered my eyes, tears welling up as a rush of pent-up feelings poured out of me.

The hours slowly crawled by, and with every passing moment, I anxiously glanced at my watch, eagerly awaiting lunchtime. My small office, enclosed in glass walls, nestled itself in the corner of a sprawling office space. To reach me, guests had to navigate through a maze of desks, enduring curious stares along the way.

Suddenly, the phone on my desk jolted me out of my reverie, its shrill ring piercing the quiet air. They informed me that I had a visitor. "Please, show her in," I said, gently placing the phone back on its receiver. It was all part of our calculated plan. From my vantage point, I could see the backs of my staff, their focused energy consumed by their work.

A collective gasp escaped their lips as Mel confidently sauntered into the room, gracefully passing by them, and finally entering my office. In that moment, she wrapped her arms around me, bestowing upon me a tender kiss, while the eyes of my colleagues gazed upon us, their curiosity clear.

Taking her hand in mine, I led her through the bustling building, our steps echoing against the polished floors. Not even an earthquake could have wiped the radiant smile off my face. I reveled in the jealous glances of those who had always dismissed me. Even to this day, I can feel the intensity of their eyes drilling into me, their envy contorting their once amiable faces into something grotesque.

But I didn't let their negativity dampen my spirits. With Mel by my side, I felt invincible. We walked past the rows of cubicles, and I could sense the whispers and hushed conversations following in our wake.

It was the most extraordinary lunchtime I've ever experienced at work. All around me, people abandoned their meals, their eyes fixated on Mel. The sound of hushed whispers filled the air as anticipation grew. A subtle click echoed as a guy discreetly snapped a photo of the moment on his phone. I felt an indescribable sense of power and reveled in the envious and covetous glances of those around us. If you were to ask me now what I consumed during lunch, I would simply shrug, saying, "Who cares? Mel was by my side," as a mischievous chuckle escaped my lips.

I stepped back into my office after bidding farewell to Mel. The sunlight filtered through the blinds, casting elongated shadows across the room. My eyes widened with surprise as I noticed a neatly written note resting on my desk, its elegant handwriting beckoning my attention. It read, "Call your mother urgently."

Instantly, the sound of alarm bells echoed in my mind, their shrillness reverberating through my thoughts. Yet, the note left me with no choice but to comply, for I feared the worst, believing that someone close to me had passed away.

It is important to note, dear readers, that this was the same mother who never once called me during my hospital stay or bothered to visit the clinic. In fact, it had been four long years since I last heard from her.

A voice in my head, always a soft whisper, cautioned me against making the call. Reluctantly, I reached for the receiver and dialed her home number from memory. The anticipation weighed heavy in the air as I held my breath, waiting for her to answer.

"Hello," her voice came through the line, laced with a hint of weariness.

"Hi mom, it's me," I hesitated, uncertain of how she would respond.

"Is it you?" she snapped, her refusal to use my name a small yet sharp sting. She rarely addressed me by my name.

"Yes," I sighed, contemplating the idea of ending the call. Deep down, I knew that some things would never change, but hope still lingered within me.

She launched into a tirade, venting about her financial burdens and accusing my brother and me of abandoning her. It was the same woman who had squandered my tuition money on a lavish trip to Europe, returning home only to threaten me with exorbitant rent or eviction. Threats seemed to be ingrained in her very being.

Nevertheless, she continued, revealing that the company she had dedicated her life to was now insolvent, unable to pay its employees' pensions. A common sight under our new government. In that moment, I realized that I had more than enough money saved up, far exceeding my own needs.

Without hesitation, I carefully noted down her banking details, my fingers gliding across the paper. I initiated a significant transfer into her account, hoping it would bring some relief to her dire situation.

* * *

As I completed the transfer, a mix of emotions flooded over me. Despite our tumultuous history, she was still my mother, and a part of me couldn't bear to see her suffer. I couldn't ignore the pang of guilt that gnawed at my conscience, reminding me that I had the means to make a difference in her life.

But as I hung up the phone, I couldn't help but wonder if my gesture would truly change anything. Would she appreciate the help, or would it simply enable her destructive behavior? It was a risk I was willing to take, hoping that perhaps this act of kindness could mend our fractured relationship.

Days turned into weeks, and I heard nothing from her. Doubt crept into my mind, wondering if she had even received the unexpected gift. I debated reaching out to her again, but my pride held me back. I didn't want to beg for her gratitude or acknowledgment.

And then, to my surprise, I discovered a neatly folded note on my desk. Hoping for a glimmer of good news, I reached for my phone and dialed my mother's number. Now, dear reader, I want to emphasize yet again. Here I was, calling the same mother who had been absent during my time in the sterile hospital room. She was the same mother who had used my intuition funds to gallivant across Europe. And once more, she was the same mother who never expressed gratitude for the previous time I deposited money into her account.

At that moment, I couldn't help but wonder if she was seeking to reclaim the money she had spent raising me, a bitter taste of betrayal lingering on my tongue. Though it takes a whole town to raise a child, I had left home during the early months of grade ten, seeking solace in the halls of a boarding school.

Please allow me to digress. The memories came rushing back with force as I reflected on my brief stay at the hospital. A mean guy had kicked me in my most vulnerable area—my dreams of having children of my own shattered.

The story, however, was far from over. Those six weeks in the hospital felt like an eternity, a blur of white walls and hushed conversations. A significant amount of time that could have been dedicated to my schoolwork, lost in the abyss of medical bills that accumulated each passing day. When the time came for me to go home and recover, my mother didn't even bother to show up, leaving me feeling abandoned and alone. Yes, I know the reasons, but please bear with me. Another lady, Auntie L, came to my rescue, her driver arriving at the hospital to collect me. Before we embarked on the journey to their opulent home, we made a detour to my house.

As I gathered my belongings, my mother stormed into my bedroom, her voice piercing the air with her furious words, assaulting me for the pain and suffering she claimed I had caused her. Let me remind you, dear reader, that it was I who was restricted to a hospital bed. She followed me outside, her voice echoing in my ears like a relentless bark, until we finally parted ways. At least for the next two years, I found solace in the warmth of my new family's home, where I was accepted for who I truly was.

Returning to the present moment, the shrill dial tone resounded in my ears, its persistent purring filling the room.

"Hello," my mother snapped, her tone dripping with her usual air of self-importance.

"Hi mom, it—"

"Oh, it is so good to hear your voice," she said insincerely, her voice dripping with feigned sadness. "I have been so worried."

"Bullshit," my mind whispered, while my heart urged me to be kind and get this conversation over with.

She continued her tirade, her voice filled with resentment, as she complained about her deteriorating financial situation and how the company had mercilessly slashed her pension fund. She painted a picture of helplessness, claiming she had no means to provide for herself. I listened attentively, as I always did, and in the midst of our conversation, I took the initiative to transfer money into her account.

"Mom," I interjected, my voice breaking through her tirade, "It's okay, I just transferred money into your account." I waited for a thank you that I knew would never come. Instead, she abruptly hung up, leaving me enveloped in a profound silence.

At the time, I had no idea that I was about to confront the most significant choice I would ever make.

Chapter Thirty-Three

While weeks slowly transformed into months, I faithfully continued to deposit money into my mother's account. It was a lonely time in my life. The days stretched on, each one blending into the next, as I carried out my duties with a heavy heart. Mel had returned to her home country, leaving me missing her terribly. The absence of her alluring presence was palpable, a void that echoed through the walls of my empty apartment.

Although we kept in touch, it was not the same as before. The sound of her laughter over the phone was a faint echo of the joy she used to bring me. But until the very end, she had kept her end of our agreement, friends with benefits. And now, only the friendship remained, a mere shadow of what we once had. Memories of our intimate encounters often flashed through my mind, like flickering images on an old film reel, fueling my longing for her.

Although I too had stayed true to our agreement, I could feel a pang of jealousy when I thought about her meeting a new "part-time lover," as she had playfully christened me. A role I had dutifully fulfilled without ever disappointing her. The bitter taste of envy lingered on my tongue, mixing with the bittersweet memories of our time together. I took pride in my ability to resist Mel's allure and protect my heart from being captivated by her.

The atmosphere at the airport was somber as we said our last goodbyes, the weight of sadness filling the space. I could see the longing for me in her eyes as she slipped through the gates, a flicker of desire that mirrored my own. I must admit that I, too, shed tears at the time. The saltiness of my own tears mingled with the scent of her perfume, a reminder of the love that once blossomed between us. Her absence left a deep mark on me, like a scar that refused to fade. Loneliness washed over me once more, like a heavy blanket.

This loneliness, I somehow think, played a part in a crucial decision, and its repercussions would soon become clear. Just like I made meticulous plans to enrich my future, my mother too schemed sinister plots to derail my life. At the time, I was oblivious to the fact that it was a trait she was renowned for. Blinded by my eagerness to impress, an unwavering determination to succeed fueled me. I truly believed that if I could prove myself to her, she would finally recognize my true character and perhaps even develop feelings for me. At that time, I was naïve and unaware of the reality that things didn't work that way, leaving me powerless to win her love. Oblivious to the valuable truth that awaited me, I pushed myself forward and upward, driven by an unyielding desire for success.

In order to counterbalance the solitude and financial strain of caring for my mother, I threw myself completely into my job. A new travel opportunity arose within the company, and seeing that I had no immediate family, I eagerly volunteered. I frequently traveled to remote cities, each one a new canvas waiting to be explored, and met interesting new people, their voices blending together in a symphony of unfamiliar accents. Despite my longing for Mel, I stayed occupied with this fantastic opportunity and remained a pillar of support for my mother.

As I pushed myself forward in my pursuit of success, unaware of the valuable truth that awaited me, I couldn't help but feel that I had traded one form of emptiness for another. The whirlwind of my job and the distractions it provided only masked the deep longing I felt for a connection that seemed impossible to recreate. I had a tendency to subject myself to difficult situations, almost as if I sought solace in the pain.

This tendency became more apparent as I continued to navigate through life. It was as if I was addicted to the emotional turmoil, finding comfort in the chaos it brought. The more I pushed myself, the more I realized that success alone was insufficient to fill the void Mel had left behind. My longing for my mother's approval continued to drive me, pushing me further into the depths of exhaustion.

* * *

During my travels, I encountered countless individuals who seemed content with their lives, despite not having achieved great success. They found happiness in the simple joys of everyday life, in relationships, and in the beauty of the present moment. Their stories served as a wake-up call, urging me to reconsider my priorities. I began to question whether my relentless drive for success was truly worth sacrificing my own happiness and the potential for genuine connections.

However, before I could fully grasp the extent of my own revelations, the inevitable occurred. One early Saturday morning, my heavy eyelids slowly lifted, revealing the stark white walls of a sterile mental health clinic. The air in the room felt suffocating, filled with the faint scent of antiseptic.

"What happened?" I croaked, my voice barely audible, as the nurse sat beside me, her presence a comforting anchor amidst the chaos within me.

"Your coworkers found you on the cold, hard floor of your office, plunged into darkness," she whispered, her voice a soothing melody for my frayed nerves.

I attempted to sit up, but the weight of the tranquilizers held me down, my body feeling like a leaden anchor. Instead, I reached out and clasped her hand, seeking solace in her touch, and asked, "What's wrong with me?"

A gentle smile graced her lips as her fingertips tenderly caressed my hair. "The doctor says it's burnout," she said softly.

My heart sank as her words echoed in my mind. Burnout. The mere mention of the term sent shivers down my spine as I realized the toll my relentless pursuit of success had taken on my body and mind.

Enveloped in a cocoon of vulnerability, I could feel the sweat on my forehead, the tightness in my chest, as the panic overwhelmed me. Each breath I took came in quick, shallow gasps, as if my lungs were desperate for more oxygen. Anxiety draped over me like a suffocating veil.

Overwhelmed, I closed my weary eyes, succumbing to the numbing effects of the medication, desperate for respite from this existence. In that moment, I cared not whether I ever opened my eyes again. From my vantage point, it was all over. My life had become a constant struggle against unyielding forces, and I felt utterly drained, unable to continue the fight.

It was the fear of rejection that had ensnared me in this convoluted web. I had been clueless on how to cope, how to sway the opinions of others. Without their approval, their simulated affection, and their impure motives, I might as well have been a lifeless shell.

In my dream, I found myself in a surreal landscape, where reality and imagination intertwined. I was surrounded by swirling colors and ethereal beings, each representing a facet of my desires and fears. They beckoned me to confront the emptiness within, urging me to break free from the shackles of external validation.

As I ventured deeper into this dream world, I stumbled upon a mirror. Its reflection revealed a distorted image of myself, shattered and fragmented. It was a stark reminder of the fractured state of my own identity, torn between the pursuit of achievements and the longing for genuine connections.

In the distance, I heard a melodic voice calling out to me, drawing me closer to a figure bathed in radiant light. It was Mel, my lost love, who had become a symbol of the deep emotional connection I had once experienced. Mel's presence filled me with warmth and a sense of belonging, reminding me of the importance of true connections over superficial success.

Together, Mel and I embarked on a journey through the dream world, encountering challenges and obstacles that mirrored the struggles of my waking life. But instead of striving for external validation, we focused on nurturing our own inner happiness and cultivating meaningful relationships.

With each step, the dream world began to shift, transforming into a vibrant tapestry of love, joy, and contentment. The void inside me gradually disappeared, making way for a profound sense of purpose and fulfillment that couldn't be quantified by worldly success.

As the dream neared its end, I awoke with a newfound clarity. The relentless pursuit of success had blinded me to the true source of happiness—genuine connections and self-acceptance. It was time to prioritize my own well-being and seek fulfillment beyond the confines of societal expectations.

In the distance, a distant siren emitted a vague, haunting wail, jolting me awake from my dream. Memories of the peculiar encounter with Mel flooded my mind, bringing a mix of emotions that left me with a bittersweet smile on my lips. It felt surreal to realize that our paths had crossed in this very clinic.

Eagerly, I bounded out of bed and hastily made my way to the bustling dining hall, ready to test my newfound theory on the countless strangers who wrestled with their own inner demons. To my surprise, fate granted me a second chance, igniting a spark of hope within me.

Chapter Thirty-Four

As I aimlessly strolled through the expansive grounds of the mental health clinic, the scent of freshly cut grass filled my nostrils. My mind wandered as I weighed the thoughts in my hand, like a delicate balance. On one side, the image of my small town, where my mother lived, filled me with a longing for tranquility. The peacefulness of the countryside beckoned me. But on the other side, the bustling, smog-shrouded city called to me, promising success and the company of cheerful people.

In the town where my mother lived, the air was heavy with tension. The presence of the Boer Maffia, a curious and unfriendly bunch, seemed to permeate every corner. Their lips were twisted into perpetual sneers, their eyes brimming with suspicion. It was a stark contrast to the vibrant energy of the city.

Both options held allure, but I knew that this decision would shape my life forever. It was a matter of choosing the lesser evil. The days dragged on in the mental health clinic, each one filled with uncertainty. Going back to my job meant facing burnout again, a risk I couldn't bear. The thought of it brought me dangerously close to the edge, a place where ending my life seemed like the only escape. Foolish as it may be, I knew I had to be cautious.

Please, dear reader, indulge me as I momentarily digress. In an earlier part of my journey, I recounted a visit to the neurologist, a memory that still haunted me. The car ride home was suffocatingly silent, the weight of the neurologist's verdict hanging in the air. His cruel words echoed in my mind like a broken record. "You lack coordination skills," he had said, his voice cold and heartless. "You will never excel in sports." His words ate away at my soul, leaving me feeling worthless. Even under the rule of my narcissistic mother and psychopathic brother, I had never felt so small.

But what hurt the most was when he insulted my very essence. He deemed me unworthy of love and companionship, declaring that I was not relationship material and not deserving of friendships.

Beside me, I could sense my mother's satisfaction, her gloating in my misery. I couldn't help but wonder if she had influenced the neurologist's decision during their private conversation. The smiles on their faces when they returned told a story I was all too familiar with, a tale of manipulation and deceit.

As we reached the halfway point on our journey home, we veered off our intended route, my mother leading us towards a small town. Questions filled my mind, and I couldn't help but ask, "Where are we going?"

Her response was silence, accompanied by a knowing smile that sent shivers down my spine. Eventually, we came to a halt in front of a weathered building resembling a farmhouse. Stepping out of the car, my mother beckoned me to join her, her high heels delicately maneuvering around the scattered piles of dog excrement. The air inside was heavy with the scent of stale beer and smoke, assaulting my senses as we traversed through to the kitchen. There, my mother engaged in conversation with an elderly lady, the words mingling with the somber atmosphere. Seated around a small table were a group of youngsters, their wide eyes fixed on me, their gaze penetrating. It was a scene filled with sorrow. It was only later that I discovered they were my family, a secret my mother had kept hidden, for they lived in severe poverty, unlike us. Their father's recent suicide was the reason behind our visit, and tragically, a few years later, we received the devastating news of one of his daughters following the same path. And above all, I never saw them again, except for that one time, even though they lived just a short distance from our luxurious home.

Now, dear reader, do you comprehend the caution I expressed? Yes, the darkness that plagued our family ran deep.

It was a darkness that seemed to seep into every aspect of our lives, tainting even the most mundane of moments. The mental health clinic, with its sterile walls and hushed whispers, became a symbol of the battles I fought within myself. The choice between the small town and the bustling city was not just about location, but about the very essence of my existence.

So, dear reader, as I stood in that mental health clinic, contemplating the choice before me, I couldn't help but feel the weight of the darkness that plagued our family. It was a caution born out of pain and understanding, a caution that urged me to choose the lesser evil, to find a path that would lead me away from the suffocating grip of despair. And so, with a heavy heart and a determined spirit, I made my decision, knowing that it would shape the course of my life forever.

I made the bold decision to sell my house and move to the Boer Maffia-Infested town where my mother resided. Naively, I saw it as an opportunity for us to mend our relationship, and for her to find forgiveness for my father through me. In her intoxicated state, fueled by the wine she happily consumed, I questioned whether she truly understood the words she spoke.

Without hesitation, I listed my house on the market and bid farewell to my job. It was an impulsive choice, one that I knew I would have second thoughts about if I had taken the time to contemplate. Little did I know what awaited me in that unfamiliar town.

However, I couldn't bear the thought of staying stagnant. This was already my second visit to the mental health clinic in less than a year. I had a plan to rescue my mother from the clutches of financial turmoil, and I was determined to see it through. Furthermore, I yearned to find my true love, knowing that the city girls lacked the qualities I sought in my dream wife. It was time to take the leap and embark on this new chapter of my life.

But for now, I had to diligently follow the structured routine of my prescribed program for the remaining duration of my stay in the serene and tranquil mental health clinic. And deep within, I fervently prayed that my choice would not subject me to the alluring temptations that had haunted me during my previous visit, just as any decision had the potential to do.

I embraced each day with the eager anticipation of a child, my heart fluttering with a mix of excitement and apprehension. As the days passed by, the grip of panic attacks loosened, and I could feel my breathing becoming easier, like a weight lifted off my chest. The fear that once consumed me when facing strangers had vanished, replaced by a new found confidence.

Engaging in creative activities, participating in group discussions, and even indulging in the rare pleasure of watching movies and playing pool at night, I discovered a side of life I had never known before. It was in this moment that I realized I was a likeable person, as the knocks on my door multiplied while I sat there reading, people seeking my presence.

For the first time in my existence, I felt a sense of peace within myself, and I began to love the person I was becoming. During one of our discussions, a counselor commended me for my refreshing perspective on obstacles, highlighting my ability to infuse humor into challenging situations. The compliment struck a chord within me, a cherished validation of my growth. I decided to put this newfound insight to the test, and I was amazed by the positive impact humor had on the outcomes I desired. In my mind's eye, I could vividly see the scenes unfolding, and I couldn't help but laugh at the imagined results.

The time had come for me to bid farewell to the familiar sights and comforting embrace of my current environment, and uncertainty loomed ahead. Yet, I embraced this new chapter wholeheartedly, knowing that a life full of possibilities awaited me beyond the boundaries of this city.

Chapter Thirty-Five

When you are young, most choices are made on your behalf. It is not fair to leave young children with the burden of tough choices and challenging life decisions. The weight of these choices can feel like a heavy burden, casting a shadow on what should be a carefree and joyful childhood.

My mother had a different outlook. She was hardly ever at home, seemingly working until late into the nights, leaving me in the company of my bullying brother. The silence in the house was deafening, broken only by the sound of my grumbling stomach. The aroma of hunger filled the air, mingling with the stale scent of neglect. I longed for a warm meal, a taste of comfort and love.

But hope often turned to disappointment. The meals my mother prepared were a reflection of her contempt for my father, and unfortunately, I found them quite distasteful. The domestic lady, her culinary surrogate, toiled in the kitchen, creating dishes that held no appeal to my young palate. The sight of the unappetizing ox liver, the pungent offal, and the overpowering hot curry made my stomach churn with revulsion.

My psychotic brother, however, seemed unaffected by the taste. He reveled in my misery, finding pleasure in my longing for our mother's favor. They would sit at the table together, savoring every morsel, while I watched, my disappointment palpable. The bitter taste of resentment lingered in my mouth, mixing with the bitter taste of the unwanted food.

The sight of them relishing every bite while I sat on the sidelines, longing for their attention and affection, intensified my feelings of bitterness and isolation. It was as if the unwanted food mirrored the unwanted emotions that consumed me, leaving a lingering bitterness that tainted every aspect of my life.

But amidst the disappointment and despair, I began to learn the art of survival. Like a stray dog searching for scraps, I found myself drawn to the enticing smells of food from neighboring houses. The aroma of sizzling fried onions became a beacon of hope, momentarily distracting me from the hardships of my own home. It was a small escape, a momentary respite from the constant hunger and emotional turmoil.

Whenever I found myself under the scrutiny of the lady of the house, I would instinctively put on my most pleading puppy dog face, hoping to appeal to her empathy and receive her kindness. I had learned that sometimes, survival meant relying on charm and cuteness to elicit a compassionate response from others. It was a skill I honed to ensure that I could find solace and nourishment, even in the face of neglect and indifference.

In those moments, as I stood there, my mouth watering and my heart yearning for warmth and belonging, I realized that even in the darkest of times, there was always a glimmer of hope. It may be found in the enticing aroma of sizzling onions or in the power of a puppy dog face, but it is a reminder that even amidst the burden of tough choices and challenging circumstances, resilience and survival can be found.

This approach, my secret weapon to quieting my growling tummy, had earned me many friends and exposed me to a myriad of culinary delights. Among them, the flavors of Italy. This approach was precisely how I had crossed paths with an Italian family who showered me with delectable treats. Through them, I forged a deep bond with their only son, Maurizio.

Our friendship flourished over the years, and today I express gratitude to the mother who nurtured my love for cooking. I can still vividly recall standing on a chair, eagerly absorbing her culinary techniques, the sight of those golden fried onions, and the aromatic spices she sprinkled with precision.

However, one fateful day, my deranged brother followed me and discovered my cherished sanctuary. He barged into the family's home, intent on assaulting me, and callously stole a valuable knife from their kitchen, leaving behind a chaotic mess. I am convinced that this was all part of my mother's sinister scheme, and unfortunately, it succeeded. The family banished me from their home, forbidding any contact with their son ever again. My best friend was abruptly torn away from me, leaving a void in my heart.

I was devastated by the loss of my friendship with Maurizio. It felt like a betrayal, not only from my brother but also from my mother, who seemed to have orchestrated this entire incident. The pain of losing someone who had brought so much joy and happiness into my life was unbearable.

In the aftermath of that fateful day, I found myself spiraling into a deep sense of loneliness and despair. The once comforting aroma of food now only served as a painful reminder of the love and connection I had lost. My hunger became more than just a physical ache; it became a symbol of the emotional void that consumed me.

Here in the sterile confines of the clinic, I've reached a pivotal decision to return to the very people who inflicted such deep wounds upon me. To most, this choice would be seen as pure madness—reuniting with a brother and a mother who had inflicted severe trauma upon my soul. However, at the time, I naively believed that my success and prolonged absence would compel them to embrace me once again. It felt like a long-awaited homecoming, a warm embrace that I desperately craved.

Yet, amidst my anticipation, I failed to realize that not once had these same people bothered to pick up the phone during my agonizing days in the hospital or the mental health clinic. The thought often haunts me, leaving me to question the driving force behind my actions. Perhaps it was because I have come to understand the power of letting go, as I discovered when I penned the story about my father. It was a cathartic experience that allowed me to release the emotions I had been holding onto for so long.

Additionally, I have personally experienced the transformative power of forgiveness. If I could find it within myself to forgive Rudi and E for their attempt to end my life, then surely forgiving my mother and brother would be a mere drop in the vast ocean of my journey.

This was something I knew had to be done, not just for them, but for my own sake as well. My conscience would never grant me peace if I were to walk away, knowing my mother was suffering financially. And I was the only one capable of supporting her during this trying time. Above all else, aside from providing financial aid, I had a grand plan to liberate my mother from the burdens that plagued her existence. I eagerly anticipated sharing this transformative plan with her, a beacon of hope in the darkness. It was time to bid farewell to this city and confront the demons that had relentlessly tormented my soul.

Chapter Thirty-Six

Instead of taking the straightforward seventeen-hour drive to my mother's town, I chose a detour through the place where I was raised. This wasn't just a journey; it was a pilgrimage of healing, a chance to close the doors I had left open when I embarked on my selfish pursuit of success.

My first stop was at my closest friend's house, where I had abandoned her during one of the darkest times in her life—when her father died. She and her family had always fed me, given me a bed during my fleeting visits when I was searching for food and belonging. This time, I didn't arrive empty-handed. Before ringing the bell, I hauled a dishwasher from the backseat of my car, placing it between me and the door, like a shield—just in case.

Her face lit up as the door swung open, and her grin widened at the sight of the dishwasher. Her laughter, pure and joyful, filled the air. With a beer in hand, her husband and I spent the evening installing it. The clinking of tools and the hum of the dishwasher filled the room. I'd never seen her so happy. She has since passed away from heart complications, but I still have a recording of her voice. When I miss her, I listen to it, and it brings back that evening—the warmth in her words and the love in her laughter.

The following day, I went to see my best friend from high school to offer condolences for his mother's recent passing. The house held a somber atmosphere, but his father was glad to see me and arranged a get-together. The smell of charcoal and sizzling meat filled the air as we gathered around the grill. It was a long-overdue barbecue, a chance to catch up with old friends. Yet, as we laughed and reminisced, I felt a strange disconnect. Most of them were married, settled into lives I hadn't chosen. I had to constantly wave off their matchmaking suggestions. The laughter and chatter mixed with the crackling fire, creating a bittersweet symphony of memories and missed opportunities.

There was one more stop I had to make before I left, but it took a bit of courage. Rather than just walking past my high school crush's house, I came up with a clever scheme to get her phone number. If I had only been aware that she had to share a cellphone with her parents, who were extremely impoverished.

To my delight, she agreed to my request for a dinner date. The anticipation filled me with nervous excitement as I drove to pick her up. I could feel a mix of anxiety and hope building within me. I lacked the courage to confront her disapproving parents, unaware that I would only make matters worse.

During my time in school, I had supported her family with insignificant gestures, and I had abandoned them when her dad lost his job because of illness. The weight of regret had burdened me for many years. To make amends, I had a plan to gift her an envelope filled with bills. On the opposite side of their home stood a lavish church, its grandeur contrasting with their humble abode. And this is where we agreed I would pick her up for our date, to avoid running into her parents.

I took her to the fanciest restaurant in town, its elegant ambiance enhanced by soft jazz music playing in the background. The aroma of delectable dishes wafted through the air, teasing our senses. Despite its reputation, the restaurant seemed ordinary compared to the lavish places I had become accustomed to.

On our way back home, the city lights illuminated the night sky, creating a romantic atmosphere. With a playful tone in her voice, she asked if we could go for a nightcap somewhere. I agreed, and we embarked on an adventure.

One thing led to another, and in the intimate space of the backseat of my car, we shared a moment of passion. The touch of her skin against mine, the sound of our hushed whispers, and the intoxicating scent of her perfume created an unforgettable experience. It was a spontaneous act, unplanned but long overdue, as I had never fully satisfied her insatiable desires when we were high school lovers.

After I dropped her off, with a warm embrace and a passionate farewell kiss, I made my way back to the bustling pub. In my intoxicated state, I sent her a message detailing hints of our intimate encounter.

My heart raced in my chest, pounding with a mix of exhilaration and trepidation. The anticipation of her response filled me with both excitement and anxiety. The weight of the evening's events hung heavy on my shoulders, leaving me feeling both elated and guilty.

Foolishly, I pressed send without a second thought.

Minutes turned into what felt like hours as I anxiously awaited her response. The constant buzzing of my phone against the wooden table only heightened my nervousness. Each vibration sent a jolt of anticipation coursing through my body, making my heart skip a beat.

As I waited for her response, a sinking feeling of regret washed over me. Suddenly, the sound of a message alert cut through the silence, and my heart skipped a beat. But instead of her reply, it was her dad who answered with a warning, his voice filled with anger and disappointment. I never felt so foolish before, my actions exposing my thoughtlessness. And to think, someone close to me is married to her sister, a constant reminder of the shame I had brought upon myself. News spreads fast, and I had become a subject of gossip and judgment.

Just before I left, the universe gave me one last chance to reconsider my decision to return to my mother and brother. Unbeknownst to me, my brother was in town, hiding in plain sight. Word of my presence spread like wildfire, and soon enough, friends and even strangers began approaching me, asking for help with their failing computers. What was supposed to be a brief visit turned into an unexpected four-day stay, as I found myself offering computer maintenance to anyone in need. Crisp, fresh bills flowed into my hands, a constant reminder of the demand for my services in this small city.

With each task completed, I saw it as a chance to make amends for those I had abandoned. My friend's little brother, who had his own business, generously offered me a place to establish my own. My closest friend even offered me free accommodation. Yet, despite these golden opportunities, I foolishly declined, choosing instead to return to a family that had treated me poorly. The scent of regret clung to me, a constant reminder of what I had just thrown away.

Looking back, I realize that I would still make the same decision, fully aware of the consequences. Eventually, I severed ties and continued on my journey, thinking I had escaped unscathed. But the universe had other plans. Just outside of town, I nearly faced a fatal accident—a clear warning sign that I failed to heed. As regret fills the air around me, I am left to contemplate the cost of my choices, wondering if I will ever learn.

Chapter Thirty-Seven

As I drove, a sinking feeling settled in my chest, realizing I had crossed the point of no return. The charred and impassable bridge, once a route of escape, was now behind me. The lingering scent of burnt wood reminded me of the irreversible choice I made. But deep down, I preferred it that way, knowing I had to forge ahead.

As I approached my destination, doubts swirled in my mind like a storm gathering strength. The silence in the car amplified the unease, intensifying the weight of my thoughts. I had been wondering why my mother had been so quiet lately, but now the truth unfolded before me.

A different home greeted me as I parked in the driveway. The absence of the boarders' cars, once a source of my mother's financial struggles, was palpable. The emptiness seemed to echo with lost opportunities. It turned out that under the new government, a university had opened, causing all white students to flee to other cities.

From the eerie silence that enveloped me, I sensed that something was off. The early stages of my decision to move back tested my resolve. I had envisioned my mother waiting with open arms upon my arrival, but instead, a heavy silence hung in the air. I turned off the engine; the quietness amplifying the racing thoughts in my mind.

As I sat in the car, memories flooded back, vivid and haunting. I could almost feel the weight of L's presence, waiting for me when I returned home late from the pub. It became painfully clear that the only wonderful memories I had of the house were unrelated to my mother.

Summoning my courage, I finally stepped out of the car, bracing myself for my mother's inevitable wrath. I expected a verbal assault for abandoning her; the words cutting like knives. Yet, deep down, I knew that if I found the right words to defend myself, she would redirect her attack, like a strategic move in a chess game.

I took a deep breath, steeling myself for what lay ahead. As I approached the front door, the sound of my footsteps seemed to echo through the empty house. The familiar creak of the porch swing, a constant companion in my early adulthood, now seemed to mock me.

Opening the door, I was met with a chilling silence. The air felt heavy with unspoken words, and I couldn't help but feel a pang of guilt for leaving my mother behind. But I had made a choice, a choice that I believed was necessary for my own happiness and growth.

Memories of bygone times rushed into my mind as I entered the living room. The walls adorned with family photos, the worn-out armchair where my mother used to read her Bible. Yet, there were no photos of me or my father, only of her with my brother, their radiant smiles hinting at a hidden narrative. It was all a stark reminder of the emptiness that had once filled this space, the echoes of silence still lingering in the air.

I called out for my mother, my voice breaking the stillness. There was no response. Panic began to creep in, and I hurriedly searched the house, hoping to find her in one of the familiar rooms. But she was nowhere to be found.

A sinking feeling settled in my chest once again. Had my decision caused irreparable damage to our relationship? Had I pushed my mother away for good? Doubt gnawed at me, but I couldn't let it consume me. I had to face the consequences of my actions and find a way to mend what was broken.

I made my way to my mother's room, the door slightly ajar. Hesitantly, I pushed it open, revealing a scene that pierced my heart. There she was, sitting on the edge of her bed, tears streaming down her face. Shattered, she sat there silently, her face pale and her hands trembling.

Her silence had not been one of anger, but of pain and sorrow. She had been struggling, not just financially, but emotionally as well. The absence of the boarders had left her feeling isolated and abandoned.

With caution, I approached her, fully aware of her unpredictable mood swings and her tendency to react impulsively. I reached out, gently placing a hand on her trembling shoulder. In that moment, words seemed unnecessary. Our relationship held a profound understanding of the depths we had reached and the pain we had inflicted upon each other.

I, on the other hand, had arrived with the intention of fixing things. And then, the truth of her charade struck me like a blow to my guts, causing a sharp intake of breath. I felt like I could scream with frustration, my chest tightening as waves of anger washed over me. Yet again, they have deceived me, leaving me in the shadows of my brother's devastation.

It suddenly made sense why he was on the run. The sight of her old car, crumbling and worn, made it clear. The news of her sleek car reached my brother, its shiny exterior tempting him with thoughts of easy money. While she was out, he and his friend took her new car for a test drive, the engine humming softly as they sped down the road. Their scenic drive ended abruptly, the screeching sound of metal against metal filling the air. Intoxicated by their reckless actions, they leaped out of the car and ran away. Or at least, this was the version shared by eyewitnesses, who described the scene in vivid detail.

And now, she looked at me with hopeful eyes, silently pleading for my assistance. Suddenly, the reason behind her silence became clear. If she had called me and told me the story, I would have declined to come. To put it mildly, I was deeply wounded and filled with rage. I had grown tired of living in my brother's shadows, constantly picking up the pieces after his malicious actions. Since our childhood, things had remained unchanged.

The memories of our childhood flooded my mind like a torrential downpour washing over me. I could see the shattered pieces of our lives, glimmering like shards of glass in the sunlight. The past surged back to me, a heavy veil lifting, revealing a collage of images and emotions.

I remembered the sound of my brother's fists landing on the pupils and teacher at our school, the echoes of their cries reverberating in my ears. I could smell the faint scent of fear and desperation that hung in the air, mingling with the unmistakable scent of anger. It was a toxic combination that left me trembling in the shadows of the teacher's and parents' wrath.

My mother's financial troubles cast a dark cloud over our lives, and I could feel the weight of her burden pressing down on my shoulders. She had moved countless times, desperately seeking a fresh start, a chance to mend her tarnished reputation. But no matter where we went, my brother's infamous deeds hung over us like a lingering shadow.

He had a way with my mother, a charm that seemed to blind her to his destructive tendencies. He always got his way, manipulating her with his silver tongue. It was a pattern that had scarred me deeply, leaving me weary and guarded.

Yet, despite the pain and the brokenness that seemed to trail behind my brother, a part of me still longed to fix things. I yearned to mend the shattered pieces of our lives, to bring light to the darkness that had consumed us.

Anger surged through my veins, causing my hands to tremble uncontrollably and my fists to tighten, turning my knuckles white. I could feel the throbbing of the veins in my temples sync with the rhythm of my heart, while my brow creased in frustration. A throbbing ache settled in the pit of my stomach, making it difficult to breathe.

I could feel the heat rising to my cheeks, a fiery flush spreading across my face, betraying the boiling anger within me. It felt as if a storm was brewing inside my chest, the raging winds of betrayal and resentment colliding with the torrential rain of disappointment. Each breath I took felt strained, as if my lungs were constricting under the weight of my emotions.

But amidst this tempest of emotions, I couldn't help but notice my mother's pleading gaze. Her eyes, once filled with hope, now held a glimmer of desperation. It was in that moment I realized the true depth of her silence. She had feared my rejection, my refusal to come to her aid. And perhaps, in her own way, she too was tired of living in the shadows of my brother's destructive choices.

Taking a deep breath, I pushed aside the seething anger and bitterness, allowing a flicker of empathy to ignite within me. I knew that I couldn't let my own pain blind me to the struggles of others, especially those who had been caught in the crossfire of my brother's actions. With a newfound determination, I looked into her eyes, silently conveying my decision.

"I'll help you," I finally said, my voice tinged with a mix of exhaustion and resolve. "But this time, things will be different. We won't let his actions define us anymore."

Chapter Thirty-Eight

If only I had truly understood the unbreakable bond between a mother and her first-born. It was a connection that no amount of money, success, or good deeds could alter. I had tried everything in my power to win her favor, even converting to Christianity, but even that had failed. The signs were unmistakable, scattered throughout my life, manifesting in the meals we shared, the photographs on our walls, and her unwavering financial support for my brother's failed pursuits.

You see, during my upbringing, my mother had a reputation for being involved with married men. I overheard her bragging to her friends about her ability to "destroy" relationships, relishing in her power. She was a master manipulator, while these men were unwitting victims. But there came a point when even she couldn't tame the wild stallion. He became the only father figure I ever knew, and she spent years trying to make him hers, but he remained loyal to his wife. Defeated, she resorted to a sly tactic.

One evening, she came home late from work, and I could sense that something had changed. But I saw through her facade, recognizing the sinister glint beneath the surface. With dramatic flair, she flung her hands up in the air, as if conducting a grand symphony, and declared, "I am reborn!" The room filled with the echo of her declaration, and I abandoned my television show to stare at her wide-eyed.

My brother, always eager to please, sprang to his feet and enveloped her in a tight embrace, showering her with effusive praise. Their joyful reunion created a harmonious melody of affectionate sounds that resonated around me. He clearly felt the need to change himself and mimic her completely. We started attending charismatic churches again, where her followers worshiped fervently, and he converted, ensuring that she would have eyes for him alone.

But no matter what I did, she would never regard me with the same intensity as she did him. Despite the crimes he had committed, the pain he had caused her, and the financial burdens he had brought upon our family, she would always welcome him back with open arms. It left me feeling utterly powerless, like a mere observer in their tumultuous dance.

I remember one particular evening, a family dinner that was supposed to be a celebration of my recent promotion. I had worked tirelessly for years, hoping to earn a sliver of her pride. As we sat down, my mother barely acknowledged my achievement. Instead, she turned the conversation to my brother's latest scheme, a venture doomed to fail like all the others. Her eyes sparkled with excitement as she spoke of his "potential," while I sat there, my heart sinking with every word.

In that moment, it became painfully clear. No matter how hard I tried, I would always be second to him. The realization hit me like a tidal wave, washing over me with a cold, bitter clarity. I was not just competing for her love; I was fighting a battle I could never win. The bond between a mother and her first-born was a fortress, impenetrable and unyielding, leaving me on the outside, forever looking in.

Looking back, I wish I had acknowledged the one vital ingredient that was absent at that moment. Blinded by my mother's false promises, my vision was clouded, unable to see the truth. My eagerness to impress her was like a wildfire, consuming rationality and reason. Despite the warning signs, I stayed, like a moth drawn to a flame. Now, as I reflect on this moment, I perceive it as a silent triumph I had surreptitiously claimed from her. Through the shimmering cascade of money she poured into my brother's fruitless endeavors, she remained oblivious to the fortitude she was unknowingly instilling within me.

If only I had known the power they unknowingly bestowed upon me, I would have turned my back on them, escaping their toxic influence. But I had a plan, a final desperate attempt to change the dynamic. Deep down, I knew this would be my last effort, my last chance to alter the course of their relationship and reclaim control of my life.

Little did I know that the crisp sound of fresh money and its distinct scent of ink and paper would lure my brother to her doorstep. As I presented my proposal to my mother, I took her trembling hands in mine, shivering under her icy touch. Her snake-like eyes, unwavering, bore into me, sending an icy chill down my spine. I ignored her frigid ways, confident that my plan would succeed.

"Mother," I said, challenging her piercing gaze, "I have a plan to change your life for the better."

She just looked at me, her eyes cold as ice, the room thick with tension. Her intimidation no longer phased me; I had outgrown it.

"What I propose is that we convert the spacious garage into a cozy cottage where you can live, while you rent out the house for additional income." To add insult to injury, I flashed my signature grin, knowing it would only further annoy her as her mouth twitched in irritation.

Her poker face almost worked, but her eyes betrayed a flicker of doubt. "And who is going to pay for all of that?" she asked, her tone as chilly as a winter gust.

"For starters," I said, squeezing her hands, feeling the roughness of her skin, "I have enough money saved up. And we can secure a mortgage if we need more."

"How much have you got?" she asked, a hint of enthusiasm in her voice, her curiosity palpable.

Her question caught me off guard, but like her, I maintained a stoic expression. "Enough," I said with a nonchalant shrug, feeling the weight of the moment.

As I sat there, I could sense an impending battle, a fierce storm on the horizon. The room was filled with an unsettling silence, broken only by the rhythmic ticking of the grandfather clock, each sound amplifying the mounting pressure. I remained silent, my heart pounding, anticipating the inevitable verbal assault. I could feel the weight of her pride suffocating the atmosphere. I had tried to save her from financial ruin, but now she would unleash her fury upon me. I whispered to myself, "Any second now."

Suddenly, her voice erupted, sharp and piercing. "You think you can just waltz in here with your grand ideas and save me? You've always been the dreamer, the one who thinks money can solve everything."

Her words echoed with the pain of abandonment, reminding me of my father, who had left her. I always believed she blamed herself, constantly questioning her actions.

I remained calm, refusing to let her words penetrate my resolve. "I know it's not just about the money, Mother. It's about creating a better life for you, a life where you can have peace and comfort."

She scoffed, her voice dripping with sarcasm. "And what about my dreams? What about my future? What's in it for me?"

I took a deep breath, steadying myself. "Mother, your dreams will always be within reach. This isn't just about you; it's about our family's well-being. We can turn this situation around and thrive together."

Her expression softened, a flicker of vulnerability crossing her face. "I don't want to be dependent."

I knew what she wanted. She wanted the money I was offering, so she could find a solution herself. But I wouldn't fall into her trap. I knew most of the money would end up in my manipulative brother's account, the primary cause of her financial distress. Once again, I was left to clean up his mess.

But I refused to let resentment cloud my judgment. I had a plan, a way to help my mother financially while giving her the independence she craved.

"I understand your need for independence, Mother," I said, my voice gentle yet firm. "And that's exactly what I want for you. But we can't ignore the reality of your situation. The debts are piling up, and if we don't act now, you'll lose everything."

Her eyes brimmed with tears, a mix of frustration and fear on her face. "I never wanted it to come to this," she whispered.

"I know, Mother," I replied, holding her trembling hands. "But we can't change the past. We can focus on the present and the future. With the resources I have, we can pay off the debts, start anew, and build a better life."

She looked at me, searching for sincerity in my eyes. "How can I trust you won't abandon me like your father did?"

I squeezed her hands reassuringly. "I am not my father."

A glimmer of hope appeared in her eyes, gradually replacing the doubt. "But what about your brother?"

She finally fell into the trap I had set. I paused, taking a deep breath before outlining my plan. "With his skills in manual work, he can help with both the building and plumbing tasks."

Silence filled the room as my words sank in. I could see the struggle in her eyes, torn between her past experiences and the glimmer of hope I presented.

Finally, she nodded, a mix of determination and vulnerability on her face. "Okay," she said softly. "I'll trust you, but promise me one thing."

I leaned in, eager to fulfill any promise that would bring her peace. "Anything, Mother. What is it?"

"Promise me you'll stick around until my new cottage is finished," she said, her voice wavering.

My eyes filled with tears as I looked at the woman who had inflicted immense pain and adversity upon me. "Mother, I give you my word." Unlike her, I made sure to honor my commitments.

The room filled with a sense of unity and determination as we shook hands. Despite the challenges ahead, I knew that with patience, perseverance, and unwavering support, we would overcome them and forge a brighter future. It was my sly strategy to fill the house with unfamiliar faces, ensuring my brother couldn't return and drain her completely, like the psychotic parasite he truly was.

Chapter Thirty-Nine

My dearest mortal reader. From my latest venture, I learned that the magic of life unfolds beyond the confines of my comfort zone. Amidst this journey, I discovered numerous aspects about myself that had remained unknown. Allow me to illustrate this with a brief analogy.

Imagine my dearest mother, who valued her own existence above all else, leading a dreary and monotonous life. In pursuit of change, I hurried to the nursery and acquired two plants, seeking ones that thrived both indoors and outdoors. It's worth mentioning that these plants were siblings, born simultaneously. I carefully placed one on the windowsill inside the kitchen, while the other I planted outside, where it could be seen from the kitchen. As I went about washing the dishes, I couldn't help but notice the remarkable disparity between the two.

The outdoor plant, exposed to the elements—gusting winds, relentless downpours, and scorching sun—stood firmly rooted, flourishing amidst the challenges. In contrast, the indoor plant stretched its tendrils towards the window pane, yearning for a world beyond, craving a space where it could truly thrive. Perhaps it simply longed for its sibling.

Suddenly, the vibrant green leaves of these plants whispered their secrets to me, highlighting the stark differences between my brother and me. He, undeniably the favored one, resembled the delicate indoor plant, seeking solace in the safety of our mother's nurturing embrace. Meanwhile, I, like the hardy outdoor plant, had to rely on my own resilience to endure the unpredictability of this world. Despite the daunting obstacles, a sense of contentment washed over me, for these challenges sculpted me into the self-reliant individual I had become. As we matured, I embraced my own identity, cherishing the person I had become, even though I had always yearned to walk in his footsteps during our formative years.

Venturing outside the familiar surroundings of my daytime job, comfortable house, friends, and steady income, I discovered hidden skills I never knew existed within me. As the construction of my mother's new cottage progressed, I adeptly managed the building teams, overseeing the intricate details of plumbing, electrical needs, painting, and the layout of the kitchen and other rooms. This journey taught me the value of meticulous planning and the rewards of stepping into the unknown.

Through these challenges, I experienced a profound emotional impact. The doubts and fears that once held me back were replaced with a newfound sense of self-reliance and growth. I embraced my own identity, cherishing the person I had become, even though I had always yearned to walk in my brother's footsteps during our formative years.

In summary, just as the outdoor plant thrived in the face of adversity, I discovered that the true essence of growth lies beyond our comfort zones. It is within these uncharted territories that we unearth our hidden talents and capabilities. So, my dearest reader, dare to step outside your comfort zone, for it is there that the magic of life awaits.

It was only then, during those moments, that the true advantages of having an absent father became apparent. As a teenager, I became my mother's reliable handyman, willingly enduring days of hardship rather than hiring a specialist. Whether it was fixing the pool pump, the borehole pump, or the vacuum cleaner, I was always there to troubleshoot. The scars of these endeavors were not just physical; I recall vividly the sensation of being electrocuted, my hair standing on end like the quills of a porcupine. The sight of my charred face in the mirror served as a stark reminder of that shocking incident. Pun intended.

Armed with the valuable lessons I had learned, I effortlessly put my skills to the test during the construction of the cozy cottage. The sight of me fixing light fixtures and fastening brackets became a familiar scene, as I was always ready to lend a helping hand. With determination, I played my part diligently, particularly when it came to the installation of the kitchen cupboards.

In stark contrast, my brother, who had initially appeared eager, quickly lost interest. Instead of contributing, he would frequently vanish with a wad of money in hand, supposedly to purchase supplies. However, the reality was that he would often find himself at the local pub, the air heavy with the smell of alcohol and stale cigarettes. Hours would pass, and he would eventually return, his bloodshot eyes betraying his misadventures.

The construction of the cottage was far from smooth. We faced delays with the arrival of crucial materials, and there were moments when the weather turned against us, halting progress. The construction teams had their own share of issues — miscommunications and mistakes that required painstaking corrections. These setbacks were a constant reminder that success was not guaranteed.

We were fortunate enough to have the help of an architect who generously designed the plans for our cottage free of charge, under the condition that I take his sister Beth out on dates. Although she was undeniably beautiful, her company came at a considerable price. In hindsight, it would have been more cost-effective to simply pay the architect for his services. Nevertheless, with each date, our connection deepened, and I soon discovered a valuable return on my investment. As an aspiring architect herself, Beth diligently monitored the construction progress, often bringing me snacks and treats. We frequently sought solace in the shadows of the unfinished building, sharing passionate kisses.

The architect's plans were nothing short of exquisite, surpassing even the most skeptical expectations of my mother. The transformation of the garage into a duplex dwelling was a stroke of brilliance, if I may say so myself. Whenever I ascended the scaffolding, I was greeted by breathtaking views of the picturesque wine lands and the majestic snow-capped mountains, a sight that never failed to leave me in awe.

As my eyes darted around, I couldn't help but notice the inquisitive gazes of the neighbors, their eyes peering at me through their windows like curious owls. The town, infested with the notorious Boer Maffia, had a reputation for prying eyes. We encountered direct confrontations with these figures, their disapproval palpable as they criticized our progress and attempted to disrupt our work. In the midst of this, my mother had chosen this place as her hiding spot after retiring early. However, fortune was on my side as a famous rugby player had purchased the house next door. The air was filled with the aroma of freshly plucked weeds as our neighbors suddenly found an excuse to tend to their neglected gardens. The blonde bombshell girlfriend of the rugby player effortlessly stole the spotlight, diverting the intense gazes away from me, like a dazzling performance captivating the audience.

As I delved deeper, my attention was drawn to an essential element overlooked by the architects. The area beneath the staircase leading to the second floor lay vacant, void of purpose. Inspiration struck, and I swiftly formulated a plan to transform this empty void into a functional spare shower and toilet. The excitement welled within me as I presented my proposal to Beth, who, with a reassuring pat on my back, enthusiastically approved. With a sense of satisfaction, we set our plan into motion, eager to bring this space to life.

As my mother's cottage neared completion, I couldn't help but feel a sense of accomplishment. The challenges we faced, the prying eyes of the neighbors, and the presence of the Boer Maffia had all been overcome. The sleepless nights, the sweat and toil, and the frustration of dealing with setbacks made the final result all the more rewarding. It was the love and support of Beth, the beauty of our surroundings, and the resilience of our spirits that allowed us to create a sanctuary in the midst of chaos.

Life may have its hardships, but it is in those moments that we discover our true strengths and the beauty that can emerge from adversity. And as I looked upon our cottage, nestled in the picturesque landscape, I couldn't help but feel a deep sense of gratitude for the journey that had led me here.

Chapter Forty

During the final stages of construction, our dwindling funds brought about a noticeable change in my brother's demeanor. The crisp scent of freshly cut wood mixed with the swirling dust, permeating the air as we toiled to complete the intricate roof assembly. It had been years since I last encountered my manipulative brother, and his presence now exuded an unfamiliar gentleness.

"Careful up there," he called out. His voice, once sharp and commanding, now held a surprising softness. "Don't want you taking a tumble."

I nodded, my heart pounding despite the familiar routine. The rhythmic pounding of hammers and the cheerful chatter of our conversation filled the air, creating a vibrant atmosphere. However, amidst the camaraderie, flashes of his past mistreatment flickered in my mind, stirring a sense of unease within me. Despite his newfound respect, I maintained a cautious distance, wary of his true nature.

My foot slipped. I teetered on the edge, heart pounding. Fingers grasping for any hold. Our eyes locked. His cold, unforgiving gaze pierced through me, a flicker of the man I once feared.

Memories surged forth like a crashing wave, transporting me back to the confines of my childhood home.

"Bring me my tea now!" my brother's bellow resonated, laced with venom. Engrossed in preparing for my forthcoming final exams, I caressed the pages of my notebook, yearning to escape the suffocating confines of my residence.

"I'm studying," I replied, voice trembling.

"Don't test me," he growled, his face contorting into a mask of rage. Before I could react, he lunged at me, knocking me to the ground. He straddled my chest, restraining my arms, and unleashed a relentless barrage of strikes, a ferocity that shook me to my core.

"Bring me my tea or face my wrath," he spat, his words mingling with the acrid sting of his saliva on my face. Summoning every ounce of courage within me, I fought back, drawing upon hidden reserves of strength. I wriggled and contorted my body, managing to break free from his grip. With a surge of adrenaline, I sprang to my feet and sprinted down the corridor, desperately seeking sanctuary. Fear coursed through my veins, my heart pounding against my ribcage as the sound of his approaching footsteps grew louder, inching ever closer with each passing second. My throat tightened, my breath caught in my chest as I darted into my mother's bedroom and forcefully slammed the door shut behind me, buying myself a precious moment to devise an escape plan.

I hurriedly entered my mother's spacious walk-in closet, the soft carpet muffling my footsteps. Desperation fueled my search for something, anything, to shield myself from his rage. As my trembling fingers explored a drawer, they brushed against a chilling, metallic surface. A gasp escaped my lips as I withdrew a pistol, its coldness sending shivers down my spine. With wide eyes, I prepared myself as his approaching footsteps grew louder, until finally, he peered into the closet.

"Found you," he sneered, his eyes glinting with malice. His hand snaked into my hair, yanking me forcefully from my hiding place. Without hesitation, I brandished the pistol, causing him to recoil in sheer terror.

"Don't touch me again," I whispered, my voice trembling at first, but gaining strength with each word. I pressed the barrel tighter against my temple, the cold metal fueling my resolve. His fear only made me stronger.

"Please," he whimpered, his voice filled with desperation. "I'm sorry. I won't do it again."

I hesitated, my mind racing. Was he truly remorseful? Or was this just another ploy to manipulate me?

"Prove it," I demanded, my voice filled with a newfound strength. "Never lay a hand on me again."

To my astonishment, he nodded, eyes filled with a mixture of fear and shame. The power had shifted. He never touched me again, and I knew, in that moment, I had reclaimed my life.

Presently, I found myself in a precarious situation, my heart pounding in my chest. My fingers ached as I desperately clung to the rough edge of the roof, feeling the gritty texture bite into my palms. The sun's rays reflected off the sweat on my forehead, blinding me for a moment as I locked gazes with my brother. Our eyes, a mixture of fear and hostility, engaged in a silent battle of wits.

A powerful gust of wind whistled through the air, carrying the refreshing aroma of freshly cut grass and the distant echoes of barking dogs. My desperate eyes pleaded for help, but my brother's stony gaze betrayed his malice, sending shivers down my spine. The scoff that escaped his lips confirmed my worst fears, a mocking sound that echoed in my ears.

With no other choice, my grip slipped, and I tumbled through the empty air, my scream mingling with his malicious laughter. The world spun in a dizzying blur as I plummeted two stories down.

To my immense luck, a leftover sandpile appeared in my line of sight, and I braced for impact. The soft grains cushioned my fall, absorbing the shock. Relief flooded my body as I sank into the summit of the pile, the fine sand caressing my skin.

I wiggled my toes, feeling the grains slip between them, and a hysterical laugh burst from my lips. The absurdity of my survival overwhelming me.

Suddenly, a heavy thud startled me, swallowing my joy. A hammer landed beside me with a metallic clang, stark against the softness of the sand. I looked up at my brother, his figure silhouetted by the rising sun, radiating animosity.

"What's so funny?" he asked, his voice dripping with malice, seeping into my bones.

I rose to my feet, shaking the sand from my shoes, feeling the grains slip away from my soles. "Can't you see?" I asked, disbelief lacing my words. "I'm okay."

His sneer deepened, and he turned away, disappearing from sight on the roof above. I muttered to myself, "Some things will never change." But as I headed back to the rooftop, determination hardened within me. This task needed to be finished—and so did my time in his shadow.

Not long thereafter, we completed the roof assembly. The cottage stood before us, a symbol of our hard work and determination. As the sun cast its warm rays upon the freshly painted walls, a sense of relief washed over me. However, the scars of the financial impact weighed heavily on my bank account, a burden that couldn't be ignored.

Standing side by side with my mother and brother, we admired the majestic details of our accomplishment. The smell of sawdust and paint lingered in the air, a reminder of the countless hours we had devoted to this project. It was time to bring her furniture from the main house to the cottage, a task my brother and I approached with enthusiasm.

As we carried the heavy pieces of furniture, the creaking of floorboards echoed through the empty rooms, blending with our excited chatter. At that moment, I failed to notice the hidden intentions behind my brother's eagerness to empty the house. It wasn't until later that I realized the truth.

With my trusty drill buzzing in my hand and the smell of sawdust in the air, I carefully secured my mother's cherished artwork to the wall. The intricate details of the piece required a delicate touch, but I persevered and completed the task in due time. As I moved on to fastening the curtain railings, the sound of metal meeting metal echoed through the room, accompanied by the rustle of fabric as I hung the drapes. The velvety texture of the curtains made my fingers tingle as I adjusted them just right.

Amidst the work, I couldn't help but reflect on the enormity of the task I had accomplished. It was then, in that moment of contemplation, that I realized something unsettling. Throughout the entire process, my mother had not once uttered a simple "Thank you." It struck me like a bolt of lightning, but I brushed it off, assuming she had a plan to express her gratitude in a grand housewarming celebration. Fueled by anticipation, I eagerly pressed on, completing each task with determination.

Little did I know, however, that this silence was not a mere oversight on her part. It was a calculated manipulation, a powerful tool she wielded against me as I tirelessly worked to impress her. It was her way of keeping me under her control, her fear of being alone driving her to exploit my eagerness to please. As this realization washed over me, I couldn't help but feel foolish for falling into her trap. *Silly me*, I thought, as I finished up the final touches, unaware of the depths of her scheme.

Before we knew it, we had finished the work. The main house, void of life, stood abandoned while my mother settled into the cozy cottage.

To my great shock, surprise, and utter disbelief, my mother didn't intend to fill the house with tenants as we had planned. Instead, my brother, his wife, and their three children moved in, leaving me without a place to call home. The weight of their decision pressed heavily upon me, and I had no other choice but to let them stay.

Neither of them had jobs, despite the daily wage I had paid my brother during the construction period. Their audacious choice left me feeling helpless and abandoned. I couldn't bear the thought of their children going hungry, so I reluctantly moved into the old living room to help with their food and boarding.

Yet, as the days went by, a sense of regret began to creep into my heart. I had never anticipated the depths of despair I would feel in this place that was supposed to be my refuge. The once-beloved countryside now felt suffocating, filled with the parasites who pretended to be my family. In that moment, I felt more destitute than ever before.

Chapter Forty-One

Every choice I had made echoed through my mind like a haunting melody, a cruel reminder of my shattered dreams. At night, I would lay in bed and stare aimlessly at the cracked ceiling, its peeling paint a visual representation of my broken spirit. My mother's betrayal gnawed at my insides with the intensity of a ravenous predator, leaving me feeling hollow and empty.

My appetite had vanished, a casualty of the emotional turmoil that consumed me. The weight loss was extreme, leaving me looking like a skeleton, a weak and emaciated version of who I used to be. The pain of my mother's deceit seeped into every dark crevice of my stomach, twisting and turning like a venomous serpent. Once again, she had cunningly robbed me of the success I had worked so hard to achieve.

And here I found myself, once more, suffocating in the shadow of my brother's actions, his failures casting a dark cloud over my life. It was a bleak and desolate moment, a suffocating darkness that enveloped my existence. I knew I had to escape their treachery, to break free from their grasp.

A part of me thirsted for retribution, to reclaim the money and efforts I had selflessly poured into my mother's newfound happiness, freeing her from the shackles of financial burden. Yet, another part of me longed to distance myself from them, to flee as far away as possible. But above all, I feared for the well-being of my brother's children, the weight of their future resting solely on my shoulders as the sole breadwinner of the family. The thought of leaving them behind filled me with dread.

But I could not stay. The added financial strain would swiftly deplete the meager savings I had left, leaving me stranded and vulnerable. Money, a concept they seemed oblivious to, became the source of my torment. I was caught between a rock and a hard place, torn by conflicting emotions.

And then, one fateful morning, the catalyst arrived, deciding for me. The air was thick with the pungent scent of marijuana as the doorbell pierced through the silence. I rushed to answer it, my heart pounding in my chest, and stared wide-eyed at a group of impeccably dressed women.

"Hello," one of them greeted, her voice laced with a mix of authority and concern, as she referenced a name on her clipboard. Each member of the group introduced themselves as representatives from the local social services center. Alarm bells blared in my mind as I hurriedly stepped outside to call my brother and his wife, who were finishing their "spliff" as they called it.

"There are social workers here to see you," I said, gesturing towards the living room, my voice trembling with a mixture of fear and apprehension. They seemed unfazed, casually finished smoking their joint, and giggled as they walked into the house.

From my vantage point, I discreetly caught glimpses of their hushed discussions with the social workers, straining my ears to hear their worried tones. The air in the room felt tense, heavy with the weight of unpaid school fees and concerns about their child's behavior and social skills. The faint scent of anxiety hung in the air, mingling with the faint whiff of desperation.

My eyes widened in disbelief as I caught sight of their smallest daughter's artwork, a shocking depiction of her parents smoking weed during an innocent art class. It was a vivid image that spoke volumes about the chaotic atmosphere within their home.

Feeling a sense of urgency, I swiftly retreated into the refuge of my bedroom. With a determined grip, I pulled out my phone, the smooth surface cool against my fingertips, and hastily dialed the number of my best friends.

Their voices on the other end of the line carried a sense of relief and familiarity, their words resonating through my ears like a soothing melody. In the midst of uncertainty, they reassured me that their offer remained—a lifeline to hold on to.

Viewing their proposition as a temporary respite, a stepping stone towards acquiring my own sanctuary and stable employment, I swiftly made a decision. Without a moment's hesitation, I gathered my belongings, hastily stuffing them into my bags.

To avoid prying eyes, I stealthily made my way through the backdoor. Moving silently along the perimeter of the property, I navigated through the shadows, my heart pounding in my chest with a mixture of anxiety and exhilaration.

Just as I thought I had successfully evaded detection, a curious dog approached, its sharp bark threatening to expose my escape. Acting on instinct, I gently stroked its head, reassuring the loyal creature with a tender touch.

Once again, I had left behind the toxicity of my family, the weight of their troubles slowly lifting from my shoulders as I embarked on a path towards freedom and self-discovery.

However, my mother was far from done with me. She slithered like a snake, her unexpected actions always catching me off guard. Yet, for the time being, I found temporary relief from her malevolence as the calmness of the surroundings drowned out her presence. Little did I know, I would soon encounter her equal—a younger version, equally filled with vengeance.

As I made the decision to leave, its benefits quickly became apparent. I secured a hybrid job and purchased a small house at a reasonable price. The only drawback was its proximity to my mother's property. Nevertheless, I devised ways to evade my toxic family and avoid chance encounters.

Whispers of my brother's crimes reverberated through the close-knit community. Sitting in the pub, savoring an ice-cold beer, I couldn't believe my misfortune on a particular evening. Two individuals settled beside me, their voices filling the air with mentions of my brother's name. Unbeknownst to me, during the construction process, my brother had squandered the money I had given him intended for plumbing and bathroom fixtures. The truth dawned on me as I overheard the respected town plumber recounting the details to his companion. My brother had deceitfully posed as the plumber's assistant, using his name and account to purchase the equipment from the hardware store. It was difficult to fathom, but I knew it to be true, as he was capable of such deceitful acts.

The revelation hit me like a powerful blow, leaving me feeling as though there was no refuge in any town that could shield me from the shame of my brother's actions. I had to take action, as I couldn't afford to have my reputation tarnished. Without hesitation, I gulped down the remaining beer and hastened to the nearest ATM. To my surprise, the strangers were still engaged in their animated discussion as I reentered the pub.

"Excuse me," I interjected, startling them and earning curious gazes that were rightfully deserved. I introduced myself and explained my familial connection to the situation. The man who had shared the story was taken aback, making an effort to offer his apologies. However, I reassured him that the fault lay with my family. Sliding the cash across the bar counter, I made my offer. He accepted, but not before generously buying me another beer. Needless to say, our friendship endured, and I had the honor of witnessing the birth of both his children, each of them named after legendary rock stars. This one's for you, Jules.

Chapter Forty-Two

During testing times, I never gave much thought to being single. I pondered whether it was better to face challenges alone or with a supportive partner. The answer would reveal itself later in life, but for now, I remained undecided. At this point in my journey, everyone I knew was married, and I often traveled long distances, fulfilling the roles of best man and occasional photographer.

But then, by pure chance (although I believe nothing is truly left to chance), I met L.

I could tell just by looking at her that luck, whether good or bad, would eventually make an appearance. And it did, sooner rather than later. Allow me to digress.

It was a lazy Sunday morning, and I found myself sitting in my favorite restaurant. The distant sound of church bells filled the air, barely registering in my mind. The waitress casually mentioned that my mother frequented this place, but my attention was captivated by the enchanting presence of a red-headed goddess seated across from me, engrossed in the morning paper. Every inch of her exuded an irresistible allure—from her long, slender legs to her luscious lips, captivating eyes, and elegant neck. As she teasingly sipped her drink through a straw, it was clear she knew the effect she had on others.

I watched her intently, eagerly searching for any sign that her eyes would meet mine. The way she bit her lip while flipping through the paper ignited deep desires within me. My plate of fried eggs grew cold, but I couldn't tear my gaze away from her, mesmerized by her allure. And then, it happened. In a fleeting moment, her eyes darted in my direction. I shifted uncomfortably, craving more attention from this

Venus-like figure, whom I playfully named in my mind, the goddess of love, beauty, sex, and everything I yearned for. My heart raced, echoing my excitement. I knew what I had witnessed, and the subtle curl of her lips confirmed that she was aware of my knowledge.

As I eagerly shoveled a forkful of food into my mouth, her intense emerald eyes locked onto mine, her gaze unwavering. With a delicate flick of her fingers, she greeted me, exuding a seductive aura that only the fairer sex possesses. My eyes widened in disbelief, and my jaw froze in place. As I forced myself to swallow the unchewed food, a wave of shame washed over me, causing my face to flush. Her piercing eyes penetrated my soul, whispering untold tales of seduction. In an instant, desire ignited within me. She muttered something inaudible, but my pounding heart drowned out any sound.

Venus directed her pointed finger, adorned with a meticulously manicured nail, towards me, inviting me to join her. Uncertain, I glanced around the small room, then pointed at myself, silently mouthing the question, "Me?"

She nodded enticingly, teasingly rubbing her foot against the leg of a nearby chair. I don't know what compelled me, but an invisible force seemed to pull me towards her.

"Hey," she greeted, introducing herself, her voice resembling the melodic tones of a rainbow, if rainbows could produce music.

"Do you mind if I call you Venus?" I asked, gently shaking her hand, reluctant to let go. The fragrance of her floral perfume, reminiscent of lotus, etched itself into my memory. She giggled and replied, "Sure, call me whatever you like."

Never before had I spent so many hours in a restaurant. We savored our cappuccinos, exchanged stories, and when the afternoon arrived, I indulged in a bottle of exquisite wine accompanied by a platter of delectable finger foods. We ventured outside, spending the afternoon on the patio, our lips aflame with shared kisses and enthralling tales.

Warning signs were scattered everywhere. Deep down, I knew she would poison my very soul, yet her allure was irresistible. From the subtle brush of our hands when pouring her wine to the warmth of her breath against my face, I sensed her lethal nature. She was a black widow, and I found myself trapped in her web. The yearning to make love to her consumed me, even though I knew she would devour me afterwards. I never imagined that a goddess like her would even consider looking my way. Yet, I was falling for her at an alarming speed, free-falling without a parachute. There was only one way out of this, a descent into my own demise.

No matter how my mind fought against the warnings and her irresistible charm, I knew I couldn't resist her requests. The wine further weakened my resolve, leaving me in a state of autopilot, with Venus as my guide into the unknown. Soon enough, we found ourselves in her lavish duplex apartment, where warning signs were scattered all around, yet I chose to ignore them once again.

With a freshly opened bottle of wine, the soft melodies in the background embraced us as we nestled on her luxurious leather couch. The flickering candlelight infused the air with the delicate scent of jasmine, creating an atmosphere of pure bliss. Leaning in close, Venus planted a tender kiss on my lips, leaving a heavenly taste of cherry balm that lingered for days. We exchanged stories, igniting our lips and moods with passionate kisses that set us ablaze. Occasionally, a mischievous smile would grace her face, as if she could sense the tremor that ran through me with every touch, finding great amusement in it.

As our bodies intertwined, a current of electricity surged through my veins, igniting a fire within me that I had never experienced before. Each touch, each caress, sent shivers down my spine, leaving my skin tingling with anticipation. The warmth of her touch against my bare skin felt both soothing and intoxicating, like a drug coursing through my system.

Her lips, soft and velvety, danced along my neck, leaving a trail of goosebumps in their wake. The rise and fall of her chest matched the rhythm of our breaths, creating a symphony of desire that echoed through the room. I could feel my heart pounding in my chest, as if it were desperately trying to keep up with the whirlwind of emotions that consumed me.

Her fingers traced delicate patterns across my body, leaving a trail of fire in their wake. With each gentle stroke, I felt my inhibitions fade away, replaced by a desperate hunger for her. The room seemed to spin around us, blurring the lines between reality and fantasy, as we surrendered ourselves to the intoxication of our desires.

But amidst the passion and ecstasy, a nagging voice in the back of my mind reminded me of the danger that lurked beneath her enchanting facade. It whispered cautionary tales of those who had fallen victim to her seductive charm, their souls left shattered and broken in her wake. Yet, in that moment, I couldn't bring myself to care. The allure of Venus was too strong, overpowering any rational thought or self-preservation instinct.

In the depths of our passion, I found myself willingly diving into the abyss, surrendering to the inevitable downfall that awaited me. The flames of desire burned brighter with each passing second, consuming any remnants of logic or reason. I was a moth drawn to her flame, willing to sacrifice everything for just a taste of her forbidden fruit.

Little did I realize that succumbing to her enchantment would be my undoing, trapped in a labyrinth of seduction and betrayal. But in that moment, as our bodies entwined and our souls collided, I couldn't resist the pull of her magnetic charm. I was under her spell, and I would willingly succumb to the consequences that awaited me.

Chapter Forty-Three

Venus surpassed every lascivious thought that invaded my depraved mind. I clung to her like a desperate limpet to a solid rock, while the prowling presence of a lion loomed nearby. Possessiveness, an unfamiliar trait, consumed me in her presence. As we strolled through the bustling mall, I unleashed deathly glares upon any man who dared to glance in her direction. And I graciously smiled at those who nodded approvingly at the beauty by my side. She became the guiding torch, illuminating the darkness of my existence. How benevolent the universe seemed, I mused.

Despite the many warning signs that surrounded me, I foolishly disregarded them. I sprinted recklessly into the relationship, blindfolded and unbothered by the inevitable pain that awaited. The adage "all good things must come to an end" held no weight in my heart, not then. The complexity of the web spun by this mastermind was beyond anything I could have imagined, manipulating me like a puppet on strings.

In no time, our bond tightened, becoming as constricting as the sucker I was for codependency. I craved someone to feed off, to stroke my fragile ego. Venus, the perfect accomplice, catered to my needs, stroking not only my ego but also my arrogance and pride.

Every day, as the clock struck five, she would glide into my driveway, clutching a bottle of wine and a captivating book. Her understanding of my vulnerabilities reached depths I could never have comprehended. However, after our intimate encounters, she never stayed the night. In a cunning manner, she played upon my longing to spend a night with her, carefully crafting her grand finale—

the ultimate act in her plan.

"Let's make plans to escape for a weekend," Venus would whisper, her voice dripping with seduction, as our bodies pressed against each other, the heat between us palpable.

My breath would catch in quick gasps as she traced a delicate nail over my chest and down my tummy, a shiver of anticipation running through me. "Okay," I muttered, unable to resist, completely ensnared in her seductive web.

My eyes widened with surprise, and I couldn't help but flinch when she casually mentioned the name of a coastal town on the West Coast that held special meaning to me.

I shot her a curious gaze, but she dismissed it with a nonchalant shrug and placed a seductive finger over my lips, silencing any questions I had. I could never have imagined how she knew it was my favorite town, but later I uncovered her secret.

"Yes!" I exclaimed, my voice trembling as her finger traced intricate circles around my abdomen, sending electric waves of pleasure through me.

"Great!" she said with a mischievous smile. "It's settled then." She gracefully rose from the bed, giving me a teasing glimpse of her exposed rear, a sight that weakened my resolve. As she dressed, she leaned down to plant a soft peck on my brow before slipping away, leaving me consumed by my yearning desires.

My eyes widened in disbelief. Her seductive allure had enticed me, fueling my cravings, before abruptly leaving me consumed by longing. I let out a frustrated grunt and turned onto my front. With the vivid images of her intoxicating beauty etched into my mind, sleep eluded me, playing a cruel game of hide and seek. In my dreams, the sandman took the form of Venus, a seductive enchantress casting a spell over me. And in that moment, I realized that even grown men could succumb to tantalizing fantasies, just like young boys and their innocent wet dreams.

Soon after, on a bright and sunny Friday afternoon, I eagerly loaded our bags into the car. From the meticulous way Venus had packed, it was clear she had something up her sleeve. Yet again, I brushed off the warning signs, oblivious to the underlying intentions. It was our first road trip together, and she radiated joy, effortlessly keeping me entertained. As we set off, her lighthearted playlist, whimsically titled "A Midsummer Night's Dream," filled the car with melodic enchantment. The road stretched out before us like a never-ending ribbon, while we joyously sang along to her thoughtfully chosen anthems. Unbeknownst to me at the time, numerous songs subtly whispered the words "wedding" or "marriage."

As we drove, the excitement mounted, and our eyes widened with awe as we beheld the breathtaking views of the azure Atlantic Ocean stretching out endlessly before us. A surge of exhilaration sent a shiver down my spine, goosebumps dancing upon my arms and neck. Every note of "Let Go" by Paul van Dyk seemed to encapsulate that very moment, transporting me back to that exhilarating thrill. Even now, when the song plays, it brings forth a flood of emotions, vividly capturing the essence of that day. Years later, when I stumbled upon the music video, the lyrics and Venus's mischievous smile fell into place, weaving a tapestry of memories and realizations. It was a surreal moment, one that happens only once in a lifetime, leaving an indelible mark on my soul.

My empty stomach growled loudly, a hungry symphony echoing through the quaint cottage. As we checked in, I couldn't help but admire the panoramic views of the ocean stretching out before us. Venus, with her playful nature, dubbed the cottage our "love nest," igniting anticipation for our first sleepover together. Despite a warning sign that stared me straight in the eye, I chose to ignore it. The bed, adorned with scattered rose petals, emanated romance, while a chilled champagne bottle awaited us in an ice bucket, reminiscent of a honeymoon suite. It made sense when Venus made a phone call, informing someone of our imminent arrival. But the alarm bells in my head remained silenced.

"I have a surprise for you," Venus whispered, her amber eyes locking onto mine, impossible to resist.

My eyes widened, knees weakening, signaling my agreement. She took my trembling hand and led me to the bathroom, where a steam shower, unlike any I had ever seen, awaited us. As she turned on the faucets, steam billowed, matching the heat coursing through my veins. With her slender fingers, she delicately unbuttoned my shirt, her sweet nothings filling my ears. My heart pounded against my ribcage, akin to a deer fleeing a lioness. Uncontrollable shivers coursed through my body as desire consumed me. I felt a sense of weakness, almost pathetic, as I willingly surrendered my life, body, and soul into her capable hands.

Before I could fully comprehend the situation, I stood undressed, exposed. Venus giggled theatrically, shedding her own clothes, providing a show that would forever be etched in my memory. With a playful gesture, she stepped into the shower, her backside enticing me to follow. My knees quivered, and I cautiously entered, panting like a racehorse.

I yearned for a love-making experience akin to the movies, fervently praying for it. However, the black widow had different intentions. She lathered me from head to toe, her touch igniting excitement within me. Her hands moved teasingly across my body, as if preparing me for some sort of ritual. Before I could react, she abruptly closed the faucets and stepped out, leaving me wet and confused.

Using a fluffy towel, she dried me off, her actions once again teasing, seductive. It seemed as if she were rewarding my patience for this sleepover, but her true motives soon became apparent. From her suitcase, she produced a perfectly tailored outfit, crisp and neat, designed specifically for me.

My brow furrowed in concern, the creases deepening on my forehead, but before I could voice my opinions, she pulled out a pair of shiny brogues; the leather gleaming under the soft glow of the room's light. It was as if she had planned to counter my questions with a surprise, a calculated move to divert my attention. Yet, the impish smile playing on her lips was there, hinting at hidden motives, the corners of her mouth slightly upturned, mischief dancing in her eyes.

As I reluctantly took the shoes, she peeled her towel off; the fabric sliding off her skin with a whisper, revealing her flawless form, rewarding my curious eyes with her allure on full display. I watched, my breath quickening, hands trembling, as she slipped into black lace lingerie, the delicate fabric teasingly caressing her curves, causing my mouth to turn dry, my throat suddenly parched.

A slap on my backside, a playful tap, was my cue to get dressed, and I sat on the edge of the bed, dressing, while I watched her slip into a velvety miniskirt, the fabric so smooth it seemed to melt against her skin, and a champagne silk blouse, the delicate material shimmering in the light. She left the top button undone, allowing a seductive peek at her flawless cleavage, accentuated by the delicate lace bra.

I must admit that I did, at the time, think of asking her to marry me. But, I knew not to push my luck. She was one of a kind, delicate like porcelain, and I had to handle her with caution, like a fragile china cup. With excitement coursing through me, I eagerly anticipated parading my girl in front of the well-to-do gentlemen meandering through this lavish coastal town. I applied the aftershave she adored, its refreshing notes mingling with the scent of her lotus perfume that made me yearn to be with her all night. Dressed impeccably, we linked arms and ventured out into the refreshing night, the sound of crashing waves echoing in our ears.

I followed her directions and parked outside a seaside restaurant. Fish netting and empty seashells adorned the outside, the salty scent of the ocean mingling with the faint aroma of freshly cooked seafood, creating an ambiance of coastal charm.

A bold sign with red lettering caught my attention, warning that entry was only permitted with a reservation. Much to my surprise, Venus tightened her grip on my hand, her confident and melodic voice as she shared my surname with the hostess, who promptly led us to our table. Another warning sign I missed, as if our relationship was already bound by the weight of my last name.

At the time, I was too consumed to even entertain any thoughts. As I walked alongside the goddess, I couldn't help but notice the intense stares from the male patrons, their eyes fixated on her. Some of them were left speechless, their jaws dropping as their eyes widened in astonishment, while others couldn't hide their envy, their narrowed eyes revealing their jealousy. And then there were those who shot me an angry stare, their resentment practically radiating off of them. I knew what they were thinking. How did someone as destitute as me end up with someone as remarkable as her? I reveled in the attention we received, the whispers and murmurs floating in the air, and pulled out a chair for Venus to sit before sinking into my seat, a sense of pride and contentment settling within me.

Once again, the table shimmered with vibrant confetti, creating a kaleidoscope of colors, while a bottle of effervescent champagne awaited, emanating a tantalizing aroma. It evoked memories of newlyweds, filling my mind with a rush of emotions. My anticipation heightened, imagining returning to our cozy cottage, consumed by a fiery, passionate love for my girl.

Simultaneously, curiosity bubbled within me, eager to witness the unfolding of her mysterious plans. Immersing myself in the present moment, I surrendered completely, locking eyes with her alluring, amber gaze. The male patrons, their disbelief palpable, couldn't resist ogling my enchanting goddess, my captivating black widow.

Chapter Forty-Four

Afrikaans people have a fitting word for a hangover: 'babbelas.' I knew what a 'babbelas' felt like, but this was different. The morning light pierced through the curtains, casting a hazy glow on the room. My eyes, heavy and weary, felt like something unseen was pushing them forward, threatening to pop out of their sockets. The sound of my breath echoed in my ears, accompanied by a dull throbbing in my temples.

As I tried to swallow, my throat burned, and my tongue clung to the roof of my mouth, parched and dry. An unpleasant taste lingered, as if I had been licking an ashtray, the remnants of a long-forgotten habit. The scent of tobacco hung in the air, wrapping around me like a persistent fog. The realization hit me like a jolt of electricity, causing my eyes to snap open.

I stared up at the ceiling, desperately searching my foggy mind for any recollection of the previous evening. But memories remained elusive, shrouded in a dark cloud that refused to dissipate.

"Mornin', hubby," Venus murmured, her voice soft and melodic, like a gentle summer breeze. She propped herself up on her elbow, delicately brushing the strands of hair away from my eyes. In the morning light, she looked ethereal, a goddess amidst our tangled sheets. The warmth between our bodies radiated beneath the covers, a reminder of our intimate connection.

"Morning," I replied, my voice groggy and hoarse, desperately needing moisture. And then it hit me, like a sudden bolt of lightning. I sat up abruptly, my eyes widening in shock.

"Hubby?" I asked, my voice trembling in disbelief.

Venus giggled mischievously, her fingers tracing circles across my chest. "Don't you remember, my husband?"

Her response, a question in return, raised a red flag in my mind. It was a classic technique to mask the truth, one I had seen countless times on crime scene investigation shows. Something was off, and I could feel it. My gaze darted around the room, and there, on the bedside table, lay the source of my pounding headache. A packet of cigarettes, my preferred brand, sat alongside a pack of slims, the type commonly favored by elegant women.

"What happened?" I asked, my voice filled with curiosity and a hint of frustration.

"Hmm," Venus groaned, straddling me and guiding me inside her with purposeful movements. Her breathless words mingled with the rhythmic sounds of our bodies coming together.

"You," she gasped, tapping my nose playfully, "and me," she continued, cupping her breasts and riding me like a wild stallion, "we got married. And then we came back here, and we did what we're doing now, over and over, until you fell asleep."

My desires consumed me, unable to dispute her claims. This wasn't how I had envisioned our marriage. The thought of marrying Venus had crossed my mind briefly, but it was far too soon. Trapped in her snare, I surrendered to the excitement of the moment, waiting for it to be over. As if sensing my disquiet, she intensified her movements, her moans and groans echoing with pleasure.

When she finished, she abruptly got up and sauntered to the bathroom, her hips swaying with each confident step. The enchantment of her beauty faded, leaving me numb. I watched her silhouette through the frosted glass, the warm water cascading over her body. I should have felt fortunate, but I was lost in a haze of confusion.

My gaze fell on our clothes scattered on the floor, and a vague memory flickered. I recalled getting dressed and driving to the seaside restaurant, but everything after was a blur. The sight of my tailored suit jolted me upright.

"Did she plan our supposed wedding?" I blurted out, then bit my tongue, realizing my mistake.

"What did you say?" Venus's voice, muffled by the running water, carried an edge of curiosity.

"Oh, nothing," I mumbled, brushing it off.

As she closed the bathroom door, I seized the moment. Her handbag sat on the kitchen table. I hurried over and rifled through it, desperate for any clue. I pulled out a sachet of white powder, only to find it was sweetener. Frustration surged, my heart racing. I found a rattling pill container and noted the name.

Filled with panic, I frantically rummaged through the cluttered room, my heart pounding in my chest. Finally, my hands landed on my phone, and I quickly realized it was in airplane mode. With a swift motion, I deactivated it, and the phone emitted a sharp beep, breaking the silence. As I glanced at the screen, a wave of shock washed over me. Messages from my brother, mother, and distant friends flooded the display, all congratulating us on our marriage. My heart raced as I opened the photos attached to the messages. There we were, Venus and I, in a dimly lit bar, proudly displaying our wedding bands. Another photo showed her holding a document, our signatures glistening as if they were a legally binding contract.

A gasp escaped my lips as I realized the implications. My mind screamed, "Wedding ring!" I stared at my finger, and there it was, an extravagant wedding ring flaunting its grandiose design. How had I not noticed it earlier? Confusion clouded my thoughts, making it difficult to comprehend the situation.

Furrowing my brow, I pondered the mystery. I had no memory of sharing these images with anyone. The names on the screen belonged to people I had long lost touch with. It seemed as though someone had randomly shared the images, reaching out to anyone who seemed relevant.

Suddenly, the sound of the toilet flushing jolted me back to reality. Time was running out, urging me to hurry my search. Closing the messages, I quickly typed the name of the medication written on the container into the search bar. As I scrolled through the results, another surprise awaited me. The medication was commonly prescribed for individuals suffering from bipolar mood disorder. I had no understanding of what it meant, but I assumed it had some connection to Venus's sudden desire to marry me.

Just as I slid the phone back into my pocket, the bathroom door swung open, and Venus emerged. The soft glow of the rising sun filtered through the sheer curtains, casting a sensual sheen on her bare skin. Her enchanting gaze fixed upon me, conveying her readiness for another round with her newfound husband. I forced a sheepish smile and climbed back into bed, hoping to engage in her seduction.

As she mounted me and writhed with snake-like grace, her moans of pleasure filled the air. Instead of surrendering to the moment, my mind wandered to darker thoughts, anticipating the depths of her capabilities. I knew I would eventually uncover the truth.

Chapter Forty-Five

Marriage was a whirlwind of emotions, a journey I never expected. The weight of the ring on my finger transformed everything. The enchantment of courtship vanished, exposing the harsh reality of our happy-ever-after illusion. Fear gripped me, and I felt adrift in a desolate landscape.

Venus, with her opulent duplex apartment, sold it and move in with me. Naively, the thought of a prenuptial agreement never crossed my mind. Little did I realize that the peculiar laws of wedlock meant that everything I owned now belonged to her as well.

Her apartment sold with astonishing speed, flooding her with a wave of newfound wealth. She embarked on a shopping spree that sent shivers down my spine. The news of her affluence reached the ears of the snakes in my life, my brother and mother. They discovered my address and became frequent visitors, eager to assist their newfound ally, Venus, in squandering her money.

Then, as if by some miraculous intervention, the true essence of Venus's bipolar mood disorder unraveled before my eyes. Every time I dared to scold her for her extravagant spending, she would descend into what she called a 'downer.' She would barricade herself in her bedroom, drowning her sorrows in cigarettes and red wine for days on end. When she finally emerged, her emaciated figure sent chills down my spine, a spectral skeleton haunting the halls of my home.

She only emerged from her self-imposed isolation when she heard my brother's voice, seeing him as her drinking companion. The sound of their unkind words gossiping about me pierced my heart. Yet I remained silent, unwilling to warn her of his ulterior motives, their camaraderie fueled by a shared love for alcohol. I knew that once her money dried up, he would vanish into thin air. And I, too, chose not to warn her.

Soon, my life spiraled out of control. This time, karma attacked me with the relentless force of a Greek siren, its consequences impossible to ignore. The haunting images of our wedding had spread through the dark annals of social media, making their way to her brother and sister, who lived nearby. Their voices echoed with disbelief and warnings, like a chorus of caution.

With suspicion clear in her voice, her sister questioned me about how we had met. Her words carried such weight that my knees grew weak, a physical manifestation of the assurance that our meeting was not a coincidence.

Reluctantly, I agreed to a dinner with them, hoping to find a way out of this tangled web. On a Wednesday afternoon, the sun hung low in the sky, casting long shadows across the room. With a bottle of wine clinking softly in the backseat, I coaxed Venus into the car.

We arrived at her brother's house, the sound of laughter and chatter drifting through the open windows. The aroma of sizzling meat wafted towards us, mingling with the smoky scent of the barbecue. My pulse quickened, unsure of what awaited us inside.

As we sat down to eat, their voices filled the room, recounting stories about Venus. Each word landed like a heavy blow, causing my jaw to drop and my eyes to widen in disbelief. The weight of their revelations hung heavy in the air, suffocating me. Venus threw a tantrum and locked herself inside a spare bedroom, the sound of her slamming the door reverberating through the house.

It was then that I learned the chilling truth. I was her fifth husband, a fact that made my heart skip a beat. The knowledge that two of her previous husbands had met their demise in motorcar accidents sent shivers down my spine. The apartment she had purchased with the money from her late husband's will now felt tainted, like a dark secret hidden within its walls. And the revelation of her neglected daughter, placed in foster care by the court, left a bitter taste in my mouth.

As their words faded into the background, a cold realization washed over me. The toxic bond between Venus and me was suffocating, devouring our souls. Our passion, once intoxicating, now felt like a dangerous flame consuming us both. I had to end it, to break free from this destructive cycle before it consumed me completely.

Venus emanated palpable hostility towards her brother and sister as we departed. She vehemently spat insults at them, venom dripping from her words while threatening them with her share of their inheritance. Undeterred, they brushed off her vitriol, their soothing whispers of encouragement resonating in my ears.

Determined to reach the safety of our house, I sped up; the cars whizzing by on the motorway, their lights streaking like shooting stars. Suddenly, a jolt shook the car, causing it to sway beneath me. Glancing at the rearview mirror, my eyes widened in alarm as I beheld Venus in the throes of a fit. It was as if an otherworldly presence had seized control of her body, akin to the chilling scenes from the movie 'The Exorcist.'

Regrettably, I made a grave decision in my panic. Activating the hazard blinkers, I pulled over to the side of the road. The area we found ourselves in was notorious for crime, including hijackings.

As I hastily exited the car and sprinted towards the back, my heart pounding in my chest, Venus swiftly bounded across the seat, commandeering the vehicle and leaving me stranded. Her sinister laughter echoed in my ears as my car vanished into the distance, seamlessly blending with the flow of traffic on the motorway. Frantically patting my pants for my phone, I realized I had left it behind, intensifying my fear and vulnerability.

The cars continued to zoom past on the motorway, their relentless honking assaulting my senses, amplifying my unease and helplessness in this disconcerting predicament.

"Shit," I muttered, the curse escaping my lips like a whisper, and started walking. Each determined step sent a resounding thud through my sneakers as I strode purposefully towards the dilapidated shacks at the end of the off-ramp.

Just as I quickened my pace, a flicker of movement caught my eye. I glanced towards the overhead bridge and noticed a group of hoodlums huddled together, their faces illuminated by the dancing flames of a makeshift fire burning in a rusty paint bucket. Their eyes glimmered with a sinister warning, sending a shiver down my spine.

Fear and adrenaline coursed through my veins as I hastily retraced my steps, realizing that the dangerous path ahead was not worth the risk. With a sinking feeling in my gut, I acknowledged that I only had one option left—to hitch a ride home. Standing on the side of the motorway, the roar of passing cars filled my ears, drowning out the thumping of my heart. I extended my trembling thumb, a desperate plea for salvation. Seconds stretched into agonizing minutes, but luck seemed to elude me.

Then, to my surprise, my very own car, driven by Venus, appeared before me and came to a sudden halt a few meters away. A flicker of hope ignited within me as I sprinted towards it, grateful that she had finally seen reason. But her true intentions soon became clear. Just as I reached out to grasp the door handle, she sped up, leaving me in a cloud of exhaust fumes. Her malicious laughter pierced through the air, a haunting soundtrack to my pain and betrayal.

Anger and regret mingled within me, a tumultuous storm of emotions. I despised myself for disregarding the warning signs, fueled by my own desires. And the hatred I felt towards Venus intensified, for reveling in the torment she inflicted upon me. My mind became a battlefield, torn between thoughts of revenge and self-pity. But I knew deep down that the darkness in the universe always seemed to favor people like her. She continued her sadistic game, stopping and speeding off, each time mocking my futile attempts to catch up. Eventually, I resigned myself to defeat, my shoulders slumping in resignation as I trudged along the desolate motorway.

To my utter relief, a police van pulled up beside me, its flashing lights casting an eerie glow upon the surrounding darkness. The officer inside looked at me with concern evident in his eyes as the passenger door swung open. "What are you doing?" he asked, his voice laced with a mix of worry and authority. "This is an extremely dangerous area."

I recounted the harrowing events to the officer, relaying the details of what had transpired. Miraculously, luck was on my side. He happened to be heading towards my hometown and offered me a ride. As we sped along the motorway, I caught a glimpse of my car parked haphazardly on the side, hazard lights blinking. Venus had stepped out, frantically searching for me. A surge of satisfaction coursed through me as I rolled down the window and defiantly flipped her the bird, a triumphant smile etching itself onto my face.

The police van eventually pulled into a nearby petrol station, the bright lights illuminating the dreary surroundings. I followed the officer into the shop, immediately greeted by the familiar aroma of freshly brewed coffee and a mix of convenience store snacks. I purchased a packet of cigarettes, my fingers trembling as I indulged in a habit I had long abandoned. The routine of opening the packet and placing a cigarette between my teeth felt oddly comforting, the nicotine soothing my frayed nerves.

Little did I know that this same motorway held a surprise in store for me, but in that fleeting moment, I allowed myself to savor the simple pleasure of listening to the symphony of traffic in the bustling city.

Chapter Forty-Six

My heavy eyelids fluttered open, struggling against the blinding glare of the bright overhead lights. As my vision cleared, I could make out the sterile hospital room around me, filled with the rhythmic beeps and urgent sirens of life-support machines. A sense of panic gripped my racing heart, mirroring the chaotic symphony of sounds. In a flurry, a nurse burst into the room, her kind smile and gentle gaze offering a glimmer of reassurance. She reached out, taking my hand in hers, offering comfort in her touch as she hushed my groggy and hoarse voice.

Confusion clouded my mind as I mustered the strength to ask, "Where am I?" I squinted, trying to adjust my eyes to the harsh illumination above.

"In a hospital," the nurse cooed, her voice soothing, as she directed a small flashlight towards my eyes. She hastily retreated, returning moments later with a doctor by her side. The urgency in their movements was palpable.

The doctor settled on the edge of my bed, his presence a calming force as he assessed my condition, checking my pulse. Meanwhile, the nurse scurried around the room, tending to the equipment with a sense of purpose.

"Welcome back," the doctor said, his voice filled with a mixture of relief and curiosity. He placed the stethoscope against my chest, his ears tuned in to the steady rhythm of my heart. With a nod of approval, he motioned for the nurse to disconnect the intricate web of wires connected to my limbs and body. The once incessant buzzing of the machines ceased enveloping the room in an eerie silence.

Perplexed by the doctor's statement, I furrowed my brow and questioned, "Back?"

Ignoring my inquiry, the doctor maintained his unwavering focus, fixated on his watch. Satisfied with the results, he draped the stethoscope around my neck and performed a series of tests, thoroughly examining my throat, eyes, and blood pressure.

"Send him for a CT scan, ASAP," he ordered the nurse, his tone authoritative and urgent.

"Yes, doctor," the nurse responded promptly, scurrying out of the room, her voice commanding as she relayed instructions down the bustling corridor.

As the doctor closed the door, a soft click resonating in the room, he pressed a button, adjusting the angle of the bed to a more comfortable position. With gentle care, he fluffed a pillow and placed it behind my back, providing support.

Leaning in closer, his tone gentle yet cautious, the doctor inquired, "What is your name?"

My lips parted, struggling to form the words, momentarily forgetting my identity. But then, with a surge of memory, I uttered my name.

Nodding in acknowledgment, the doctor held up three fingers before my eyes. "How many fingers do you see?"

Confusion clouded my thoughts as I struggled to focus, before finally responding, "Three."

Continuing his assessment, the doctor moved on to the next question. "When is your birthday?"

Providing him with the information, including the year, I hoped to shed some light on the situation.

With a knowing smile, the doctor posed another question, his gaze filled with a mix of curiosity and concern. "What year is it?"

Recalling the current year, I answered with certainty, hoping to ease any worries.

He nodded, his expression grave, and then asked, "What is the date?"

Providing him with the requested information, I watched as a flicker of realization passed through his eyes.

"Yes," he murmured softly, his voice filled with a mix of

understanding and concern, "But the day you mention was weeks ago."

"I am not sure I follow?" I said, my gaze fixed on the doctor, pleading for answers. The overpowering scent of disinfectant permeated the air, causing a wave of nausea to wash over me.

The corners of his mouth twitched, and he fired another question at me. "What is the last thing your remember?" he asked, his voice calm and reassuring. "Take your time."

With urgency, the nurse rushed back into the room, carefully holding a glass filled to the brim with a vibrant pink liquid. The sound of her footsteps echoed softly on the linoleum floor as she sat on the edge of the bed, next to the doctor.

She held the rim of the glass to my lips, and I could feel the coolness of the glass against my skin. I raised my arms to clutch the glass, but the weakness in my muscles betrayed me. I managed a small sip, surprised by the sweet taste and the sensation of the liquid gliding down my throat.

While I took small sips, my mind wandered, trying to remember. A surge of electricity coursed through me, and suddenly, a vivid memory of being air-lifted in a helicopter flooded my mind. I quickly shared this information with the doctor. His eyes lit up with genuine interest, and a spark of hope flickered within me.

"Yes," he said, his voice filled with encouragement, "and can you remember anything before that?"

I told him how I left from work, and traveled home eagerly, because it was a Friday. A triumphant smile played on his lips, and he nodded at the nurse. She connected a drip to my arm, and I could feel the slight pinch of the needle as it entered my skin. It was only then when I noticed how frail and bony I had become.

"There was a terrible accident as you traveled home," the doctor said softly, taking my hand in his, his touch warm and comforting, "and you have been in a coma for weeks."

I couldn't tear my eyes away from him, my gaze wide and filled with astonishment. "You were one of the lucky ones," he said, with a nod at the nurse. She opened the bedside table drawer, pulled out a newspaper, and placed it on the bed. The photograph of the mangled car wrecks caught me off guard. I couldn't help but have my gaze immediately drawn to the headline that read, "Tragic accident on M5 results in multiple fatalities." The words in the article danced before my eyes, and I strained to make them out. And there, between the twisted metal and shattered glass, I spotted the lifeless bodies scattered across the cold, unforgiving tarmac.

A porter rushed into the room, the sound of his hurried footsteps echoing against the sterile walls. With the gentle guidance of the doctor and the nurse, they carefully lifted me from the soft hospital bed and settled me into the wheelchair. The porter, a kind-hearted man named Dumisani, had a warm smile that reached his eyes, instantly putting me at ease.

As we made our way through the long corridors, the wheels of the wheelchair squeaked, harmonizing with Dumisani's merry whistle. His cheerful tune filled the air, mingling with the soft beeping of medical equipment and the distant chatter of staff. The scent of antiseptic lingered, a constant reminder of the hospital's sterile environment.

"Hold on tight," Dumisani said, his voice laced with excitement, as we suddenly veered off course. The wheelchair jolted, taking a sharp detour, abandoning the signs that led to "Radiology." The sight of women clad in soft pajamas, cradling their infants and nursing them, captivated me. My eyes eagerly darted around, savoring the scene like a thirsty vampire spying a drop of blood.

"Do you like what you see?" Dumisani exclaimed, his mischievous chuckle filling the air and drawing the attention of the young mothers. Feeling a pang of embarrassment, I lowered my head, pretending to be engrossed in the pristine, gleaming tiles.

"Dumisani!" the young mothers playfully exclaimed, their hands lightly slapping his backside. Their laughter echoed through the corridors, accompanying us all the way to radiology. A grin etched itself onto my face, impossible to erase.

While we waited for my CT scan, Dumisani sat beside me, offering a comforting presence that eased my anxiety. He shared his wisdom, his voice gentle yet full of conviction. He spoke of his own journey, the decision to leave behind a successful career in the corporate world to dedicate his life to helping others. His words touched my soul, and tears welled up in my eyes as he held my hand.

In that moment, I realized how much I needed his presence, his guidance. It was as if he was an angel, sent to provide support during this difficult time. His kind words stirred deep emotions within me, igniting a desire for change. The pursuit of wealth no longer held the same allure. For the first time in a long while, the universe seemed to smile upon me, offering a glimmer of hope.

Though I could not walk or care for myself, a surge of encouragement rippled through my body. It was a feeling of strength and determination, a belief that I could overcome any obstacle. Dumisani's words had ignited a fire within me, sparking a resolve to transform my life for the better.

I did not know what awaited me beyond these sterile walls—a life filled with exciting new encounters and sensory delights. If only.

Chapter Forty-Seven

Sitting beside me on the sterile hospital bed, I turned to my mother, my voice weak and uncertain. "Who is Lizelle?" The sterile scent of antiseptic mingled with the faint fragrance of flowers from the small vase on the bedside table.

Her voice, as cold as the clinical surroundings, replied, "Your wife." A jolt of recognition struck me. "Venus!" I exclaimed, the name resurfacing from the fog of my memory.

My mother's gaze was as frosty as ever. "Yes." Her curt response and the smirk that played on her lips hinted at her satisfaction. This was her revenge on my father, the man who had left her. Now, in my weakened state, I depended entirely on her, a role reversal that seemed to please her immensely. The doctors and physiotherapists had deemed me fit to leave the hospital, but the road to recovery would be long and arduous.

"Venus had to sell your house to cover the hospital and medical expenses," she announced, her voice cutting through the silence like a knife. Her satisfaction at delivering this blow was palpable. I could barely mask my shock, feeling the impact of her words like a punch to the gut.

"Where is she now?" I asked, my voice betraying my desperation. My mother, fiddling with her bangles, revealed, "No one knows. She disappeared. I spoke to her parents and checked at The Bistro, but she's vanished."

The shock was overwhelming. "What?" I stammered, struggling to process her words. Her nonchalance about my wife's disappearance was chilling.

"At least she had the decency to divorce you before leaving," she added, her voice indifferent, as though recounting an unimportant detail. The scent of lavender mingled with the tension between us, creating a stifling atmosphere.

It dawned on me that my mother's mention of "The Bistro" and her knowledge of Venus's true identity meant one thing: she had orchestrated our meeting. The realization was a gut punch. The mother, who had always seemed distant and aloof, had meticulously planned every detail of my life, including the most intimate aspects. As I absorbed this revelation, I whispered under my breath, "You conniving witch."

The room felt as though it was closing in on me. My mother's manipulation had turned what I thought was a chance encounter into a carefully orchestrated meeting. The shock of it all left me reeling, struggling to piece together the truth.

"Where is his holiness?" I asked, referring to my brother, as I noticed the unfamiliar cars parked in the driveway. The vibrant hues of the flowers in the garden danced before me, their sweet fragrance mingling with the breeze. With each step, the crunch of gravel beneath my feet sent a tingling sensation through my weary body. Weak and unsteady, I clung to the wall for support, every movement a struggle as I made my way toward the front door.

"No!" my mother warned, her voice sharp with urgency. "Not that way. Through here." Only then did I realize she had finally taken my advice and rented out the house to tenants.

"Where is the golden calf?" I tried again, my exhausted body leaning against the coolness of the wall. My breaths came heavy and labored, as though I were a lion after the chase.

"I got rid of them," she said, unlocking the door without looking at me, her tone as cold as the metal key she turned.

"But he has a wife and children!" I protested, but my voice was weak, barely more than a whisper.

"And?" she scoffed, pushing the door open with a brisk shove. "He didn't pay his rent."

The words I wanted to say died in my throat, choked back by the fear of being cast out onto the streets. I followed her inside, my stomach churning as the musty scent of old furniture and forgotten memories wrapped around me. The living room, once filled with life, had become a cluttered storage space. A single, unkempt mattress lay on the dusty floor beside a worn suitcase.

"Venus left that for you," my mother said, pointing at the suitcase with a dismissive wave. The familiar plaid pattern brought a flood of memories crashing down on me. My entire existence seemed contained within that old, battered case. Tears welled up in my eyes, a deep ache burning in my chest, but I had no words left to express the overwhelming sorrow that gripped me.

Overcome with exhaustion, I collapsed onto the mattress. The pungent stench of cat urine hit me immediately, but I was too tired to care. With a heavy sigh, I let the fatigue pull me under, slipping into a deep, dreamless sleep.

My eyes slowly blinked open, struggling to pierce the suffocating darkness. The blackness felt thick, almost tangible, pressing down on me like an oppressive weight. My muscles groaned in protest as I forced myself upright, the effort leaving me dizzy and off balance.

The air was heavy with the acrid stench of cat piss, clawing at my throat and triggering a memory I'd tried hard to bury. I coughed, the foul smell bringing me back to my mother's cottage—a place that was more trap than home. My stomach growled loudly, a twisted reminder of how long it had been since I'd eaten anything substantial. The hunger gnawed at me, sharp and relentless, echoing the emptiness inside.

The silence around me was broken only by the faint creak of old wood settling, a ghostly sound that sent a shiver down my spine. My mind, still foggy with sleep, stirred, unraveling a tangled mess of thoughts and regrets. Accusations swirled like a storm, each one stinging like a lash. I couldn't escape them, just as I couldn't escape her —the witch who had given me life and then twisted it into something barely recognizable.

I squeezed my eyes shut, blocking out the darkness and the memories that clung to it. I needed to get out of here, but my body was weak, and my mind was even weaker. Her voice, that cold, manipulative tone, had been the soundtrack of my life since I returned from the city, and no matter how hard I tried, I couldn't drown it out. She had ensnared me in her web, and there was no easy way out.

I knew why my father had left without a trace. Facing her wrath was a fate worse than death, and he had chosen the coward's way out, leaving me to withstand her vengeance. I could almost hear his voice, a faint echo of a memory: *"Son, some battles aren't worth fighting."* But I wasn't him. I wouldn't run. I'd learn the lessons life was forcing on me, even if the cost was high.

I took a deep breath, trying to steady myself. This wasn't the life I'd envisioned, but it was the one I had to survive. Slowly, I let the visualization technique I used to teach my students take hold. I pictured a different world—one where the darkness didn't follow me. A cozy house, a warm meal, the sound of laughter instead of silence. I clenched my fists, holding onto the image like a lifeline. *This isn't forever,* I told myself. *It's just for now.*

As I lay there, the realization hit me with the quiet force of dawn. I couldn't drag anyone else into this nightmare until I'd found a way out myself. My family's darkness wasn't something I wanted anyone else to see. Not now, maybe never. I was done with dating, done with the corporate world. My mother had taken so much from me, but she couldn't take my skills, my will to rebuild.

With a newfound resolve, I forced myself to move. My legs wobbled as I pushed myself upright, my hands grabbing onto anything within reach for support. A stack of boxes toppled over, their contents spilling across the floor, but I barely noticed. I shuffled towards the kitchen, the cold tile against my feet a sharp contrast to the warmth I was trying to summon in my mind.

"Mom?" I called out, my voice hoarse and unsteady, but there was no answer—only the hollow echo of my voice bouncing off the walls. My stomach twisted in hunger, but the fridge held nothing but a wilted salad. I slammed the door shut, frustration boiling over. The microwave and oven were empty too, as if mocking my desperation.

Leaning against the countertop for support, I stared at the empty space around me, the reality of my situation sinking in. *She's not here,* I thought, half relieved, half fearful of what that meant. The silence was deafening, filled only with the faint hum of the refrigerator and the distant chirping of crickets outside.

I stumbled towards the front door, my movements clumsy but determined. The cool night air hit me as I stepped outside, and for a moment, I just stood there, letting it wash over me. I reached into my pocket, pulling out a crumpled cigarette. The first drag was harsh, but familiar, and as I exhaled, the smoke curled into the night, a minor comfort in an otherwise chaotic world.

This was my sanctuary, the only place where I could think clearly, plan my escape. And I would escape—no matter what it took. I took another drag; the nicotine calming my nerves, and let my thoughts drift. Somewhere out there, a new life awaited, far away from this darkness.

Chapter Forty-Eight

My eyes shot open, jolted by the distant hum of my mother's voice mingling with unfamiliar chatter. My heart raced, thudding in my chest, a hot wave of embarrassment flushing my face as her voice grew louder, more animated. The door to my cluttered storage room flew open, revealing me sprawled on the unkempt mattress. The visitors, wide-eyed, gasped, their hands flying to their mouths as murmurs of astonishment floated through the room. My mother stood there, a smirk tugging at her lips, her eyes gleaming with a mischievous sparkle that only deepened my irritation.

"What's going on?" I snapped, my voice sharp with frustration.

With a dismissive wave, she gestured as if orchestrating a grand performance. "I've decided to put the house on the market," she said, her voice dripping with satisfaction.

"Why would you do that?" I asked, struggling to keep the disbelief out of my tone.

Her gaze was cold, snake-like, as she met my eyes. "Because it's my house, and I'll do whatever I want with it," she hissed, her pleasure evident. With a final glance, she tapped the windowpane, spun on her heel, and rejoined her friends. Their laughter rang out, a cruel reminder of my predicament.

Curled into a fetal position, I grunted in frustration. I recognized some of these people from before, their faces a painful reminder of my fall from grace. To add to the sting, she would later call the real estate agency and retract her decision, leaving me in a state of limbo.

As days passed, my strength slowly returned, only to be met with her escalating charade. At night, as I drifted into uneasy slumber, her lover's moans and groans pierced through the walls, a constant reminder of her betrayal. During these moments, I used the opportunity to borrow her car and sneak out to buy cigarettes.

Eventually, I abandoned driving, my strength fading. I navigated the darkened streets on foot, each lamppost a distant beacon. As I shuffled from one to the next, people I knew drove past, their eyes deliberately avoiding mine. My struggle was a stark contrast to their indifference, each step a testament to my determination to escape, even if only for a moment.

And then, out of nowhere, something completely unexpected occurred, catching me off guard and leaving me bewildered. PTSD (Post-Traumatic Stress Disorder) violently invaded my mind, a consequence of the car accident that had tragically taken many lives.

The memories surged back with brutal clarity, an unrelenting flood of fear and despair. The screeching tires, the twisted metal, and the blood-curdling screams replayed in my mind like a relentless nightmare. The once familiar streets I navigated daily now seemed to pulse with hidden dangers, their shadows harboring echoes of past terror. Each jarring noise, every sudden movement, became a trigger that sent me spiraling back into those harrowing moments.

Daily life transformed into a battleground against the relentless flashbacks and paralyzing anxiety. Simple tasks became monumental obstacles, and my world felt like a precarious house of cards, ready to collapse with the slightest tremor. My mind, once a place of refuge, now resembled a chaotic battlefield.

In the absence of therapy, I turned inward, searching for the inner resources to find strength. Armed with my inner strength and a mindset focused on positivity, I took on the challenge of confronting my fears head-on. I immersed myself in practices that helped me regain a sense of control: meditation, journaling, and focusing on small, manageable goals. Each day, I reminded myself of my strength and the capacity for healing within me.

Gradually, I developed coping strategies that allowed me to navigate through the turmoil. The path to recovery was neither straightforward nor easy, but I was determined to persevere. Nightmares continued to wrench me from sleep, leaving me drenched in cold sweat, heart racing, but I fought back with every ounce of resolve I had.

With each deliberate and precise step through the dimly lit streets, the lampposts gradually lost their enchantment, their once inviting glow fading into insignificance. They transformed into symbols of my strength, guiding me toward a future where peace and happiness were within reach. The road ahead remained treacherous, but I faced it with newfound resilience, ready to embrace whatever lay ahead.

Although I was grateful for healing, I felt trapped and suffocated in the witch's lair. The longer I remained confined, the more the walls closed in on me, squeezing me tightly. And besides, my tastebuds craved the refreshing taste of an ice-cold beer in the company of vibrant, healthy people. Well, almost, because most of the patrons at the local pub were either divorced, contemplating divorce, planning it, or getting married with the option of divorcing one day. And now, I found myself among them. So much for my earlier criticisms. Now, I rowed along the river of denial, feeling the resistance of the water against the oars.

As I approached the pub, the thumping music of the live band grew louder, reverberating through the air. Goosebumps spread across my arms as the melodies felt like a personal serenade, especially when they flawlessly performed "Eye of the Tiger" by Survivor. I quickened my pace, eager to immerse myself in the lively atmosphere, and stepped through the doors, greeted by smiles and nods from unfamiliar faces.

Here, unlike at my mother's house, I was a stranger. Everyone present was oblivious to my fall from grace and my family's tarnished reputation. Seeking solace, I purchased an ice-cold pint and found solace in a cozy corner, basking in the warmth radiating from the crackling fireplace, a stark contrast to the frigid storage room that had become my temporary abode.

My foot instinctively tapped to the rhythm of the music as I closed my eyes, tears streaming down my cheeks. A surge of pent-up emotions flooded out, releasing the weight that had burdened me for months. The taste of that first beer after what felt like an eternity was pure bliss. I savored each sip, perhaps a bit too eagerly. Combined with the medication, it ignited my mind like a powerful stallion.

Opening my eyes, I noticed a blonde woman staring at me, her brow furrowed in deep contemplation. Avoiding her gaze, I focused on the band, anticipating their next song. Suddenly, a young man seated beside the blonde jumped up and approached the lead singer, whispering a suggestion into his ear.

The speakers blared with the chosen song, igniting a surge of energy within the crowd as they enthusiastically moved to the lively beat. The blonde woman approached me, taking my hand and leading me towards the makeshift dancefloor. We twisted and bounced, surrendering ourselves to the infectious rhythm.

Amidst the exhilaration, she introduced herself as Beatrice, shouting her words into my ears with a rough British accent. I reciprocated with my own introduction, losing myself in the moment. She then introduced the man who had requested the song as her fiancé, Alexander, who exuded an air of regality. Together, they represented a lineage of nobility, with Beatrice's elegant finesse perfectly complementing Alexander's regal stance.

The next morning, I awoke with a throbbing ache at my temples, the pain pulsating like a drumbeat. Squinting against the bright light, I flung myself out of bed, my bare feet sinking into the plush carpet. The air was filled with the tantalizing aroma of sizzling bacon and eggs, guiding me down the unfamiliar corridors with each breath.

"Hey sleepy head," Beatrice greeted me as I sauntered into the dining room of the opulent house, her voice melodic and soothing. My eyes darted around, taking in the majestic details of the room. Sunlight streamed through the grand windows, casting a warm glow on the ornate furniture. The gentle flow of a nearby river reached my ears, accompanied by the harmonious melody of birds chirping in the lush landscape.

"Mornin'," I mumbled, my voice groggy and hoarse, the words escaping my lips like a whisper. "Where am I?"

Beatrice greeted me in the early morning with a tight, affectionate hug and a gentle kiss on my cheek. "You're at our estate," she breathed, her voice filled with kindness. "We'll give you the grand tour once you've had something to eat. Come, sit down and relax."

I sank into a plush chair, its velvety fabric enveloping me in comfort, as she poured freshly brewed coffee from a steaming pot into a large cup. The rich aroma filled the air, mingling with the scent of morning dew and freshly cut flowers. I took the cup, feeling its warmth seep into my hands, providing solace to my frayed hangover nerves.

Alexander emerged from the shadows, rubbing the sleep from his eyes, his movements slow and languid. He greeted me with a grunt, his touch gentle as he caressed his temples, sharing in my pain.

We savored a full English breakfast, the clinking of silverware and the tinkling of laughter filling the room. Our conversation turned to the crazy adventures we had the previous evening, and we couldn't help but grin at the recollection. The food on our plates, a feast for the senses, tantalized our taste buds with its savory flavors.

It was then that they shared their true intentions, their voices filled with sincerity. They had been searching tirelessly for someone who could speak the local language and manage the guest house while they tended to the spa. After hearing my story the previous evening, they had decided that I was the perfect candidate.

In that moment, a sense of belonging washed over me, my English roots resonating with theirs. I drenched my bacon and sausages in brown sauce, the tangy aroma enveloping me, and spread berry jam on my toast, savoring its sweet taste. The bitter tea, cup after cup, warmed me from the inside out.

I listened intently, my head nodding in agreement, as they detailed the perks of the job—a weekly salary, a vehicle, accommodation, and meals. With each word they spoke, my grin grew wider, my heart filling with relief. Lady luck had finally smiled upon me, her kind eyes shining down on my weary soul. Her timing could not have been more perfect, as I could sense a looming disaster awaiting me at home.

My gaze darted back and forth between Beatrice and Alexander, their eager eyes fixed upon me, awaiting my response. The difficulty lay in discerning the genuine intentions of others. I pondered on the stark contrast of my current circumstances, from the frigid storage room I called home to the warmth of the crackling fire in the fireplace. The soft melody of a jazz tune wafted through the air, further enhancing the tranquil atmosphere. There was little to deliberate upon. Beneath the table, a lively border collie let out a spirited bark, causing me to startle. My mind refocused on the present, a dreamy smile gracing my lips.

Without hesitation, I agreed wholeheartedly to their proposal, my voice filled with gratitude. "I can start today." Their grins mirrored my own, impossible to erase, as we embraced the promise of a new beginning.

Following the grand tour of the opulent estate, guided by Beatrice and Alexander, we settled onto the vast porch, leisurely savoring our tea. Their border collie found comfort at my feet, his soft fur brushing against my ankles. The gentle breeze carried the scent of freshly cut grass and blooming flowers from the meticulously maintained landscape.

My eyes scanned the breathtaking view, taking in the vibrant colors of the swimming pool, the quaint cottages nestled among the trees, and the serene river with its inviting pier and rowing boats. The warm sun kissed my face, filling me with a sense of tranquility. Just as I wondered where I would find my place in this grand estate, Alexander seemed to read my thoughts.

Excusing himself, he trudged towards the primary residence while I reached for a cigarette, sharing a sneaky drag with Beatrice. Our laughter mingled with the sweet melodies of chirping birds, creating an atmosphere of pure joy.

"I believe this belongs to you now," Alexander said as he returned, tossing a pair of keys my way. The jingling sound of the keys resonated with excitement as I caught them in my hands. The keys unveiled a room number, 12, and a key specifically designed for a Volkswagen. My eyes darted around, and I spotted the sleek white car, gleaming in the sunlight, parked nearby. With a surge of gratitude, tears welled up in my eyes, silently thanking Beatrice and Alexander for their generosity.

"Go fetch your things," Beatrice encouraged, her voice filled with warmth. "We'll be waiting for you when you return."

Eagerly, I leaped up from the porch, playfully saluting them with an exclamation of, "Aye, boss!" I sprinted towards my new car, feeling the excitement coursing through my veins. But my faithful companion refused to let me out of his sight. His paws clicked against the cobblestone courtyard as he followed closely behind me.

"What's his name?" I shouted back towards Alexander, the words carried by the gentle breeze.

"It's Guinness!" Alexander called out with a chuckle, his voice filled with affection.

"Hello Guinness," I greeted him as our eyes locked, a connection forming between us. I sensed his silent plea to join me, and I opened the back door, allowing him to jump onto the comfortable back seat. His enthusiastic panting filled the car as he poked his head through the open window, his tail wagging with excitement.

The scenic drive back to my former residence was filled with breathtaking views as the lush countryside rolled by. I savored every moment in the company of my loyal companion, feeling a sense of freedom and belonging.

As we approached my mother's house, a mix of anticipation and apprehension filled my senses. The engine's purr faded as I parked in the driveway, my tummy churning with nervous energy, and my hands trembling with anticipation. Little did I realize, the snake of fate slithered its way into my plans, sensing my intentions and plotting its own course. "I'll be right back," I whispered to my faithful canine companion, his tail wagging in understanding, as I caught my breath.

Stepping out of the car, the crisp air enveloped me, carrying the distant murmurs of my mother's conversation with a man. Their voices traveled through the air, their tones filled with deliberation, mingling with the subtle rustling of leaves in the gentle breeze. Taking a deep sigh, I approached the door, its worn wood creaking under my touch, and with a gentle push, it swung open, revealing a figure that resembled a Jewish rabbi. A halo of silver framed his face as his piercing gaze met mine, sending a shiver down my spine.

"Come inside," he said, his voice cold and unwelcoming, without bothering with a formal introduction. From the way he clenched his jaw and avoided eye contact, I could sense his deep-seated animosity towards me, and instantly knew my mother had poisoned his mind before my arrival.

He sank into a worn-out seat beside my mother, his fingers intertwining with hers. She sat there, her back straight and her lips curled into a smug smirk, believing herself to be a divine deity.

"Hey," I said firmly, trying to assert myself, "I came to fetch my—"

With a swift motion, the rabbi raised his hand, his eyes narrowing in authority, as he cut me off and took control of the situation. His gaze shifted towards my mother, awaiting his cue, and she nodded with an air of superiority. He unleashed a torrent of scathing words, berating me for my perceived inadequacies as a son, his voice cutting through the air with venom. He went on and on, his tirade seeming endless. When he finally finished, they both stared at me, their eyes filled with anticipation, waiting for an explosive reaction.

I couldn't help but burst into boisterous laughter, the sound echoing in the room, fueling their anger even further. Providing no explanation, I nonchalantly sauntered into the dimly lit storage room, retrieving my belongings. For months, I had eagerly anticipated this moment, envisioning it in vivid detail in my mind. Little did I know it would unfold quite differently. As I packed my modest belongings into my tattered plaid suitcase, a merry whistle escaped my lips. The sound mingled with the hushed surprise emanating from my mother and Rabi. With my suitcase firmly in hand, its worn handle pressing against my palm, I turned around, ready to face their astonishment one last time.

Little did I know that Guinness, my loyal companion, had come searching for me. As I stepped back into the living room, he positioned himself beside me, his teeth bared and a low growl emanating from deep within his chest, aimed directly at my mother. The sight brought me immense satisfaction. Their faces contorted with fear, their knuckles turning white as they clung desperately to each other's hand.

"You know what?" I said, fixing the rabbi with a piercing, unwavering gaze. He nodded, silently urging me to continue, but I could see the tremor in his knees.

"You can have your way with my mother all you want," I declared, causing them to gasp in shock, "But you won't lay a finger on her fortune. She loves her wealth more than life itself." His eyes widened, his cheeks flushing crimson with embarrassment. He muttered something incoherent and shifted uncomfortably in his seat. My mother simply glared at me, her eyes burning with pure hatred.

"Good luck," I said as I walked out, clutching my suitcase tightly, with Guinness faithfully by my side.

Chapter Forty-Nine

The dimly lit pub, with its wooden furnishings and cozy atmosphere, had become our sanctuary. The sound of laughter and clinking glasses filled the air, creating a vibrant energy that was palpable. Beatrice and Alexander effortlessly mingled with the crowd, their magnetic personalities drawing the gaze of wealthy patrons who eagerly backed their ventures. Unbeknownst to me, this pub had also become my haven, but for different reasons.

The pub buzzed with excitement as the locals marveled at Beatrice's and Alexander's larger-than-life reputations. People eagerly gathered, captivated by their presence, hanging on their every word. Meanwhile, I found solace in conversing with the rare Afrikaans-speaking individuals, effortlessly switching between languages. It was through these interactions that I formed connections with new friends, eager to be associated with Beatrice and Alexander, but unable to socialize with them as intimately as I did.

Little did I realize, this was an extra advantage that came along with our undisclosed conditions. It worked like magic—free drinks flowed generously, courtesy of the bustling pub filled with people yearning to meet my almost noble friends. They exuded an air of regality, commanding attention without the official title to accompany it.

On one memorable evening, the pub throbbed with life. The music reverberated through the air, creating an infectious beat that matched the high spirits of the crowd. The Springboks, our national rugby team, had emerged victorious over England in the world cup finally, igniting a wave of celebration. The sounds of high fives and back pats echoed throughout the pub, mingling with the cheers and chants of jubilant fans.

As the night wore on and our glasses emptied, my newfound friend and I made our way to the counter, seeking a refill. For the sake of formality, let's refer to my friend as Bennie. The barman seemed overwhelmed by the demand, but we patiently waited, soaking in the lively atmosphere. It was then that Bennie pointed towards a group of attractive women, referring to them in the typical Afrikaans slang as "hot chicks."

As my gaze followed his direction, the vibrant colors of the surroundings seemed to blur together. The sound of my pounding heart drowned out the chatter of the crowd. A strange, yet comforting scent filled the air, bringing with it a wave of nostalgia. My knees trembled, threatening to give way under the weight of the moment.

And then, a wave of familiarity washed over me, like a gentle breeze on a warm summer day. It was as if I had lived this exact moment before. The same conversation, the same surroundings, even the same clothes adorned our bodies. It was a surreal echo of a memory that I couldn't quite place, a sensation of Déjà vu that left me momentarily bewildered.

And there she sat, my dream girl, her infectious smile illuminating the world around us. The sight of her caused a whirlwind of butterflies to dance within my stomach. It was undeniably her, the girl who had graced my recurring dreams throughout my life. Her short, highlighted hair framed her flawless porcelain face, and her soft blue eyes sparkled with a touch of mischief. Every detail mirrored the girl of my dreams with impeccable precision. There was not a shred of doubt in my mind. I had finally found her.

Allow me to emphasize, dear reader, that I am not a confident man. Approaching a stranger in a public place had never been within my comfort zone. Yet, in that moment, without even the slightest hesitation, I mustered the courage to walk up to her. I could feel the disapproving glances of her friends, their scorn prickling my skin, but I remained undeterred. I locked my gaze with hers, my eyes shining with anticipation.

"What?" she asked, her voice filled with shyness as she averted her eyes.

A surge of joy coursed through me as memories of the girl in my dreams flooded my mind, her smile mirrored in reality.

"One day," I declared with a glimmer of certainty, "I am going to marry you. Because you are my Déjà vu."

A chorus of coos and surprised gasps escaped the lips of her friends, but I paid them no mind. In that moment, I reveled in the sheer magic of it all.

Marna, the girl in my dreams, and I drove home from an outing exploring the picturesque little towns on the outskirts of the Cape Winelands. The soft hum of the car engine filled the air as we cruised along the winding roads.

"Elmo," she said, her voice filled with affection, using the nickname she had given me, a term of endearment that always made my heart skip a beat.

"I'm all ears, Princess," I replied, using the nickname I had lovingly bestowed upon her, a term of endearment that never failed to bring a radiant smile to her face.

As she turned sideways in her seat, her scent of lavender and vanilla filled my senses, beckoning me to lean in closer and kiss her. I nodded, lowering the volume of the music, giving her my complete attention. Her delicate fingers gently tapped against my elbow, demanding my undivided focus, a playful reminder of how much she valued my presence.

Adjusting the rearview mirror, I stole glances into her captivating baby blue eyes, marveling at their beauty as I navigated the meandering road ahead. Even after months of being together, my stomach still fluttered with butterflies whenever I witnessed her enchanting smile, grounding the girl of my dreams firmly in the present.

"I have something to ask you," she said, her voice tinged with caution. My eyes widened in anticipation as I awaited her words.

"I don't want to have children one day," she confessed, her words laced with uncertainty. Now, for those who may have forgotten, or perhaps missed, my earlier revelation that I am unable to have children, I must reiterate it once again. Yes, I cannot have children. This truth had led to many rejections in the past. But let's not digress any further.

I watched "my bird," as I often playfully teased her in the rearview mirror, my heart pounding with disbelief. Without a second thought, I pulled over abruptly, the screech of the tires echoing through the air. In a rush of adrenaline, I darted around the car and flung open the passenger door.

On the gravel surface, I sank to my knees, feeling the roughness beneath me. With fervor and love pouring through every fiber of my being, I asked her to marry me, a ringless proposal that held all the sincerity in the world.

To my sheer delight, astonishment, and surprise, her response rang out, startling not only me but also the nearby birds. Their wings fluttered as they took flight, carrying my heart along with them. And with uncontainable joy, she exclaimed, "YES!"

In the depths of my dreams, the image of the girl I longed for materialized into my reality. Our connection was undeniable, evident by the admiring whispers of those around us. They marveled at the unique and enchanting bond we shared, unlike anything they had ever seen. If I had to describe it in just two words, it would be a "silent understanding."

As twilight settled upon us, I would lie in bed, contemplating the words to convey our story, my mind wandering. And just as the perfect words formed in my thoughts, she would stir beside me, emitting a soft murmur in her slumber. Her gentle touch, caressing my back, seemed to acknowledge and comprehend my unspoken emotions.

In the realm of mundane tasks like preparing meals, our conversations would veer away from the necessities at hand. Yet, without uttering a single instruction, our dinner would magically manifest on the table, adorned with precisely what we required. My cousin once witnessed this marvel, her astonishment mirrored by her young children's agreement.

A profound connection binds us, one that sends shivers down my spine as I reflect upon its depth. To put it simply, it feels like telepathy. She understands my joys, my sorrows, and my needs without me voicing them. And likewise, I possess the same intuitive understanding of her. In the presence of others, I would abruptly dart into the house, retrieving an item she anticipated, placing it delicately into her waiting hands. Our guests, bewildered, would inquire, "How did he know?" In response, we would share a knowing smile, our shoulders shrugging in unison, concealing our secret understanding.

With a mischievous wink, I can only imagine the vivid imagery that dances through your mind when you ponder the intimate moments shared by individuals like us. Should I delve into the intricacies, or simply describe it as an ethereal experience? Ah, my cherished reader, I have discovered my very own wonder woman. The universe, in all its glory, has ultimately bestowed upon me the most precious reward one could ever desire—true love.

Our wedding, in all its enchantment, resembled nothing less than a fairy tale. Despite my limited funds, I transformed the occasion into a cherished dream for my beloved bride-to-be. As she gracefully glided down the aisle, the mellifluous melody of the organ's chimes filled the air, resonating with our hearts. Her eyes, locked on me, shimmered like the celestial stars above, while the whispers, sniffs, and gasps of awe from the onlookers created a symphony of astonishment. In the blink of an eye, the ceremony concluded, culminating in our joyous and resounding "yes!" And what truly made our wedding extraordinary was the absence of my mother. Even before I had the chance to reveal her true nature, my soon-to-be wife, of her own accord, confessed, "Your mother gives me the creeps." It was in that profound moment that our bond solidified, and I knew without a doubt that I desired a lifetime with my princess.

EPILOGUE

My dearest mortal reader. This story is far from over. I encourage you to please leave a review and a comment. There are still many untold stories about my life that I wish to share. If there is anything you want to hear or know, please reach out to me.

In between motivational talks and travels, I will make time to respond. I promise. Until then, farewell, but only for now.

While I worked on this memoir, I made a startling discovery. You can read the full story on positive thinking here. Harness the power of Your Mind.

THANK YOU

Thank you for taking the time to read *Growing Slowly Nowhere*. Your support is invaluable, and I'm deeply grateful for your engagement. To everyone who has been part of this journey—family, friends, and all my readers—this achievement is as much yours as it is mine.

If you enjoyed this memoir, I'd love to hear from you! Please consider leaving a review or. Your feedback not only helps me improve but also aids in reaching more readers who might find inspiration in these pages.

For updates on new releases and to stay connected, follow me on social media and join my mailing list. Your continued support and engagement are deeply appreciated!

Iwan Ross is a renowned storyteller from South Africa whose fascination with human emotions shines through in his writing. With his debut novel, *Elm Brook Manor*, Ross garnered acclaim and fame for his unique ability to intertwine love, danger, and suspense.

Despite his success, Ross remains grounded, channeling his boundless imagination into every story. His work blurs the lines between reality and illusion, making each narrative a thrilling journey. As an author, Ross doesn't just write; he crafts immersive worlds where secrets are hidden, and nothing is quite what it seems.

Reading a book by Iwan Ross is an invitation to live the story itself—experience the intrigue, the suspense, and the emotional depth firsthand.

Printed in the USA
CPSIA information can be obtained
at www.ICGtesting.com
CBHW021019101024
15373CB00071B/826